Imagined States

EDINBURGH CRITICAL STUDIES IN LAW, LITERATURE AND THE HUMANITIES

Series Editor: William MacNeil, Southern Cross University
Senior Deputy Editor: Shaun McVeigh, University of Melbourne
Deputy Editor: Daniel Hourigan, University of Southern Queensland

With a global reach, this innovative series critically reimagines the interdisciplinary relationship between legal and literary (or other aesthetic) texts through the most advanced conceptual frameworks and interpretive methods of contemporary theory available in the humanities and jurisprudence.

Editorial Board
Dr Maria Aristodemou (Birkbeck, University of London)
Associate Professor Fatou Kine Camara (Université Cheikh Anka Diop de Dakar)
Professor Daniela Carpi (University of Verona)
Dr Susan Chaplin (Leeds Beckett University)
Professor Andrew Clarke (Victoria University)
Dr Stella Clarke (University of Melbourne)
Professor Penny Fielding (University of Edinburgh)
Mme Justice Hon Jeanne Gaakeer (Erasmus University Rotterdam)
Professor Peter Goodrich (Cardozo School of Law, Yeshiva University)
Professor Elizabeth Hanson (Queen's University at Kingston)
Associate Professor Susan Sage Heinzelman (University of Texas at Austin)
Professor Bonnie Honig (Brown University)
Professor Rebecca Johnson (University of Victoria)
Dr Orit Kamir (Hebrew Union College)
Associate Professor Lissa Lincoln (American University Paris)
Professor Desmond Manderson (Australian National University)
Professor Panu Minkkenen (University of Helsinki)
Dr Anat Rosenberg (IDC Herzliya)
Professor Renata Salecl (Ljubljana/Birkbeck, University of London)
Professor Austin Sarat (Amherst College)
Dr Jan Melissa Schram (University of Cambridge)
Professor Karin Van Marle (University of Pretoria)
Dr Marco Wan (University of Hong Kong)
Professor Ian Ward (University of Newcastle)
Professor Alison Young (University of Melbourne)

Available or forthcoming titles
Imagined States: Law and Literature in Nigeria, 1900–1966
Katherine Isobel Baxter

Judging from Experience: Law, Praxis, Humanities
Jeanne Gaakeer

Schreber's Law: Jurisprudence and Judgment in Transition
Peter Goodrich

Living in Technical Legality: Science Fiction and Law as Technology
Kieran Tranter

edinburghuniversitypress.com/series/ecsllh

Imagined States

Law and Literature in Nigeria, 1900–1966

Katherine Isobel Baxter

EDINBURGH
University Press

For Chris

Edinburgh University Press is one of the leading university presses in the UK. We publish academic books and journals in our selected subject areas across the humanities and social sciences, combining cutting-edge scholarship with high editorial and production values to produce academic works of lasting importance. For more information visit our website: edinburghuniversitypress.com

© Katherine Isobel Baxter, 2019, 2021

First published in hardback by Edinburgh University Press 2019

Edinburgh University Press Ltd
The Tun – Holyrood Road
12 (2f) Jackson's Entry
Edinburgh EH8 8PJ

Typeset in 11/13pt Adobe Garamond Pro by
Exeter Premedia Services Pvt Ltd., Chennai, India

A CIP record for this book is available from the British Library

ISBN 978 1 4744 2083 9 (hardback)
ISBN 978 14744 8756 6 (paperback)
ISBN 978 1 4744 2084 6 (webready PDF)
ISBN 978 1 4744 2085 3 (epub)

The right of Katherine Isobel Baxter to be identified as author of this work has been asserted in accordance with the Copyright, Designs and Patents Act 1988 and the Copyright and Related Rights Regulations 2003 (SI No. 2498).

Contents

Acknowledgements	vii
Introduction: Literature, Imagination and the State of Exception	1
1 'Natural Justice, Equity and Good Conscience': History, Politics and Law in Nigeria, 1900–1966	12
2 'I Am the Law': District Commissioner Fiction and the State of Exception	26
3 'Seeking a Legal Form': Joyce Cary's *Mister Johnson*	54
4 'Beast of No Nation': Bribery, Corruption and Late Colonial Administration in *No Longer at Ease*	85
5 'Written in the Interest of the People': Representing the Law in Cyprian Ekwensi and Market Literature	107
6 'Sensational Coverage of a Sensational Trial': Treason, Journalism and the State	130
7 Violence and the Law in *A Man of the People*	157
Conclusion: Imagined States	181
Bibliography	195
Index	201

Acknowledgements

This book has been a long time in the making and I have carried it around the world with me. On my travels I have had the good fortune to explore my ideas with colleagues, friends and students over several years.

Initial thanks therefore go to colleagues at Hong Kong University, where this project started, whose support and interest gave me the confidence to keep going: Kelvin Au, Wendy Gan, Elaine Ho, Chris Hutton, Douglas Kerr, Julia Kuehn, Yeewan Koon, Tina Pang, Q. S. Tong and Marco Wan. Thanks also go to Julia Chan, Nin Chan and Owen Graham who provided assistance in the early stages of my research. Formal thanks are also due to Hong Kong University whose funding supported initial archival research, as well as attendance at the School for Criticism and Theory, where I consolidated my thinking for this project through discussion with my peers in the 'Bilingualism' seminar, led with characteristic generosity and verve by Haun Saussy. I owe them all my gratitude.

At Stanford University I received valuable feedback from colleagues in the PWR research group and through conversations with colleagues from the Workshop in Poetics. Special thanks are due to Kathryn Hume, Noam Pines and Molly Molloy, whose kindness was boundless. In addition, thanks are due to Stanford University Library and to Carol Leadenham at the Hoover Institution Archives and Library, where a good deal of the research for this project was undertaken.

Thanks are likewise due to colleagues at Northumbria University, in particular Clark Lawlor and Julian Wright who both patiently read drafts of the manuscript. An early draft of Chapter 2 received valuable feedback from colleagues in Northumbria's English and Creative Writing seminar series. In addition, thanks go to Ian Davidson, Ann-Marie Einhaus, Adam Hansen and Richard Terry whose conversations with me about this project have been inspiring; and to Hannah Gregory, who provided companionship in our shared deadlines. Formal thanks are also due to Northumbria, which has supported this project through research leave and funding to enable me to complete my archival research. Thanks also go to the Literary and Philosophical Society of Newcastle and to the British Library, whose collections have supported this project.

Portions of this research have been presented in seminars and conferences where I have invariably received very useful feedback. Thanks therefore go to Birmingham's Centre for the Study of Cultural Modernity, Durham's 'Inventions of the Text' seminar series, and the ASLCH annual conference. In addition I am tremendously grateful to Marco Wyss and Shaun McVeigh who have both been generous in providing commentary and suggestions. An earlier version of Chapter 4 was published in a different form as 'Judging Judgement in Chinua Achebe's *No Longer at Ease*' in Marco Wan (ed.), *The Legal Case: Cross Currents between Law and the Humanities* (Routledge 2012).

Edinburgh University Press has been fantastic to work with and I am particularly grateful to Eddie Clark, Sarah Foyle, Jackie Jones, John Watson and Laura Williamson, and copy-editor Cathy Falconer. Special thanks, moreover, are due to Bill MacNeil. His generosity, patience and unstinting enthusiasm have been an extraordinary support. I could not ask for a better editor.

Thanks are due to two others whose conversations and interest in this project have kept me going. The provocation to this project emerged from conversations many years ago with David Johnson. His friendship and the critical challenges he has offered to it along the way have made the project stronger than it would otherwise have been. Likewise, Madhumita Lahiri has been an inspiring friend and has similarly challenged me to keep pushing my thinking.

My final debt of gratitude is to my family and, in particular, to Chris. Without his boundless patience, care and friendship, his willingness to challenge my thinking, to read and reread my work, and to remind me when to stop, this project would never have reached its conclusion.

Introduction: Literature, Imagination and the State of Exception

This book takes as its starting point Adigun Agbaje's observation that 'no other area vividly illustrates the enduring character and pervasiveness of the colonial inheritance in the Nigerian post-colony more than its system of laws'.[1] I want to expand on this to claim that it was the imaginative space of the state of exception, that is to say the suspension of that 'system of laws', which was the pervasive experience of colonialism and its most significant inheritance in the post-colony. Moreover, I will argue that inasmuch as the law was seen by the British administration as the 'sum and substance' of its civilising mission, it was the language of civilisation that enabled a systematised erasure of the distinction between the rule of law and the suspension of the rule of law under colonial rule.[2]

In pursuing this argument I focus my attention on a range of fiction written by British and Nigerian authors between the turn of the twentieth century and the outbreak of civil war in Nigeria in the mid-1960s. These works, some of them literary, some of them popular, dramatise in fascinating ways and from distinct perspectives the operations of the law in colonial and postcolonial Nigeria. My choice of fiction, and of newsprint in Chapter 6, is not accidental. As Benedict Anderson reminds us, in *Imagined Communities*, it is 'the novel and the newspaper' that provide the 'technical means for "re-presenting" the *kind* of imagined community that is the nation'.[3] Unlike Anderson, my interest is not in nationalism per se; nonetheless, in what follows I demonstrate why we should add 'the law' to Anderson's list of institutions that 'profoundly shaped the way in which the colonial state imagined its dominion'.[4] Moreover, if the novel

---

[1] Agbaje, *The Nigerian Press*, p. 40.
[2] James Fitzjames Stephen quoted in Hussain, *The Jurisprudence of Emergency*, p. 5.
[3] Anderson, *Imagined Communities*, p. 25.
[4] Ibid. pp. 163–4. Anderson names three such institutions: 'the census, the map, and the museum'.

and the newspaper provide the means to imagine 'the nation', whether colonially or independently understood, it follows that Agbaje's observation might be usefully illuminated by attending to their 're-presentation' of the law.

As the title of this book suggests, my interest diverges from Anderson's insofar as my focus is on the relationship between imagination and statehood, legally understood, more than the relationship between imagination and nation, socially understood. Admittedly, this distinction is not a neat one. Ideas of nationhood and statehood are frequently entangled: rhetorically, politically and emotionally. Consequently, some of the same issues of language, race and geography that preoccupy Anderson arise here too. My concern, however, is not to trace the emergence of the Nigerian nation and Nigerian national consciousness. Rather, in using the term 'states', I invoke ideas not only of statehood but also of the state of exception.

Giorgio Agamben's exploration of this concept at the turn of the millennium provides a suggestive reading of its origins in Roman law and its theorisation in the twentieth century, most extensively in Carl Schmitt. Nonetheless, despite his attention to its European applications, notably under National Socialism, Agamben appears scrupulous in avoiding acknowledgement of the colonial context to which his explication of the state of exception appears so apt. Indeed, as Marcelo Svirsky and Simone Bignall note in their introduction to *Agamben and Colonialism*, Agamben's work has been frequently criticised for its 'disregard for the specific histories and social circumstances of present states of exception, or relations of abandonment in colonial frameworks, and of colonial and imperial relations'.[5] Agamben might thus be understood to provide a valuable set of terms, but not a direct model for approaching the state of exception in the colonial context. Furthermore, despite gesturing to the role of imagination in the suspension of the law, Agamben never fully explores the place of imagination in *State of Exception*. Taking my lead from Anderson, in what follows I want to draw attention to the significance of that role of imagination, and in doing so to reconfigure our ideas about the state of exception in a colonial context.

---

[5] Svirsky and Bignall, *Agamben and Colonialism*, p. 6. See also Motha's 'Colonial Sovereignty, Forms of Life and Liminal Beings in South Africa'.

Whilst Agamben's name has been synonymous with thinking about the state of exception over the past two decades, he has not been alone in wanting to reconsider the implications of the state of exception. Interestingly in 2003, the same year that *State of Exception* was originally published as *Statio di eccezione*, both Nasser Hussain and Achille Mbembe very explicitly explored the relationship between colonialism and the legal exception.[6] In contrast to Agamben's resounding silence, Hussain argues that 'colonialism is the best historical example for any theoretical study of norm and exception, rule of law and emergency'.[7] Like Agamben, Hussain invokes Schmitt's definition of sovereignty as a starting point from which to unpack the paradoxical logic of exception. Schmitt declared that the 'sovereign is he who decides on the exception'.[8] This definition distinguishes sovereignty from the law as the power or force by which the law can be suspended. In a practical and political sense this is the force permitted to the state as sovereign power to suspend the rule of law in order to protect its sovereign interests. As Hussain points out, the fact that provision is made for this suspension of the rule of law in most modern constitutions highlights the intriguing propensity of 'legal systems in their theoretical and practical formulations ... [to] deliberate upon the conditions of their own failure'.[9] For, the conditions of 'emergency' on which any state of exception is presumed to rest must only arise as a consequence of the failure of the rule of law to maintain civil peace. In the colonial context this propensity (to 'deliberate upon the conditions of [the law's] failure') was at the heart of what became a defining characteristic of the law: its indeterminacy. Moreover, the propensity that Hussain highlights was crucial in underpinning the provisions made in the colonial legal system for creative latitude in administering both the law and its exception. As Hussain explains, '[if] a rule of law was the settled theoretical standard

---

[6] See Hussain, *The Jurisprudence of Emergency*; Mbembe, 'Necropolitics'. Mbembe observes that '[t]he colony represents the site where sovereignty consists fundamentally in the exercise of a power outside the law' (p. 23). A year earlier Robert Eaglestone noted the similarity between Agamben's camp and colonial legal practice. See 'On Giorgio Agamben's Holocaust'.
[7] Hussain, *The Jurisprudence of Emergency*, p. 31.
[8] Schmitt, *Political Theology*, p. 5; quoted in Hussain, *The Jurisprudence of Emergency*, p. 15 and in Agamben, *State of Exception*, p. 1.
[9] Hussain, *The Jurisprudence of Emergency*, p. 17.

of colonial politics, the institutional practices of the colonial state constantly fell short of such a standard.'[10]

Hussain presents the rule of law as associated inextricably with the civilising mission of empire, quoting James Fitzjames Stephen's emphatic declaration that '[o]ur law is in fact the sum and substance of what we have to teach [colonial subjects]. It is, so to speak, the gospel of the English, and it is a compulsory gospel which admits of no dissent and no disobedience.'[11] Nonetheless, the law's propensity to accommodate its own failure through the state of exception tempers the force of Stephen's declaration.[12] In fact we can go further than this: what the rhetoric of civilisation provided was exactly that 'new conception of sovereignty ... that was neither despotic nor democratic' which Hussain argues the British Empire required.[13] What the language of civilisation enabled was the erasure of the distinction between the rule of law and the state of exception. For, if rule of law and civilisation were indivisible, the declaration of the state of emergency under the sovereign authority of 'civilisation' could no longer be distinguished from the rule of law it ostensibly suspended. When we recognise this elision for what it is, we begin to see more clearly how the fabrication of the rule of law obscures the reality that the state of exception is always *a priori* to the law.

In the colonial context of Nigeria this elision was made possible in part by the consecration of legal actors as figures of legal creativity charged not with *following* the law but with *making* it, whether warrant chiefs (in the customary courts), alkalai (in the Islamic courts), or District Commissioners (in the English law courts, and charged with superintending customary and Islamic law too). As we shall see in Chapters 2 and 3, the figure of the District Commissioner in particular, both in fiction and in practice, came to embody the colonial administration's sovereign authority precisely. More generally, the provisionality and indeterminacy that characterised the application of English, customary and Islamic law (whose differences were themselves preserved on the premise of exceptional circumstances) during colonial rule frequently enabled the substitution of something with the force of law in the place of the rule of law itself.

---

[10] Ibid. p. 6.
[11] Quoted in Hunter, *A Life of the Earl of Mayo*, vol. 2, pp. 168–9; quoted in Hussain, *The Jurisprudence of Emergency*, p. 5.
[12] Lyndall Ryan similarly reminds us of the 'fragility of authority' that coincides with the frequent application of emergency powers. 'Martial Law in the British Empire', p. 93.
[13] Hussain, *The Jurisprudence of Emergency*, p. 25.

INTRODUCTION   5

As the foregoing account suggests, the state of exception's *a priori* relationship to the rule of law makes visible in the colony the imaginative fiction of the law. For whilst the state of exception remains undeclared, in the civility of the imperial metropole for example, the prosthesis of the rule of law remains undetected.[14] In the colony, however, the fiction of the rule of law emerges as just one form of legal invention amongst several that serve the sovereignty of a power that is neither state nor despot but itself a medium for other forces, not least commerce.[15] When the rule of law is suspended it is not that the state of exception is imposed, *on top of* the rule of law so to speak; rather the suspension of the rule of law is like the drawing back of the stage curtain to reveal behind it the state of exception that was always already there.

In what follows I take Agamben, Agbaje, Anderson, Hussain and Mbembe as my initial coordinates from which to chart my own exploration of this terrain. And, whilst the state of exception remains throughout a guiding focus for these explorations, my aim is not to provide a specifically 'Agambenian' or 'Mbembian', say, reading of the works under discussion. As I have suggested already, I hope instead to provide new configurations for thinking through the legal exception by attending to the lesser-commented role of imagination, and its literary corollary fiction, in the operations of the exception. I want to show how British and Nigerian fiction writers, sometimes consciously and sometimes not, attended to and made visible the inventive force of the law, not least in the suspension of the rule of law. For, although the conversations between law and literature studies on the one hand and postcolonial studies on the other have expanded over the past two decades, there have been no full-length studies of law and literature in West African and Nigerian fiction. Instead scholarly attention has tended to favour regions with historically particular legal systems, such as South Africa, and settler colonies, such as Kenya and Australia. Moreover, the majority of studies in law and colonialism/postcolonialism do not engage extensively with literature at all.[16] Where they do, attention tends to be given to contemporary literary fiction rather than earlier twentieth-century and/or popular fiction.

---

[14] Conrad's narrator, Marlow, alludes to this when he chides the apparent certitudes of his fellow mariners aboard the *Nellie* in 'Heart of Darkness': 'How could you [understand] … stepping delicately between the butcher and the policeman, in the holy terror of scandal and gallows and lunatic asylums.' 'Heart of Darkness' in *Youth and Two Other Stories*, pp. 132–3.
[15] Hussain makes a similar observation. See *The Jurisprudence of Emergency*, p. 25ff.
[16] There has been a gradual increase of attention to law and literature in Nigerian fiction in recent years. See, for example, Kortenaar, 'The Rule, the Law, and the Rule of Law in

A recent exception to this trend is Stephen Morton's *States of Emergency*, which explores the relationship between the state of exception, as Giorgio Agamben presents it, and colonial states of emergency as they appear in historical record and literary fiction in a variety of geographical contexts. Morton's interest, however, lies primarily in the extent to which these texts reflect the reality of the social, political and psychological effects of the application of the state of emergency.

In the following chapters, I examine the significance of the law in colonial and postcolonial fiction from the revocation of the Royal Niger Company's charter and the establishment of the Northern and Southern Protectorates in 1900, through to the military coups of 1966, which led to civil war. In the discrete period of the final half-century of British colonialism in Nigeria into the early years of independence prior to the civil war, the law provided a key site for the administration and for contemporary writers in their negotiations with the increasingly complex realities of the colonial project. As Morton has shown us, attending to the representation of the law in such fiction can provide important insights into the realities of the historical period. Equally importantly, such an analysis helps us to unpack the dominant and emergent discourses and ideologies that shaped those realities.

I have already noted Anderson's observation about the value of the novel and the newspaper. Focusing primarily on prose fiction also allows for a coherent discussion of the legal discourses and representations that emerge across high- and lowbrow publications. Indeed, whilst drama and poetry are interesting in their representations of the law, they have very particular modes of production and circulation distinct from prose and the novel. Any discussion of drama, for example, would require a very different critical framework to accommodate questions of performativity, situatedness and the politics of space. The same can be said for poetry, whose circulation and audience is frequently diffuse and diffused by publishing practices, whereby poems appear in widely varied journal and magazine venues prior to collection. These patterns of circulation, which also differ from newsprint, create considerable complications for the kind of historical-contextual approach taken here.

In the ensuing chapters, therefore, I explore a range of prose texts including popular, middlebrow and literary fiction, as well as newspaper

---

Achebe's Novels of Colonization'; Manji, '"Like a Mask Dancing"'; Osinubi, 'Abolition, Law and the Osu Marriage Novel'.

stories and memoirs, by both British and Nigerian authors in order to assess their representations of the law, and in particular the state of exception. In some instances the state of exception is foregrounded, in others it underpins a broader engagement with the indeterminacy of the law. In each case, however, my aim is to tease out how these texts reveal imagination's fundamental relationship to the law. This generally entails an examination of context first, followed by close analysis and finally theoretical explication. These explorations are organised chronologically and thematically, moving from the law 'upcountry' (focusing on pre- and inter-war British representations of the District Commissioner), through the law in the city (focusing on late colonial and early postcolonial Nigerian fiction), to law and politics (focusing on postcolonial Nigerian representations of treason and violence).

I start, however, in Chapter 1 with the historical context to these texts. Here I explain the processes of legal administration under colonialism and give an account of the political landscape of Nigeria before and after independence. As we shall see, the legal and political realms were frequently intertwined, not least in relation to suspensions of the law and declarations of emergency. Indeed, Obafemi Awolowo, a leading Nigerian politician of the era, opens his memoir with an account of precisely the legal indeterminacy I have outlined above: the District Commissioner's 'word was law' and 'the word of the Oba ... also became *something* of a law'.[17] Awolowo's choice to start here, with the elision of the rule of law and sovereign will under the rhetorical cover of 'civilisation', is made political by the memoir's publication date – 1960, the year of independence. A trained lawyer himself, Awolowo reminds his readers from the start of the legal inheritance of colonialism and calls for a new precedent of law and politics at independence, dedicating his book 'to a new and free Nigeria where individual freedom and a more abundant life are guaranteed to all her citizens'.[18] Drawing on Awolowo among others, the brief account given in Chapter 1 of the historical, legal and political context of Nigeria in the years under consideration provides the frame of reference for my discussion in the ensuing chapters.

Chapter 2 opens my engagement with fiction by examining early British representations of the law embodied in the figure of the District Commissioner. In the nineteenth century heroic action in West Africa had been represented by the freebooting adventurer, the missionary and

---

[17] Awolowo, *Awo*, pp. 8, 9; emphasis added.
[18] Ibid. frontispiece.

the trader.[19] Fiction took its cue from the explorations of independent figures like Henry Morton Stanley, whose exploits had captured the public's imagination at home. With the revocation of the Royal Niger Company's charter in 1900 and the establishment of the Northern and Southern Protectorates, however, an interesting shift occurs in the adventure tradition in which the District Commissioner comes to the fore. Indeed, we can discern what amounts to a new subgenre, District Commissioner fiction, in the first years of the twentieth century. This subgenre is significant because, while in the nineteenth century the colonial hero was typically represented one way or another as outside or beyond the law, District Commissioner fiction repositions the hero within and *as* the law. Edgar Wallace's Sanders of the River series is a classic example of this form, in which the series's eponymous hero, Sanders, embodies the civilised and civilising exceptionalism of colonial romance. Wildly improbable in their content, Wallace's novels were nonetheless hugely popular and drew on the exultant language that characterised the early accounts and memoirs of administrators, published in the same period. They thus provide a fascinating illustration of how the law was characterised in the imagination of the British public in this period.

By the 1930s, when Joyce Cary published *Mister Johnson*, attitudes were changing and Cary taps into some of the scepticism about the colonial project that emerged in the later inter-war years.[20] Cary, like his contemporary Evelyn Waugh, uses comedy to highlight the inefficiencies and incongruities of indirect rule. Setting the novel in the North of Nigeria, where he himself had served, Cary caricatures the complexities and arbitrariness of operating Islamic, customary and English law together under the will of the District Commissioner. Nonetheless, as I go on to show in Chapter 3, despite the novel's ironic critiques of the figure of the District Commissioner and the policy of indirect rule, Cary finally reinstates the heroised exceptionalism of earlier popular District Commissioner fiction.

Characteristic of almost all British colonial fiction about Nigeria from the pre- and inter-war years is the way in which it erases the urban settings

---

[19] For an early example of adventure fiction see Ballantyne's *The Gorilla Hunters*; for an example of missionary literature see [Freeman,] *Missionary Enterprise No Fiction*; for a late example of trader fiction see Shirley, *Up the Creeks*. Stephanie Newell identifies a particular subgenre of the trader adventure in 'Ruffian-Writing'. See 'Dirty Whites'. For a useful if incomplete checklist of West African adventure fiction in this period see Miller, 'Colonial West African Fiction, 1823–1914'.

[20] See, for example, W. R. Crocker's scathing memoir of colonial service, *Nigeria: A Critique of British Colonial Administration*.

of the coast. Comic or romantic in presentation, the action takes place upriver and upcountry on the edges of the 'known' geography. District Commissioners are presented as isolated or at most supported by a limited cast of one or two other white professionals (a doctor, say, or a missionary) and one or two more loyal African (but not always Nigerian) staff.[21] Moreover, in District Commissioner fiction at least, women are rarely present and tend only to be introduced as a problem or complication in the plot. Romance is eschewed or else displaced on to a secondary character, leaving the District Commissioner's sovereignty absolute. By contrast, Nigerian fiction from the inter-war years tended to focus on urban and romantic experience, and many of the first anglophone titles published internationally in the post-war period reflected these interests, despite the attention attracted by novels that represented 'traditional' culture such as Amos Tutuola's *The Palm-Wine Drinkard* (1952). Chapter 4 looks at Achebe's first urban novel, *No Longer at Ease*, in which a young Nigerian civil servant in the colonial administration is reduced to accepting bribes under the competing pressures of modern, urban life. I contextualise these pressures through reference to archival records of civil service life, the stories and advertisements that appeared in the contemporary popular press, and popular 'market literature' of the period. These points of reference reflect the pressures that Obi experiences in the novel: the pressures of love, sex, ambition, commodity culture and familial expectations. Achebe frames the novel with Obi's trial and in doing so draws attention not only to the challenge of judging Obi's case, given the incompatible pressures of late colonial urban life, but also to the larger challenge of how the state and the law can proceed after independence.

Exploration of these concerns is continued in Chapter 5, where two early novels by Cyprian Ekwensi are examined alongside a selection of market literature texts. Like District Commissioner fiction in Britain, Nigerian market literature provided an important locus for popular explorations of the law, although this fact is rarely commented upon in scholarship of the form.[22] Whether as a feature of plot, a meta-textual trope or a subject in its own right, the law appears repeatedly in market literature in the late colonial and early postcolonial period, often in surprisingly

---

[21] Arthur E. Southon's West African fiction frequently teams up a District Commissioner with a missionary. See, for example, *A Yellow Napoleon* and *The Taming of a King*.

[22] See Dodson, 'The Role of the Publisher in Onitsha Market Literature'; Newell, 'From the Brink of Oblivion'; Nwoga, 'Onitsha Market Literature'; Obiechina, 'Market Literature in Nigeria'. Stephanie Newell, however, does discuss the role of the law in late twentieth-century Nigerian popular fiction in 'Petrified Masculinities?'.

audacious and inventive ways. Like Achebe in the same period, Ekwensi draws on market literature to highlight the challenges that arose from the fundamental incongruities of colonial and postcolonial urban life, not least in the repeated abandonment of the law. *People of the City* and *Jagua Nana* depict the rapidly changing urban experience of the 1950s and 1960s in Lagos, and the ways in which the law intrudes itself upon men and women as they try to negotiate the expectations of city life.

The final section turns to representations of the law and politics in the immediate postcolonial period. Chapter 6 opens this section by looking at the press coverage of the treason trial of Awolowo and twenty-four others in 1962–3, the second major treason trial after Nigeria's independence. The trial ran for almost a year and was covered by Nigerian newspapers of every political persuasion on a daily basis. Focusing here on reportage rather than fiction, I show how journalists tried to engage their readers in the stakes of the trial using a variety of tropes, not least humour and pathos. As I demonstrate, the trial was ideologically freighted, coming as it did on the eve of Nigeria's declaration of the first Federal Republic. The creation and exclusion of the treasonable felon at this crucial moment was necessary to establish the state as such, through the legal identification of what was beyond its limits. The trial therefore reflects the continued negotiation between politics and the law inherited from the colonial administration at the point of independence. At the heart of this negotiation is the paradox that while Awolowo and his fellow defendants were charged with treasonable felony against the sovereign body of Queen Elizabeth, who remained the head of state following independence, Nnamdi Azikiwe's government were going through the ritual process of abrogating the Queen's sovereign power over the state in order to give that power to themselves in the declaration of the Republic.

Chapter 7 builds on the previous chapter's analysis to read Achebe's *A Man of the People*, focusing on the novel's engagement with the political corruption and foment of the years leading up to the Nigerian civil war, epitomised in the Awolowo trial. Achebe set the novel in an unnamed African state and thereby sought to represent the larger problems of newly independent African countries in general. Nonetheless, the coincidence of its publication with the military coups of 1966 led many to assume Achebe's involvement in or at least commitment to the initial Igbo uprising. Achebe's novel dramatises how the colonial dispersal of the law through a constant state of exception is replicated rather than resolved in the newly independent state. As had been the case under the colonial administration, commerce and individual power divert and defuse the rule of law, now under a new rhetoric of nationalism. This rhetoric is epitomised in the ironic national branding of OHMS – 'our home made stuff'. Whilst the politicians of the novel exhort the public to buy OHMS in the cause of national prosperity, they demand for themselves in private the products of the multinational companies they publicly condemn. Moreover, the reworking of the acronym signposts its familiar origin, 'on her majesty's service', thereby reinstating the sovereign power of colonial trade at the very moment of its apparent rejection.

As this synopsis makes clear, the scope of the following chapters is wide-ranging. In bringing together British and Nigerian works, popular and literary fiction, newspapers and novels, my aim is to demonstrate how concerns about the law in Nigeria permeated multiple narrative forms in the late colonial and early postcolonial era. What the ensuing discussions also make clear is the role of invention and imagination not only in the representation of the law but also in its operation and in its suspension. As Mbembe reminds us, 'the colony represents the site where sovereignty consists fundamentally in the exercise of a power outside the law (*ab legibus solutus*) and where "peace" is more likely to take on the face of a "war without end."'[23] This fact was to have repercussions beyond independence. Each of the narratives examined here, whether romantic, comic or critical, articulates the crisis point at which the prosthesis of the rule of law becomes evident and the imagined state, the state of exception, is revealed.

---

[23] Mbembe, 'Necropolitics', p. 23.

1

'Natural Justice, Equity and Good Conscience': History, Politics and Law in Nigeria, 1900–1966

In his autobiography the Nigerian politician Obafemi Awolowo tells a story from his childhood of listening to his father and his father's friends discussing 'the white man's regime':

> I remember quite vividly that father in particular and some of his friends strongly condemned what they used to describe as *'Mashai-Lo'*. My understanding was that *Mashai-Lo* was a Yoruba phrase the English rendering of which is: 'It is compulsory to go.' Father held the strong view that with all he [the white man] had done in suppressing intertribal war, slavery and slave-trade, and in introducing Christianity, it was a blemish on his record for the white man to introduce *'Mashai-Lo'*. My childish brain and imagination could not quite puzzle out what the compulsion was about. When I grew older and became literate in English, however, I understood the phrase to mean 'Martial Law'.[1]

Martial law is a state of exception in which the rule of law is suspended by the declaration of a state of emergency. In place of the legislative bodies of government, the military act with the force of law without recourse to the law. In some instances such a state of exception might last days, in others martial law becomes the norm and, as Achille Mbembe suggests, '"peace" ... [takes] on the face of a "war without end"'.[2] In fact, Awolowo suggests that his father used the phrase 'in an entirely inappropriate context'. Before 1914, he explains, Ijebu Remo, the district from which he hailed, 'was administered as part of the Colony District of Lagos, and Remo people were regarded as British subjects'.[3] In 1914 indirect rule was introduced to the Southern

---

[1] Awolowo, *Awo*, p. 17.
[2] Mbembe, 'Necropolitics', p. 23. For a useful discussion of the history of British imperial martial law, see Ryan, 'Martial Law in the British Empire'.
[3] Awolowo, *Awo*, p. 17.

provinces of Nigeria, and with it Ijebu Remo's Nigerian inhabitants were reclassified before the law. It was this reclassifying that Awolowo's father had in mind when he used the term '*Mashai-Lo*'.

In his autobiography, Awolowo reflects on the problem of *Mashai-Lo*, and his memory of his father's conversations expands into a reflection on society and the law:

> The society into which I was born was one which was riddled with fear, uncertainty and suppression. There was the fear of the white man who was the supreme lord of any area placed under his jurisdiction. *His word was law*, and his actions could never be called in question ... The sources of the people's fear of him were his strange colour, his uncanny power to shoot people down at long range, and his obviously unimpeachable authority. There was the fear of the white man's carriers and messengers who were *a law unto themselves*.
>
> There was the fear of the local chieftains who were more or less agents of the British Government ... In due course ... the word of the Oba [Chief] and his Chiefs also became *something of a law* ... It required a good deal of guts to write petitions criticising the Oba and his Chiefs. It was regarded by many white men, then in the Administrative Service, as gross impudence bordering on sedition to write critical letters, petitions, or remonstrances about an Oba. During the first five years of this century, two educated citizens of Ijebu Remo who summoned up enough courage to call attention in a petition to what they regarded as glaring cases of injustice and misrule on the part of one of the Remo Obas, were arrested, tried summarily, and sent to gaol for some months for their impertinence.[4]

Not technically martial law, the *Mashai-Lo* against which Awolowo's father complained was nothing less than the systematisation of the state of exception. Awolowo's youthful mishearing of the phrase '*Mashai-Lo*', and his association of it with the Yoruba phrase 'it is compulsory to go', serendipitously echoes the acts of legal mistranslation at the foundation of indirect rule. More than this, though, Awolowo's unwitting substitution of martial law, the legal sanctioning of the suspension of the law, with an anonymous injunction gestures to the indeterminacy of the law that the state of exception introduced under colonial rule.

---

[4] Ibid. pp. 7–9; emphasis added.

Nigeria and Colonisation

Prior to the imposition of British colonialism, theories and practices of statehood and jurisprudence varied across the territories that are now circumscribed by Nigeria's legal borders. In the nineteenth century the North was predominantly ruled by the Sokoto Caliphate, which held together a large number of independent but loyal emirates extending from present-day Burkina Faso to the Cameroons under the leadership of the Sultan of Sokoto. Islamic law consequently predominated throughout the Caliphate. In the Southern and Western regions the Yoruba were organised in city states ruled in some instances by kingship and in other instances elected leadership, but in all cases with a strong culture of elders' councils which provided checks and balances to governance. Here Yoruba religion was practised alongside Islam, introduced from the North by the Fulani in the fourteenth century, and later with the coming of European, Liberian and Sierra Leonean missionaries Christianity took hold. In the South and East governance was managed locally through republican assemblies led by a council of elders, with a few notable exceptions such as the major trading hub, Onitsha, where an Oba or king ruled. Odinani, Igbo religious practice, predominated until the coming of the missionaries in the nineteenth century and the region remained almost untouched by Islam until the twentieth century. Alongside these differences of governance and social organisation, differences of language, cultural practice and traditions distinguished communities between the Northern, Western and Eastern regions and also within them. For example, whereas twins were generally treated as a taboo in Igbo culture, requiring ritual abandonment by their parents, in Yoruba culture twins were considered to be protected by the thunder god, Shango, and were celebrated.[5]

As this cursory outline makes clear, pre-colonial geographies, statehoods and cultural identities do not map coherently on to the boundaries which the British imposed and repeatedly recalibrated during the colonial administration. Indeed, the diversity of the region was a continual challenge to Britain in establishing and maintaining colonial rule and in due course became the primary challenge to stability for Nigeria following independence. The story of Nigeria's colonisation is thus inevitably shaped by this diversity as much as it is by the varied and at times conflicting aims of colonial administration in the region.

---

[5] For a literary example of the taboo of twins in Igbo culture, see Chinua Achebe's *Things Fall Apart*.

British interests in West Africa were established through the slave trade and for much of the eighteenth century the British presence in the region was directed to that end. This trade fuelled and was in turn fed by regional and ethnic conflicts in the interior of West Africa, often characterised by the capture and sale of neighbouring populations. Thus although certain traditions of slavery were already indigenous to West Africa, the extraordinary volume of European demand inevitably undermined political stability in the region and exacerbated rivalries. As a consequence, by the end of the eighteenth century several of the old empires such as the Edo and the Oyo were on the verge of collapse. Thus, even before legal control was exerted over the region, imperial actions had had wide-ranging political consequences. With the British abolition of the slave trade in 1807 (slavery in the Empire was not abolished until 1833) Britain's trading interests changed but did not recede. The Delta region's high productivity in palm oil was rapidly tapped to supply the manufacture of everything from soap to industrial lubricants. Moreover, following the 1807 bill of abolition, the establishment of the West Africa Squadron of the Royal Navy in 1808 and the ensuing international treaties that the British government established to allow the squadron to stop and search not only British but foreign ships suspected of slave trafficking gave Britain a new and specifically legal role in the region. Vice-Admiralty courts and mixed commission courts were established along the coast and Sierra Leone became home not only to the squadron but also to the Governor of the Gold Coast.

By the mid-nineteenth century the transatlantic slave trade from West Africa had been all but stamped out; however, Britain's reliance on the region's commodities, not only at home but also across the Empire, entrenched its colonial presence. The river Niger, in particular, was a site of repeated exploration with the aim of opening up the interior of the region for trade. To do so, it was hoped, would enable British businesses to bypass the local traders on the coast who had become hugely successful in their control of the supply of palm oil from the interior. As trade and exploration increased Britain expanded its legal jurisdiction, establishing a Court of Equity at Bonny in 1850 to adjudicate trade disputes and the Lagos Crown Colony in 1861. Competition between British traders and adventurers in the region nonetheless increased in the second half of the nineteenth century as demand for palm oil continued unabated. In an attempt to resolve the negative financial impact of commercial rivalries the entrepreneur George Taubman Goldie (later Sir George Goldie) began to amalgamate leading companies in the region with the aim of establishing a guaranteed monopoly through chartered company status.

Following the scandal and demise of the East India Company, chartered companies had been a less common form of administration in the British Empire, and Goldie met with initial resistance from Gladstone's government. At the Berlin Conference (1884–5), however, Goldie argued successfully to bring his company's holdings under a British sphere of interest and the following year, in 1886, he was finally granted a charter for the Royal Niger Company. Under its charter the company took responsibility for administration of the areas it controlled along the Niger and the Benue as well as monopolising trade in those areas. Both these ends were met through hundreds of treaties established with local leaders and councils conferring sole trading rights and sovereign powers to the Company. To ensure compliance the Company also established its own militia. The Company's chartered status did not last long, however. Changes in government policy at home, the threat of increasing encroachment by French and German trading interests, and the complexity for the British government of attempting to coordinate across three different forms of administration (chartered company, protectorate and colony) led to the revocation of the Royal Niger Company's charter and the establishment of two protectorates (North and South) in 1900. In 1906 Lagos Colony was added to the Southern Nigeria Protectorate, and in 1914 the Northern and Southern Protectorates were amalgamated into the colony of Nigeria by Frederick Lugard following his appointment in 1912 as governor of both protectorates simultaneously.

As this brief account indicates, nineteenth-century British colonial interests in West Africa generally, and Nigeria in particular, transformed over the years: at times these were opportunistic, at times juridical, at times expedient, and often informed by other transnational interests (international treaties concerning the policing of the slave trade; demands for West African commodities in other regions of the Empire). Moreover, rarely did these interests demonstrate a consistent concern for the political, financial and social well-being of the indigenous populations. Consequently British activities in the region repeatedly met with violent resistance, whether to the resettlement of freed slaves in Sierra Leone in the late eighteenth century, or to the monopolistic administration of the Royal Niger Company at the end of the nineteenth century.

At the start of the twentieth century the colonial administration began to use the pretext of internecine strife and inter-tribal oppression to justify military responses to local resistance. This was the case, for example, in the Anglo-Aro War of 1901–2 where liberation of the Igbo from Aro subjugation was the justification provided for repeated military excursions into the Eastern region. Significantly, we see here the rhetoric of benevolent civilisation enter into the discourse of colonial governance in Nigeria. Military action was no longer explained as a necessity to protect commercial interests, as it had been in the nineteenth century, but rather as a liberating intervention to establish political freedom for the Igbo and thereby to bring them and the Aro under the civilising influence of colonial rule. This shift in rhetoric signals the shift in governmental approach to the nexus of civilisation-exception that was to shape policy over the following sixty years.

The exact extent of this civilising influence was to prove as liable to revision and general tinkering under colonial rule as were the geographical boundaries of the protectorates and regions that came to make up Nigeria. Nonetheless, recognising the significance of this shift in rhetoric from one of commercial interests to governance is crucial to understanding how the law was conceptualised imaginatively in the first half of the twentieth century, up to and beyond independence in 1960. And this imaginative apprehension of the law in Nigeria would emerge as much from fiction as from the practical responses of lawmakers and law enforcers. The law no longer operated simply to protect British commercial interests or to secure the safety from enslavement of West African populations; now the law aimed to initiate change within those populations. That change was summed up in a word that became almost totemic in the literature about the colonial mission in West Africa: civilisation. Indeed, this word, 'civilisation', came to justify an astonishing legal freedom and inventiveness for the colonial administration. This freedom turned the will of the colonial administrator (most commonly the District Commissioner) into law, or rather into something that was not, but acted as, the law.

Government and Politics

The prime architect of the colonial system of government in Nigeria was Frederick Lugard, whose paradigm of indirect rule was to shape the legal and political character of Nigeria definitively. Indirect rule was a system of local government whereby an individual local ruler was appointed by the colonial administration to rule over a given community or cluster of communities answerable only to the colonial administration and responsible not only for implementing colonial regulations (such as the collection of tax) but also for administering 'customary law', that is to say settling legal disputes according to local tradition. Lugard's initial experience in Nigeria was as governor of the Northern Nigeria Protectorate between 1900 and 1906, the region that had previously been administered by the Royal Niger Company. Here the Sokoto Caliphate provided a more or less ready-made Islamic legal system that lent itself to indirect rule. The relative familiarity and stability of the Islamic system (monotheistic, essentially feudal, hegemonic) suited the needs of the administration particularly well.[6] In the North this model enabled the limited number of British colonial administrators to rely upon local rulers to keep the peace and support colonial governance. The emirate structure of the Caliphate thus provided Lugard with a template which he attempted to reapply in the Southern regions on his return as governor in 1912.

As we have seen, however, the Southern regions of Nigeria were far more diverse in their systems of governance and often eschewed the model of a single ruler. As a consequence, indirect rule mapped far less easily on to these regions. District Commissioners were obliged to identify suitable leaders to be made into warrant chiefs and inevitably in doing so often chose unwisely and/or stirred up local rivalries, creating and fuelling civil discord. In *Arrow of God*, Chinua Achebe dramatises exactly such a situation when the Commissioner, Winterbottom, decides with no local consultation to appoint Ezeulu as warrant chief for the villages of Umuaro. Ezeulu, chief priest of the god Ulu, has been a respected voice among the elders of his village for a long time but he has begun to fall from favour, in part because he has sent one of his sons to a mission school but also because of his decision to side against his own village in a long-running land dispute. Ezeulu is summoned to Winterbottom's station to be offered the chieftaincy. When he refuses, on the grounds that it is contrary to Umuaro's custom, he is locked up and remains imprisoned for several weeks. His imprisonment means he is unable to fulfil the particular rites necessary to the declaration of the yam harvest and as a consequence a famine sets in amongst the community. Eventually the new Church promises to protect the villagers from the taboo of harvesting without Ulu's permission. The novel thus ends with the Church reaping the harvest of converts with their yams whilst Ezeulu and his god are abandoned.

Winterbottom's intervention is such that whether Ezeulu agrees or not, the social cohesion of Umuaro in its 'customary' state is bound to be destroyed. Were Ezeulu to agree to the chieftaincy the increasing disfavour of the villagers towards him would no doubt be enflamed to crisis

---

[6] It was also a system familiar to administrators from their experience in other African colonial regions such as Sudan. Indeed, as Allan Christelow points out, '[m]any of the key British personnel in Nigeria in the 1950s had transferred there from Sudan after that country's independence in 1952 … and naturally took Sudan as a model of modernization within an Islamic framework.' See 'Islamic Law and Judicial Practice in Nigeria', p. 194.

point. Ezeulu's refusal instead garners Winterbottom's disfavour and leads to the disruption of the local agrarian calendar with disastrous results. Achebe carefully underwrites this narrative with the particular irony that early on in the novel Winterbottom himself expresses a lack of faith in the system he attempts to impose: 'What do we British do? We flounder from one expedient to its opposite. We do not only promise to secure old savage tyrants on their thrones ... but we now go out of our way to invent chiefs where there were none before.'[7] Even where the self-awareness that Achebe permits Winterbottom was present, however, faced with 'the cultural resistance of the African population to the policy of assimilation, the British understood better than any other colonial power the need for a policy that would harness culturally legitimate political allies', as Mahmood Mamdani argues.[8] Indirect rule thus sought to work within the customary, and where the customary did not map helpfully on to the needs of the administration, new traditions were imposed prosthetically in order to shape the customary to the colonial will.

As well as the moral rhetoric of preserving cultural integrity and independence, another argument frequently made for indirect rule was practical and numerical necessity. Mamdani suggests that in the Northern Nigerian Protectorate in 1906 'the ratio of European civil officers was something like 1 to 2,900 square miles and 1 to 45,000 Africans'. By 1921 the ratio for Nigeria was one British administrator to 100,000 natives.[9] Thus, it was argued, the decentralisation of indirect rule was a necessity in order to ensure effective management of the colony. Mamdani reminds us, however, that 'the key argument in this logical construct [the scarcity of trained administrators] was artificially created; it was not inevitable'.[10] This is because throughout the nineteenth century in the coastal colonies a large, highly educated and well-trained workforce of Africans had developed, contributing to the legal and commercial administration of the region. Rather than handing over further control, however, the turn of the century saw colonial policy turn away from the African elite, who were thought to be alienated from the customary by their education, in favour of 'traditional' leaders identified locally through District Commissioners like Winterbottom.

---

[7] Achebe, *Arrow of God*, p. 36.
[8] Mamdani, *Citizen and Subject*, p. 76.
[9] Ibid. p. 73.
[10] Ibid. p. 74.

The consequences were predictable. The administration's preference for 'traditional' – which often meant uneducated – local rulers set the intellectual elites of coastal cities like Lagos against the chieftaincy cultures of the interior. Moreover, by making these local rulers answerable to the administration rather than the communities over whom they were set to rule, abuses of power were common. Rulers, unfettered by a sense of responsibility to their community and often with no tradition of monarchical good practice on which to draw, could all too easily see the role as an invitation to extortion through their function as tax collectors and legal authorities. When complaints, such as those Awolowo records in his autobiography, were made to the British administration they were often left unresolved, in part because the administration wanted to avoid appearing to have made mistakes or to be open to partisan persuasion, but also because the large areas covered and the frequent relocation of officers by the administration resulted in a singular lack of consistency in the governing of any given area. At the same time, the administrative bypassing of the intellectual elites understandably fed their aspirations for independence, prompting a well-organised and articulate resistance movement that spoke out regularly through its own press and publications in Nigeria and through the Nigerian student unions overseas. As we shall see, the political parties of the post-war years that led the country to independence emerged out of this pre-war intellectual elite and remained closely tied to the press both ideologically and financially.[11]

At the end of the Second World War the colonial government imposed a new constitution in 1946 without consultation. This established three regional legislatures in the Northern, Eastern and Western provinces (the South having been divided into Eastern and Western provinces in 1939). It also established a Nigerian legislative council. The constitution was resisted, however, not least because the various legislatures were to be populated by colonial appointment rather than election, meaning that their representational force was essentially symbolic. Following considerable lobbying by Nigerian politicians and activists, including a delegation of the National Council of Nigeria and the Cameroons to London in 1947 spearheaded by the journalist and party leader Nnamdi Azikiwe, a new constitution was instated in 1951 and a third in 1954. These new constitutions introduced democratic elections and a federal organisation of the legislatures, which remained tied to the three regions established

---

[11] For a detailed account of Nigeria's political landscape prior to and at independence, see Sklar, *Nigerian Political Parties*.

in 1939 (North, West and East). These constitutions effectively replaced Lugard's system of indirect rule by making Nigerian representation in government responsible to the electorate rather than the colonial administration. In 1957 self-government was granted to the Eastern and Western Regions, while the North, where political support for independence had been comparatively reluctant, finally gained self-government in 1959, the same year in which federal elections took place to establish the members of the federal government who would lead the country into independence in 1960.

In this process the three parties to dominate Nigerian politics between the end of the Second World War and the disintegration of the first Republic into civil war in 1966 were consolidated. These were the Northern People's Congress (NPC) led by the Sardauna of Sokoto, Alhaji Ahmadu Bello; the National Council of Nigeria and the Cameroons (NCNC) led by Azikiwe; and the Action Group (AG) led by Awolowo. What distinguished these parties was less their ideological differences than their regional and ethnic affiliations. Thus although each party sought election across Nigeria, the NCNC came to be associated with the Igbo and the Eastern Region, the AG with the Yoruba and the West, and the NPC with the Hausa-Fulani and the North. While ideological distinctions were limited (the NPC was more conservative than the AG and the NCNC; the AG was more radical than either the NPC or the NCNC), political discourse came to be increasingly characterised by regional and ethnic rivalries and mistrust. In 1966 these tensions boiled over in a coup and counter-coup that led rapidly and inexorably to civil war between the Eastern Region, which declared itself the Republic of Biafra in 1967, and the Western and Northern Regions.

Legal Practice

At independence in 1960 Nigeria took over the legal structures that it had inherited from the colonial administration. 'English' law had been practised in the coastal cities by both British and Nigerian lawyers at the end of the nineteenth century and the law continued under colonial rule to be a popular choice of degree for those Nigerians well-placed enough to study overseas. Whilst it was undoubtedly a male-dominated field, Nigerian women also trained in law during this period, notably Stella Thomas, who was called to the Bar in 1933 and became Nigeria's first female magistrate a decade later, and Modupe Omo-Eboh, who was called to the Bar in 1953 and became Nigeria's first female high court judge in 1969. At independence English law was adopted with minimal adaptation under the new federal constitution and continued to be practised by both Nigerian and British members of the Nigerian Bar.[12]

Whilst the introduction of democratic elections under the various constitutions of the 1950s curtailed the powers of warrant chiefs by making their positions essentially ceremonial, in the Eastern and Western Regions the dual legal systems of customary and English courts remained, albeit with customary courts limited in their responsibility to regional, rather than the central federal, legislatures. It was only following the military coup in 1966 that the role of customary courts in the various regions was significantly reviewed.[13] Throughout colonial Nigeria the customary and Islamic courts had been subject to oversight and intervention by the administration. Customary law was famously subject to the limitations of the repugnancy test, which required that customary law was not 'repugnant to natural justice, equity and good conscience' and that it was not incompatible with any other law concurrently in force (that is to say the English law of the colonial courts).[14] In practice this meant that as well as referring serious crimes from customary courts to colonial courts (although different rules applied in the North, where Islamic courts were allowed more latitude), both what was permitted under customary law and customary punishment for transgression were scrutinised for their adherence to English legal norms. In ideological terms the elision of these three criteria with English legal norms was a declaration of the civilising force of the legal process, since 'natural justice, equity and good conscience' were imagined as indistinguishable from civilisation as/and the English legal norm.

Christelow's description of the impact of such intervention on the Islamic courts is equally relevant to the Southern customary courts: 'While the British insisted that the native courts administer new legal principles, they offered no Islamic rationale for it. Traditional rulers and their legal advisors were left to improvise their own rationale.'[15] Particularly frustrating were the 'structures of appeal or revision' created by the British (and later federal judicial) authorities, whereby appeals against a ruling in customary or Islamic courts were referred to the colonial and later 'English'

---

[12] As we shall see in Chapter 6, the question of British members of the Nigerian Bar practising in the Nigerian courts after independence became a matter of serious contention in the treasonable felony trial of Obafemi Awolowo in 1962.

[13] See Nwogugu, 'Abolition of Customary Courts'.

[14] For a more detailed discussion of the repugnancy test, see Taiwo, 'Repugnancy Clause and its Impact on Customary Law'.

[15] Christelow, 'Islamic Law and Judicial Practice in Nigeria', p. 190.

law courts.[16] In response, despite British demands that records be kept in Roman-scripted Hausa, Islamic courts regularly recorded their proceedings in Arabic, thereby limiting British oversight since few administrators read the language even if they could speak a little.[17]

Thus, three bodies of law were inherited from the colonial administration: customary, Islamic and English (statute, common law and equity). The application and inheritance of English common law, in particular, was a matter of discussion at independence. Firstly, the phrasing of the colonial ordinance (originally issued in 1876 and modified in 1900) made it possible to interpret this inheritance in several ways. While it was clear that 'the statutes of general application which were in force in England on [1 January 1900]' were to be applied, the phrasing makes it unclear whether common law and equity were to be governed strictly by that date as well or whether developments in English common law after 1900 (or in common law taken as a universal system) would provide precedent for application in Nigeria. Secondly, there was discussion about the extent to which, in retaining English common law at independence, Nigeria could develop its own body of common law. Ghana, for example, had explicitly abandoned English common law as precedent in 1960, importing 'the concept of common law and equity as a world-wide system of law' instead.[18] Nigeria's federal regions chose to interpret this inheritance more or less explicitly, so that while the Eastern Region retained the old phrasing, the Western Region replaced it with phrasing that explicitly linked its common law to current English common law.[19]

The debates over common law in Nigeria in this period reveal an important underlying issue: as a result of the regular reconfigurations of legislatures and interventions in legal custom that took place during colonial rule, there was little opportunity for a specifically Nigerian body of precedents necessary to common law to develop. This fact, in turn, reminds us that the practice of law under colonial rule in the twentieth century was inherently inventive since even where precedent could be invoked or was nominally encouraged (as under customary law) it was nonetheless subject to relentless revision in the service of 'civilisation', which was in turn underwritten by the repugnancy test.

---

[16] Ibid.
[17] See ibid. p. 192.
[18] Bennion, *The Constitutional Law of Ghana*, p. 405; quoted in Allott, 'The Common Law of Nigeria', p. 37.
[19] Allott, 'The Common Law of Nigeria', p. 40.

In *The Image of Law*, Alexandre Lefebvre argues that the law is inherently creative, particularly when faced with a case for which there is no precedent to which that case can be subsumed. The judge, argues Lefebvre, must exercise creativity in resolving the facts presented into a recognisable case that can make itself available for judgement. Whilst Lefebvre develops his argument in relation to North American law and European philosophy, his paradigm of creativity in the process of formulating a case for judgement in the absence of precedent illuminates the importance of creativity, inventiveness and the imagination in colonial law, where the bodies of precedent available were limited and always at best provisional.

Indeed, the provisionality of the law in this period is evident in the implicit flexibility written into the legal handbooks to which administrators were advised to refer (and yet were expected to ignore). Thus in Edwin Arney Speed's introduction to the 1908 edition of *Richards's Table of Offences*, he explains that the crown's jurisdiction 'is exercised subject to certain limitations, ill defined and in many cases almost indeterminate'.[20] This provisionality is matched in the phrase used by the Muslim courts in the North to describe the force of law under colonial rule, 'hukm zamanna': 'the law of our times'. Christelow glosses this phrase with the explanation that 'British overrule was seen as a sort of temporary deviation which would soon pass', allowing Islamic law to return to its path undisturbed.[21] Thus District Commissioners applying English law, alkalai (judges) applying Islamic law, and warrant chiefs applying customary law were equally subject to the necessity of invention, repeatedly adapting their legal practices to the changing demands of the administration.

There is a challenge here, of course, as to how far the law can operate inventively and remain recognisable as the law per se: at what point does such invention become an exception to the law – an action with the force of law which nonetheless is no longer within the bounds of the law? Agamben suggests that where exceptional measures 'find themselves in the paradoxical position of being juridical measures that cannot be understood in legal terms ... the state of exception appears as the legal form of what cannot have legal form'.[22] Concurrently, he proposes an alternative model for understanding the state of exception, where 'the law employs the exception – that is the suspension of the law itself – as its original means of referring to and encompassing life'.[23] In this model 'the state

---

[20] Speed, *Richards's Table of Offences*, p. v.
[21] Christelow, 'Islamic Law and Judicial Practice in Nigeria', p. 190.
[22] Agamben, *State of Exception*, p. 1.
[23] Ibid.

of exception is the preliminary condition for any definition of the relation that binds and, at the same time, abandons the living being to law'. In both instances the state of exception is located 'at the limit between politics and law'.[24]

The constructed necessity of legal invention, imposed by indirect rule, created what was in essence a perpetual state of exception. I say 'constructed' because legal invention was only necessary because of the imposition of indirect rule: legal invention might have been avoided had the administration chosen to impose a single legal code consistently across the colony, for example. Instead, law's inherent indeterminacy in the colony posited the exception as originary, the 'preliminary condition' of the law's operations, to borrow Agamben's phrase. This construction legitimised the collapsing of the law into the body of those charged with its administration, most commonly the District Commissioner. The District Commissioner *became* the law. Moreover, in the longer term the impact of this construction, in which the state of exception stands *a priori* to the law, reverberated all the way into Nigerian independence.

In the following chapters we see how the legal invention, indeterminacy and exception outlined here were variously valorised, satirised and critiqued in fiction and the press during this period. In British fiction particularly, the state of exception is foregrounded; elsewhere it forms part of a larger interrogation of the law, as, for example, in the early urban fiction of Achebe and Cyprian Ekwensi. Following independence the specific inheritance of indirect rule emerges concretely once again in the press coverage of Awolowo's trial and in Achebe's *A Man of the People*. In each case, however, we can see how the law was consistently a key site for British and Nigerian writers to think through the history, politics and inheritance of colonial rule in Nigeria.

---

[24] Ibid. See also *Homo Sacer*, where Agamben aligns these two versions of the state of exception with the thinking of Gershom Scholem and Walter Benjamin respectively (p. 53).

2

'I Am the Law': District Commissioner Fiction and the State of Exception

In this chapter I want to examine a significant subgenre that emerges from popular colonial adventure fiction at the turn of the century: District Commissioner fiction. This form of adventure fiction places the figure of the law, embodied by the District Commissioner, at its heart and in doing so enables us to appreciate the significance of the law as a pre-eminent site for popular culture's engagement with the colonial project in the period.

As we have seen in the Introduction, postcolonial critics have drawn attention to the way in which legal and political theories of the state of exception map in compelling ways on to the structures of colonial administration.[1] What has been discussed less is the way in which popular fiction reflected and perpetuated a view of the colonial project as one built upon a self-justifying paradigm of legal exceptionalism. District Commissioner fiction was one such popular form that celebrated the enabling legal paradox of the state of exception through repeated narratives of the Commissioner's capacity to step outside the law in his enforcement of the law. At the same time, the romance of District Commissioner fiction lent a rhetorical structure to colonialism's ideological teleology. In the romance of colonialism's teleology, civilisation triumphs as a result of the heroic law-giver who is able to enforce his will fantastically. Thus, the romantic heroism of the lone white man, ruling single-handedly great swathes of primitive Africa through a 'floating *imperium*', infiltrates the memoirs, diaries and letters of those associated with the colonial administration of Nigeria as much as it defines a subgenre of fiction.[2]

Colonial adventure romance, like the state of exception, creates a space devoid of law, a 'non-place' for the reader in which actions that might otherwise be understood to be transgressive, not least an inventive

---

[1] See, for example, Hussain, *The Jurisprudence of Emergency*; Mbembe, 'Necropolitics'; Morton, *States of Emergency*; Svirsky and Bignall, *Agamben and Colonialism*.
[2] See Agamben, *State of Exception*, p. 51.

approach to the law, are sanctioned because they occur within this exceptional realm of romance.³ For Agamben, this non-place in which actions can take on the force of law whilst exempting themselves from the law and, indeed, whilst erasing the possibility of recourse to the law is frequently figured as geographical space: the camp, the nation state and the city state. In adventure romance the non-place of exceptionalism is similarly imagined in terms of colonial geography, even where that geography is itself fantasised.

The non-place of the state of exception, however, is also a state of mind. Coleridge, in a famous passage of *Biographia Literaria*, describes how Wordsworth and he divided up their subject matter when preparing material for *Lyrical Ballads*: while Wordsworth was 'to give the charm of novelty to things of every day', Coleridge was to write about 'characters supernatural, or at least romantic, yet so as to transfer from our inward nature ... a semblance of truth sufficient to procure for these shadows of imagination that willing suspension of disbelief for the moment, which constitutes poetic faith'.⁴ If the pleasure of romance, not least adventure romance, can be located in a willingness to suspend disbelief in order to grant truth to 'shadows of imagination', the state of exception is likewise brought into being through a more or less willing suspension of disbelief, what Agamben calls a 'fictional lacuna', that aims to secure the legal norm through its revocation.⁵ The state of exception, adventure romance and twentieth-century colonial administration in West Africa, then, share this reliance on a knowing (if not directly willed) suspension of disbelief as foundation and fulcrum to their counterfactual structures.

It is this striking alignment of the rhetorical and narrative structure of adventure romance with colonial administrative ideology and the state of exception that I wish to explore here. To do so I start by providing a genealogy of sorts for District Commissioner fiction, outlining its literary and historic context. I then move on to consider the typical features of the genre, before showing how these novels represent the District Commissioner as the embodiment of both civilisation and the authority that underpins the state of exception. Analysing the fiction in this way reveals how the genre's own history and modes enable it to promote an imaginary figure of the exception who is both fantastical and yet closely tied to the ideals of the colonial administration.

---

³ Ibid.
⁴ Coleridge, *Biographia Literaria*, p. 174.
⁵ Agamben, *State of Exception*, p. 31.

The District Commissioner as 'Newbolt Man'

In 1921 a young woman named Margery Perham went out to Africa to visit her sister and brother-in-law, the latter a District Commissioner in British Somaliland. The trip was to transform her life completely, instilling in her a fascination for Africa and a passionate interest in colonial administration for the rest of her life. Perham would go on to become one of the most influential voices in Britain on matters of colonial administration in general and of Africa in particular. As a Research Lecturer and later a Reader in Colonial Administration at Oxford University she trained a generation of colonial officers, often staying in touch with them for many years afterwards. At the same time she was a prolific writer, publishing books over a forty-year period on colonial policy and African politics, as well as her own travel writing and a two-volume official biography of her colleague and mentor Frederick Lugard.

Her first publication, however, *Major Dane's Garden*, was a novel, directly inspired by her visit to British Somaliland and commenced soon after her return. The book, published in 1925, follows Rhona Cavell to that protectorate where she falls in love with Major Dane, a District Commissioner modelled closely on Perham's brother-in-law, Harry Rayne. Dane is a caring maverick administrator, loved by those over whom he rules. He is rugged, 'altogether a weather beaten but reflective person' for whom 'lonely and difficult work had seemed to become his by a natural law'.[6] He also keeps a pet cheetah. In a passionate scene, Dane confesses to Rhona his love for England and a faith in Empire that he has nurtured since boyhood. 'You hear it said on all sides that this talk about our holding power in trust for the native people is all humbug. That sort of talk doesn't help,' he exclaims, 'every bit of honest work done all the world over in fulfilment of our trust justifies our country and redeems our mission.'[7] In his reticence, his love of Africa, and his devotion to service even above his devotion to Rhona, Dane comes to embody all that Perham later sought to inspire and instil in her colonial office students.

Major Dane's Garden was received favourably in the press and sold well when it appeared in 1925. No doubt this was at least in part a response to Perham's lively prose and the novel's passionate love story, which encompasses scenes of domestic and military violence, storms at sea and

---

[6] Perham, *Major Dane's Garden*, pp. 61, 65.
[7] Ibid. p. 262. The idealism of Perham's Major Dane is tellingly contradicted by Achebe's District Commissioner, Winterbottom, who, as we saw in Chapter 1, is far less confident in the civilising capacity of colonial administration. See Achebe, *Arrow of God*, p. 36.

in the desert, famine, political intrigue, murder and passionate if unconsummated love. Nonetheless, in 1925 Perham's subject was not unusual, although her focus on the love story provided some novelty. By this time the way had already been paved for her by others, who had carved out for themselves a new niche in adventure stories – District Commissioner fiction. These novels and short stories narrated the heroic exploits of men in the colonial service in the remotest parts of the Empire, commonly in colonial Africa. Foremost amongst those writers engaging with West Africa was Edgar Wallace. Wallace initially made a name for himself as a journalist and author of military and crime fiction, self-publishing his first book, *The Four Just Men*, in 1905. In 1911, however, he turned his hand to colonial adventure fiction and in doing so created his most popular hero, Commissioner Sanders. Wallace published four more Sanders books between 1914 and 1918 and went on to publish a further four by 1928, when his final volume in the series, *Again Sanders*, appeared.[8] Wallace was hardly alone, however, and others, such as Arthur E. Southon, published novels throughout the 1910s and 1920s featuring the heroic deeds of District Commissioners in Nigeria and elsewhere in West Africa. In the same period some of the first memoirs by those employed in the colonial service also appeared, such as A. C. G. Hastings's *Nigerian Days* (1925), which further fed the appetite for publications that depicted the colonial enterprise in the inter-war period. By the time that *Major Dane's Garden* appeared, then, the figure of the District Commissioner was a familiar one to the reading public. Thus Major Dane's unique capacity for colonial rule ('you can do what no other man can do,' exclaims Rhona[9]) was, ironically, already the stock-in-trade of his literary precursors, and his quiet magnetic charisma, which Perham presents as distinctive, was in fact a trait shared with many other fictional Commissioners of the period.

If Major Dane finds his immediate forebears in the fiction of Wallace and Southon, District Commissioner fiction itself has its own lineage, appearing as it does at the intersection of several emergent and dominant genres of the early twentieth century. In *Play Up and Play the Game* Patrick Howarth delineates the archetypical hero of the late Victorian adventure novels out of which District Commissioner fiction emerges:

---

[8] *Bosambo of the River* (1914), *Bones* (1915), *The Keeper of the Kings Peace* (1917), *Lieutenant Bones* (1918), *Bones in London* (1921), *Sandi the Kingmaker* (1922), *Bones of the River* (1923), *Sanders* (1926).
[9] Perham, *Major Dane's Garden*, p. 359.

> Imbued with a strong sense of institutional loyalty, upper middle class by background, conformist in belief, dedicated to a concept, not simply of 'my country right or wrong', but of a nation enjoying a natural moral prerogative, accepting ungrudgingly the demands of service and duty, inclined to treat women either as companions or as unmentionable; add to this a natural power of command, some degree of worldly success, a distrust of latter-day politicians and a tendency towards philistinism in artistic taste, and we have the species *homo newboltiensis* or Newbolt Man.[10]

Howarth traces Newbolt Man back to the mid-Victorian muscular Christianity of Thomas Hughes and Charles Kingsley, whose child protagonists were taught by challenging circumstances the virtues of loyalty, conformity and heroic self-restraint. The didactic model for young readers that youthful or adult Newbolt Man presented was balanced by the gripping adventures in which he became embroiled. These adventures might be domestic (as in the case of schoolboy fiction), historical (such as Conan Doyle's Sir Nigel novels) or imperial (as with Rider Haggard). Whatever the context, however, the ethical content of each was always sincere, offering the hero ample opportunity to hone and to deploy his Newboltian attributes to the benefit of himself and others.

At the start of the new century, Howarth notes, the challenges that Newbolt Man faced took on an additional cerebral facet, so that his powers of detection and deduction became as valuable as his physical prowess, giving rise to a rash of detective heroes from Sax Rohmer's Nayland Smith to Buchan's Hannay. These men, however, are rarely straightforward figures of the law. In many cases they are private detectives, whose superior powers of intelligence are set off to their best advantage by implicit and explicit comparisons with the distinctly lower-middle-class mediocrity of the metropolitan constabulary. Others, like Nayland Smith, are ex-servicemen whose exact roles and relations to the institutions of the law are hazy but taken for granted. In either case these Newbolt Men are characterised by an exceptionalism that places them outside the regular legal machinations of policing and investigation. In the case of Holmes, as Douglas Kerr has pointed out, that exceptionalism applies to his very reason for solving crimes in the first place. Holmes's activities are presented as diversions, brain teasers that once solved require no justice. Punishment, if it occurs at all, tends to take place off-stage, undertaken by the police and judiciary once the mystery of the crime has been laid

---

[10] Howarth, *Play Up and Play the Game*, pp. 13–14.

bare. Holmes pays little attention to the fate of those he catches once they have been caught. As Kerr explains, the point of these stories 'is hermeneutic only: interpreting the facts, uncovering the underlying story' is their focus, not the restitution of social equilibrium.[11] To a lesser extent we find a similar model in Rohmer's Fu Manchu series, in which Nayland Smith is often racing against time to stop a crime occurring rather than to solve the mystery of how it happened. Moreover, insofar as Fu Manchu evades capture at the end of each episode, *both* crime and punishment are endlessly deferred while the exciting action of detection and pursuit is foregrounded. Thus the scaffolding of socially sanctioned legal systems is rendered all but invisible.

Out of this fertile ground of maverick detection on the one hand and wholesome adventure on the other, the genre of District Commissioner fiction emerges. The Commissioner embodies all the sincere virility and virtuousness to which the schoolboy adventurer of Victorian boys' fiction might aspire, combined with the powers of analytical thinking that mark out the modern detective hero. Commissioner Sanders, for example, of Wallace's popular series, 'knew the native mind better than any man living' and has an ascetic sturdiness that keeps him going where weaker men fall foul of tropical diseases and madness. But, as Howarth emphasises, the 'closest link between the harsh, professional Sanders and Newbolt Man in his purest form is not … in resistance to the lures of women or even a cultivated philistinism, but dedication to service'.[12] Sanders's actions are not driven by a Holmesian desire to relieve boredom but by a sense of 'service given wholeheartedly, not only to a crown, but to a system', and that system is the legal infrastructure of indirect rule in West Africa.[13] In this important respect the District Commissioner stands apart from his contemporaries and forebears in that his exceptionalism is constructed from within the legal system rather than outside it. The Commissioner is no freebooting adventurer, such as we find in Rider Haggard, exploring the African continent in the absence of European systems of government and civilisation (the policeman and the butcher that Conrad's Marlow, in 'Heart of Darkness', claims restrain his metropolitan audience from the madness that threatens in the 'uncivilized' environment of sub-Saharan Africa[14]). The District Commissioner is significant because he represents

---

[11] Kerr, *Conan Doyle*, p. 140.
[12] Howarth, *Play Up and Play the Game*, p. 118.
[13] Ibid.
[14] See Conrad, 'Heart of Darkness', in *Youth and Two Other Stories*, p. 130.

the incorporation of the adventurer's spirit, the detective's acumen, and the soldier's loyalty into a figure of the law and the force of law.

This might at first seem too fine a distinction to make, not least since the District Commissioner was flanked in popular West Africa fiction by other stock figures of white male adventure, notably the missionary and the trader.[15] Nonetheless, the fact of his emergence and his enduring popularity points up a subtle but important change in the location of Newboltian values in the first three decades of the twentieth century. Moreover, it draws our attention to a change in how those values were deployed in fiction to valorise particular professions. Whilst Howarth doesn't make this connection, the development of the District Commissioner hero supplies Newbolt Man with his zenith, enabling transnational adventure to combine with patriotic service to a global mission for enlightened government, and thus embodying the crucial concept of 'civilisation'. This elision of the ideal patriotic man and the District Commissioner evidences the privileging of the figure of the law in the popular colonial imagination at the start of the new century.

We need to understand this genre shift in the context of Britain's changing political outlook towards its West African colonies at the turn of the century. As M. E. Chamberlain points out in *The Scramble for Africa*, the argument for maintaining and developing colonies in West Africa was driven as much by powerful commercial lobbying as by missionary lobbying.[16] In the mid-nineteenth century the British government had expressed a goal in West Africa for 'ultimate withdrawal from all, except, probably, Sierra Leone'.[17] However, as we saw in the previous chapter, as other European nations pressed in upon the borders of British trading regions on the west coast a strong lobby developed, arguing that British trade would be decimated by the protective tariff policies that would come into play if other nations, such as Portugal and France, took control of the region around the Niger. In the latter half of the nineteenth century, then, it was traders from exploratory companies rather than government officials that were associated with the opening up of the African continent,

---

[15] For an example of the latter see Edward Shirley's *Up the Creeks: A Tale of Adventure in West Africa* (1900), in which a young trader takes charge of an upriver trading post, and is promptly kidnapped; see also Arthur E. Southon's *The Taming of a King: A West African Story* (1927), in which Commissioner and missionary work closely together to install a system of indirect rule through Christian converts.

[16] Chamberlain, *The Scramble for Africa*, p. 46ff.

[17] *Report from the Select Committee on Africa (Western Coast)*, Parliamentary Papers, v (1865), p. iii. Reproduced in Chamberlain, *The Scramble for Africa*, p. 120.

and this is reflected in the characteristically independent gentlemen who bestride the pages of late-nineteenth-century African adventure fiction. With the new century and the shift in control of Nigeria from the Royal Niger Company to the British government, the centrality of the traders was usurped by the colonial service. This change in policy is reflected in fiction so that despite the continuing popularity of Haggardian freebooters, the District Commissioner emerges at the beginning of the twentieth century as *the* hero of the colonies.

Although, as R. B. Cunninghame Graham notes, the District Commissioner in West Africa was often cast as the unsung hero of the British colonial endeavour, early publications such as Flora Shaw's *A Tropical Dependency* (1905) and George Douglas Hazzledine's *The White Man in Nigeria* (1904) drew attention to the role of the District Commissioner as an essential feature of indirect rule under Frederick Lugard.[18] Flora Shaw was Lugard's wife and George Douglas Hazzledine was his private secretary, and thus both were eager advocates of the District Commissioner's heroised function within the system of indirect rule. Their accounts informed the popular fictional representations of the colonial service that emerged in their wake, providing a paradigm of conditions and personalities that was to be echoed again and again over the following three decades. Moreover, the paradigm of these early texts was also repeated in the memoirs that began to appear soon after, written by colonial officers who had served upcountry. These only reinforced what were becoming key tropes in both fictional and factual accounts of colonial service: isolation, unruly natives, governance by ingenuity and on a shoestring, and above all, as we have already noted, devotion to service. Moreover, in both fiction and non-fiction we find a sincerity in the framing of colonial idealism with the characteristic features of romance. These characteristic features include the threat of personal danger to the hero, a testing of his moral fortitude, his capacity for endurance (not least in challenging terrain), and his inventiveness when faced with apparently insurmountable challenges.

With this context in mind, Perham's decision to turn to the sincere romance of District Commissioner fiction as the genre in which to express her first ideas about colonial rule in Africa is an obvious choice. The Newboltian figure of the District Commissioner allowed Perham to

---

[18] Cunninghame Graham, 'Introduction', p. x.

imbue her hero with the characteristics she would herself later attempt to instil in her colonial service students at Oxford and Cambridge. Today, Perham's novel is perhaps the least known of her African writings; however, her choice of District Commissioner fiction for her initial foray into presenting and justifying the colonial enterprise demonstrates the significance of the genre as a touchstone for not only popular but also intellectual thinking about colonial rule in Africa in the first decades of the twentieth century.

Upcountry with the District Commissioner

Before exploring a few of the stories themselves it is worth taking time to examine the stock contextual detail that authors like Southon and Wallace gave to their narratives. First and foremost of these is the fact that the District Commissioner is always upcountry and almost invariably upriver. While British interests in Nigeria stretched many years back into the nineteenth century, British influence had taken hold primarily along the coast and around Lagos. These established regions, with their urban development, education systems and centralised power, were nevertheless shunned by adventure authors, who instead sought to fling their heroes as far from 'civilisation' as credibly possible. That distance is emphasised by a repeated claim of isolation. Thus, for example, in Southon's *The Taming of a King*, 'Belfort was the District Commissioner in sole charge of a territory with nearly half a million inhabitants, the first representative of a Government which was still hardly a name to most of his people.'[19] Within this territory the District Commissioner is prey to various natural hazards, from swamps infested with dangerous insects to the ever-present threat of malaria, all of which are the more hazardous because of the Commissioner's distance from medical aid. In his introduction to A. C. G. Hastings's memoir *Nigerian Days*, Cunninghame Graham notes that 'in the multitude of negroes a solitary white man is just as much alone as on a desert island, exposed to frequent fevers in a climate hostile to North Europeans, and with no single ray of limelight turned upon any one throughout the colony'.[20] Such claims of isolation are repeated again and again in fiction, in memoirs and in travel writing throughout the first half of the century.

Furthermore, in the fiction at least, rivers, rather than roads or railways, are the main mode of access to the interior, and much early fiction

---

[19] Southon, *The Taming of a King*, p. 10.
[20] Cunninghame Graham, 'Introduction', p. x.

of this period depicts the hero at the mercy of the river Niger and its tributaries, despite the fact that most administrative transportation in Nigeria used railways, as contemporary factual accounts attest. No doubt the insistence on rivers was a response to the popular and persistent fascination with African rivers, most famously the Congo, reflected in the media frenzy around the exploits of Henry Morton Stanley. Wallace himself had visited the Congo Free State in 1907 in order to report on the conditions there, whose brutality was coming to British and international attention following reports by E. D. Morel and Roger Casement in the first half of the decade. Indeed, he began his Sanders series in response to a request for copy about his experiences in the Congo from Isabel Thorne for the *Weekly Tale-Teller*. However, Wallace's stories are no 'Heart of Darkness' and, instead of exposing the abuses committed along the Congo River, he paints in rosy hues the early years of colonial administration up the Niger. Sanders's reach seems to range across much of Northern Nigeria as well as down towards the coast, that is to say covering several hundred miles of the Niger and its tributaries, although, as with much in Wallace's oeuvre, the details are hazy. Nonetheless, while Wallace clearly did not intend his readers to concern themselves too much with the realities of Sanders's excursions, their extensiveness, measured by the river's reach, once again underscores his extreme isolation.

If the District Commissioner's isolation increases the threat from his natural environment, it also compounds the danger posed by his social environment. Writing in 1905, Flora Shaw described the incursion of the Royal Niger Company, in the 1880s, into the territories that would become Nigeria:

> The disturbed condition of the territories and the hostile attitude of the native chiefs, combined with the difficulties of penetrating to the interior, through unknown tropical country, laid waste in many districts by centuries of slave-raiding and inter-tribal war, rendered these missions in most cases expeditions of no little danger, which had to be conducted at the personal risk of the leaders whose services were secured to command them.[21]

This condition of hostility and disorder amongst the natives remains a standard characteristic, following the transition to government administration, in District Commissioner fiction and in colonial memoirs: 'Millions of

---

[21] Shaw, *A Tropical Dependency*, pp. 356–7. Note here the use of 'slave-raiding and inter-tribal war' to justify the civilising mission of the colonial enterprise.

men and women lived within the vast forest-belt and amongst the towering hills of the Hinterland, savage and cruel as the gods they worshipped,' writes Southon in his preface to *The Laughing Ghosts*.[22] Southon's preface, in which he claims his story is drawn from personal experience, echoes what was by that time a common dramatisation of the Briton's upcountry experience. Whether wily, brutish or petulant, the native communities administered by the Commissioner are resistant and operate according to agendas that fail to coincide with the civilising mission of the colonial service. Hastings, for example, who joined the service in 1906, introduces the area in which he is to be Assistant Resident as home to 'forty different pagan tribes ... all ... ready to fight at a moment's notice'.[23] In the fiction, moreover, the reasons for resistance are addressed in far less detail than in memoirs or in Flora Shaw's account. 'Slave-raiding and inter-tribal war' are presented less as historical causes and more as causeless yet inherent ways of life for those over whom the Commissioner rules. Where cause is given it is often traced to the vanity of a tribe or a chief, that is to say to a moral flaw, rather than to a larger socio-historical context. This impression contributes to the sense of the Commissioner as the isolated, still point of reason at the centre of a vast whirl of chaos and constant danger.

Despite the frequent characterisation of the Commissioner as the lone white male, however, once the stories (and memoirs) get under way we discover that they are supported in their duties by a variety of British and Nigerian subordinates and colleagues. Familiar characters include the Hausa captain, the doctor, the missionary, the Assistant Commissioner and the native ally. In Cunninghame Graham's introduction to *Nigerian Days* he notes that Hastings has 'to assist him in his work ... an interpreter, three Government paid messengers and six native police, though on occasion he could draw on the Emir for more soldiers or police', yet in the very next sentence he claims he is 'Absolutely alone' because he is 'without another European at his station'.[24] Alongside this cast of subordinates we also find, in many of the Sanders stories in particular, visiting Europeans, Americans and other West Africans, although their appearance at Sanders's upriver outpost inevitably signals the start of some misadventure or another. Sanders and his fellow Commissioners are not, then, as isolated as they might at first seem. Their subordinates and colleagues consult over plans of action, carry messages, deliver medical assis-

---

[22] Southon, *The Laughing Ghosts*, p. iv.
[23] Hastings, *Nigerian Days*, p. 34.
[24] Cunninghame Graham, 'Introduction', p. xiv.

tance, and provide companionship. Nonetheless they remain subordinate to the Commissioner inasmuch as his word is law. Even the camaraderie, in *The Taming of a King*, between Commissioner Belfort and his 'best pal', the missionary Gorton, for example, acknowledges the responsibility that the Commissioner inevitably has for Gorton while he operates his mission in Belfort's territory.[25]

These groups of men – for men they almost invariably are – echo the original formation of colonial government described by Flora Shaw in *A Tropical Dependency*: 'The civil staff allotted for the purpose of founding an administration was very small', she explains, 'and its numbers were liable to be reduced by illness and leave.'[26] She goes on to quote one of Frederick Lugard's dispatches, which quivers with St Crispin's Day pride for

> the indefatigable efforts and the enthusiasm for their task which has been shown by the Political Staff. By their ceaseless devotion to duty they have not only increased the revenue ... but have brought order, peace and security out of chaos, have established an effective judicial system, and have substituted progress and development for misrule and stagnation.[27]

Both Shaw and Lugard thus paint for their readers a picture steeped in Newboltian rhetoric: an isolated, unprofessionalised group of men, whose esprit de corps and natural talents enable them to achieve successes against the odds in their civilising mission.[28] Over the next two decades this particular narrative, optimistic and rosy as it certainly is, was reflected in memoirs, such as that of Hastings, and repeated endlessly in District Commissioner fiction, creating mutual reinforcement between the genres through a shared rhetoric of the romance of the civilising mission.

'Fear of the Law [Is] the Beginning of Civilization'[29]

First and foremost the District Commissioner was responsible for the law. Understandably, following the exposure of atrocities in Leopold's Congo, the rhetoric of British colonialism in West Africa was 'civilisation' rather

---

[25] Southon, *The Taming of a King*, p. 11.
[26] Shaw, *A Tropical Dependency*, p. 419.
[27] Ibid. p. 425.
[28] Shaw notes that 'Their experience of Africa was mostly nil' (*A Tropical Dependency*, p. 424) and Cunninghame Graham presents Hastings as 'ignorant of Hausa at the first' ('Introduction', p. xiv).
[29] Wallace, *The People of the River*, p. 78.

than trade, although trade remained the driving force behind increased British governmental engagement in the region. What is significant is that the mode through which civilisation was to be established was not primarily missionary work, education or even trade, but the imposition of legal systems. These other modes of instituting Western culture were available to the British government, and in the case of trade the Royal Niger Company was already in place. The government's assumption of the company's territories in 1900, however, although a practical response to the border encroachments of France and Germany, also resituated responsibility for the civilising mission from commerce to the law. Moreover, insofar as the law was what was to be imposed, the law in a very significant way was understood *to be* civilisation. It was not simply a means to an end but both means and ends in and of itself: the establishment of the rule of (colonial) law would bring about civilisation because it *was* civilisation.

This elision of law and civilisation goes some way to explain the minimal training, and limited regard for training, that characterised the early administration. Whilst there were in fact official guides to crimes and sentencing, these were slim and judging by accounts irregularly consulted. *Richards's Table of Offences* was originally published in 1889 for application on the Gold Coast and was adopted in the Southern Nigerian Protectorate and Colony. In his introductory notes to the 1908 revised edition, Edwin Arney Speed, Attorney-General of the Colony, notes that 'His Majesty's jurisdiction' is on the one hand 'supreme and absolute' and on the other 'is exercised subject to *certain limitations, ill defined* and in many cases almost indeterminate'.[30] Speed goes on to clarify that in the Western province this jurisdiction only extends one hundred yards either side of the railway line up to Ibadan, and whilst some other territories had limited or plenary jurisdiction, others were not subject to the Supreme Court at all. In such a situation, and where the Attorney-General's guidance was couched in phrasing that was distinctly and purposefully hazy, it is no wonder that Commissioners and other colonial officers chose to interpret the law according to their own judgement. Moreover, insofar as Speed characterises the law in this way, he indicates a confidence in the capacity of the Commissioners to do so whilst at the same time embodying the requisite civilisation. That the

---

[30] Speed, *Richards's Table of Offences*, p. v; emphasis added.

Table is reprinted at all, Speed explains in his introduction, is 'largely ... to prevent District Commissioners *unwittingly* imposing upon accused persons illegal penalties'.[31] The assumption that penalties might be imposed 'unwittingly' implies that the Commissioner will never consciously overstep the bounds of civilised judgement. We see here how the fictional ideal of the District Commissioner who perfects the genealogy of Newbolt Man coincides with the District Commissioner of the administration Speed imagines for his ideal reader.

In the North, Hastings recalls that the 'copy of the Northern Nigerian laws, such as had been promulgated up to that time ... together with a curious little official effort, called the West African pocket-book, comprised my only literature on the country'.[32] In the following sentence he explains that 'the one has long since mouldered into dust upon some office shelf, the other, misleading me completely on most subjects, was very soon thrown upon the fire'.[33] The clear implication that thus emerges in memoirs, in fiction and in the hazy rhetoric of Speed's introduction to the 1908 *Richards's Table* is that the colonial officer is imagined to be civilised himself and that as such he is attributed with an innate capacity to enforce the law without additional guidance, since his judgement and civilisation are one and the same.

Hazzledine, in his 1904 account of Northern Nigeria, provides a model narrative of the new colonial officer that exemplifies the elisions and blind spots inherent in this assumption: his young officer comes straight from training at the Temple Bar but his instruction in relation to legal practice in the Protectorate is imparted while dining at the mess, where he learns 'the scheme of legislation', gets 'a general idea of the line where English law gives ways to that of the Mohammedan' and 'hears much of the native courts'.[34] Nonetheless, despite his training in English law and apparent lack of training in 'that of the Mohammedan', Hazzledine insists in a later chapter on the fact of the officer's 'compulsory attention to native law' and dismisses as 'palpably absurd' the charge of a 'system of English law substituted for and overriding the one already existing in the land'.[35] This narrative of an English trained lawyer, who picks up the niceties of colonial law over the mess table and is able as if by magic to

---

[31] Ibid. p. iv; emphasis added.
[32] Hastings, *Nigerian Days*, p. 2.
[33] Ibid.
[34] Hazzledine, *The White Man in Nigeria*, p. 40.
[35] Ibid. p. 93.

understand 'native law', relies upon the assumption of an innate capacity for civility *as* legal practice in the colonial officer. That assumption is summed up in Hazzledine's concluding argument against critics of the colonial legal system: '*Special laws* must also be made for the people themselves on the introduction of conditions not provided for by their own.'[36] Under these terms the Commissioner can create the law or 'special laws' guided by his own judgement of the circumstances he finds presented to him. This provision for 'special laws' is echoed in Agamben, who characterises this situation as one 'in which on the one hand, the norm is in force ... but is not applied ... and on the other, acts that do not have the value ... of law acquire its "force."'[37] Both Hastings's and Hazzledine's accounts model this paradigm in the inventiveness of the colonial officer in his enforcement of the law-as-civilisation, but also in the way in which the legal norm is set aside (whether the norm of English law or of customary law) in favour of acts that stand as and yet are not law. Significantly, it is exactly these aspects of the District Commissioner's activities that are presented imaginatively, time and again, in District Commissioner fiction of the period.

One version of this state of affairs, which appears in both memoirs and fiction, is the story of the District Commissioner's exaction of swift justice. In such stories the Commissioner metaphorically sets aside his *Richards's Table of Offences* and chooses his own punishment for the offender, usually death. Thus, for example, in Wallace's story 'The Eloquent Woman' the woman in question, whose demagogic powers have brought strife to Ochori country, is dispatched as her canoe flees the Maxims of Sanders's steamer, her attack already routed. Sanders orders her execution by observing 'gravely' to his Hausa sergeant, Abiboo, 'It seems to me that this woman would be better dead.'[38] This observation, as well as reducing the Eloquent Woman to someone who had forfeited her right to life, and thus to bare life ('she would be better dead'), also suspends the law according to *Richards's Table of Offences*, whereby she should stand trial. Sanders's observation is particularly striking in the way that it passively aggregates judgement to his person: 'it seems to me'. In this construction the law is set aside and Sanders's own will takes its place with a violent force that stands in for the law but is not the law.

---

[36] Ibid. p. 94; emphasis added.
[37] Agamben, *State of Exception*, p. 38.
[38] Wallace, *The People of the River*, p. 35.

Swift justice is also implicit in the 'length of thin, strong rope' that Arthur E. Southon's Commissioner Calverly finds 'worth more than its weight in gold' as he patrols his district.[39] And ends justify means later in the same collection when Calverly chooses to suspend the overarching creed of the repugnancy test in the hope of information to foil a plot by the 'Leopard Men': Calverly allows 'that torture should be used to one who practised torture; that African cruelty should meet African cruelty' in order to obtain information from his detainee, although he delicately delegates the physical exertion of the job to his willing Hausa sergeant, Achmed.[40] Such examples of 'special laws', or more precisely the suspension of the law and its replacement with actions that carry the force of law, are stock features of District Commissioner fiction's repertoire. They dramatise how the District Commissioner's will becomes substituted for the law (as the force of law), as when Calverly chooses to allow torture to extract information; and how, at the same time, that process of substitution is justified through the Commissioner's imagined embodiment of civilisation.

Whilst the summary justice of execution without trial is the most common example of the suspension of the law in District Commissioner fiction, we also find creative responses to judicial practice that fall within the 'special laws' category. Thus whilst *Richards's Table* advises that 'it is hardly necessary to remark that before passing sentence the Commissioner should in every case be careful to ascertain what punishment may be legally awarded', in the fiction there is no mention of Commissioners checking their *Tables*.[41] In his sketch of the first days of a newly appointed Commissioner Hazzledine claims that he 'will worry a little over the first few sentences he inflicts, and wonder whether they were just', implying that the young Commissioner has to rely as much on his own judgement as on the detailed guidelines of *Richards's Table*.[42] Hastings provides more details, recalling that he 'awarded sundry punishments which possibly did not fit the offence in all cases; but my efforts were subject to superior revision, and little harm resulted in the end'.[43] Hastings's gloss about 'superior revision' refers to the fact that Commissioners were required to send monthly tabulated reports on court proceedings to the Chief Justice

---

[39] Southon, *The Laughing Ghosts*, p. 129.
[40] Ibid. p. 242.
[41] Speed, *Richards's Table of Offences*, p. xii.
[42] Hazzledine, *The White Man in Nigeria*, p. 41.
[43] Hastings, *Nigerian Days*, p. 36.

or Provincial Judge, enabling the Chief Justice to modify punishments where they were deemed inappropriate. Hastings also recalls his conformity to *Richards's Table*, noting that his Court minute-book stands as a record of 'anxious poring over the Nigerian Laws'.[44] By contrast, Sanders, Calverly and company are rarely presented as keeping up their paper trail. Wallace, for example, notes that 'Sanders never consulted constitutions' and that his dispatch for the Under-Secretary of Colonial Affairs 'was a monthly nightmare'.[45]

Likewise, in 'Brethren of the Order' we find Sanders banning gin despite the fact that there was 'no law prohibiting the sale of strong drink in the territory under his care'.[46] When challenged on this very restriction Sanders responds, 'I am the law.'[47] Once again Sanders incorporates the law to his literal body. This self-substitution of the law with the person of the Commissioner is repeated in almost every story, whether in Sanders's self-presentation as the King's representative or his assumption of customary codes of honour, as when he assures his dying spy, Bogoro, 'I will carry your blood upon my hands and at my hands [your murderer] shall die; all gods witness my words.'[48] In this latter example, Sanders sidesteps the requisite trial by taking Bogoro at his word, without questioning his assailant, and choosing summary execution rather than recourse to the Supreme Court as required in *Richards's Table*. The language he uses to do so, calling on all 'gods' rather than a Christian 'God' to witness his promise, might initially imply that Sanders here moves from the code of justice administered by the colonial government to a 'native' or customary code of justice, that is to say that his actions might at first seem sanctioned as an accommodation of indirect rule. And yet, were that so, Sanders would of necessity have to hand over the case, formally at the very least, to the customary court that presided over the town in which Bogoro was attacked. Instead, Sanders's promise ignores both English and customary codes and retains the power of restitution within a *personal* bond that can only be fulfilled outside the law.

This suspension of regular legal procedures goes some way to explain the surprising scarcity of trials in District Commissioner fiction. Where trials do appear they tend to be brief and, rather than dramatising the construction of the case itself, they serve as vehicles for showcasing the

---

[44] Ibid.
[45] Wallace, *The People of the River*, pp. 68, 64.
[46] Ibid. p. 68.
[47] Ibid. p. 67.
[48] Ibid. p. 70.

Commissioner's spontaneous wisdom. The focus is on judgement and sentencing rather than on the giving of evidence, despite the common characterisation of district court sessions as full of tall tales and wild accusations. *Richards's Table*, for example, advises that 'If the witness be a native, it will probably be difficult to make him confine himself to [the] facts. The best way is to let him tell his tale in his own way, and by subsequent questioning to elicit from him how many of these facts took place in his presence.'[49] Wallace and Southon, if they show any of the trial beyond sentencing at all, tend to skip over native evidence to the 'subsequent questioning' in order to maintain attention on the Commissioner's Solomonic wisdom. In 'Guns in the Akasava', for example, all we are told of the trial of the 'crestfallen chief, Ofesi' is that 'both sides lied fearfully, and Sanders, sifting the truth, knew which side lied the least'.[50] Likewise Wallace and Southon also avoid presenting the parallel legal system of the Islamic courts in the North, which District Commissioners were expected to oversee. This is again surprising given the sensational accounts that appeared about Fulani punishments. Hastings claims that '[p]unishments were barbarous in the extreme' and lists '[m]utilation, the lopping off of hands and feet for repeated stealing, impalement on long sharp stakes of wood – the sufferers sometimes living for two days or more before their release in death – burying alive and stoning'.[51] Such violence would no doubt have lent itself to the taste for the lurid that characterises many District Commissioner stories; however, removing the Islamic legal system from view focuses the power of the law into the person of the Commissioner more absolutely, as does the silence already noted on guidelines, checks and balances in the process of administering the law.

Instead, fictional District Commissioners operate with an inventive freedom in their juridical choices, quite at odds with the formal codes by which colonial officers in real life were expected to enforce the law, whether colonial or customary. Thus, for example, when the local chief, Bosambo, encourages Medini, Queen of the N'Gombi, to imagine that Sanders will marry her, Sanders punishes him by requiring that Bosambo marry Medini himself, despite Bosambo's protestations that as a Christian he can only have one wife. Sanders justifies this response to himself by reflecting that Bosambo 'had brought that insult upon himself'.[52] In 'The Tax-Resisters'

---

[49] Speed, *Richard's Table of Offences*, p. ix.
[50] Wallace, *Bosambo of the River*, p. 166.
[51] Hastings, *Nigerian Days*, p. 56.
[52] Wallace, *The People of the River*, p. 132.

we find Sanders indirectly imposing a standing army upon the Kiko, who despite their wealth request a reduction in their taxes.[53] The cost of hosting Bosambo and his men is such that the chief of the Kiko agrees to pay full taxes, explaining that 'in the end I think it would be cheaper than Bosambo and his hungry devils'.[54] The Kiko's initial request is not without justice since Sanders taxes them to the hilt. However, Wallace justifies this heavy taxation by explaining Sanders's concern that 'people who grew rich in corn were dangerous'.[55] Sanders thus keeps their wealth in check through taxation to avoid them going on the war-path.

The relationship between tax and keeping the peace was a fraught one for District Commissioners, and it is one that Wallace depicts from time to time throughout the Sanders series. Hastings describes how he frequently collected taxes in kind rather than in coin. The store-room would gradually fill up with lengths of cloth, livestock, grain and so on, each item provided in lieu of tax. These various wares were then auctioned off to those in the region who could pay in currency, thus generating the necessary cash (and presumably at times a surplus) to be sent back to the colonial office. This system worked to exclude the poorest in the community from entering into the currency system by encouraging them to trade in kind with the tax collectors rather than selling that surplus on the open market to generate the necessary currency to pay their taxes. More generally, taxation alongside the demand for unpaid labour to support public works placed pressure on families to produce more crops and livestock with less manpower. To some degree this had been the case under the Fulani, and the British certainly played up at home the cost to the local peasant of corruption under Fulani rule (where it was claimed each point of exchange in tax collection involved embezzlement[56]) as compared with the new efficiencies the colonial administration sought to introduce. However, not only did corruption continue, the administration of Northern Nigeria, at least, ran at a deficit, creating even greater need for tax revenues and unpaid labour. Add to this the colonial administration's definition of land 'as a customary and communal possession', so that peasant freehold became essentially impossible, and the conditions were created for livestock raids and land disputes between neighbouring

---

[53] Michelle Gordon provides an interesting account of the violent tax resistance in Sierra Leone at the turn of the century. See 'The Dynamics of British Colonial Violence', pp. 157–60.
[54] Wallace, *Bosambo of the River*, p. 39.
[55] Ibid. p. 28.
[56] See Hastings, *Nigerian Days*, pp. 51–3.

communities (particularly in times of poor production).[57] Rather than using these disputes to call into question colonial taxation and labour practices, however, the Sanders stories present them as evidence of the need for the civilising presence of the District Commissioner and the colonial administration.

In Wallace's first Sanders book, *Sanders of the River*, such disputes are reconfigured to highlight the superstitious and craven character of the local communities whilst throwing into relief the Commissioner's ingenuity and fairness. For example, the Akasava come to Sanders complaining of the loss of 'three score of goats, twenty bags of salt, and much ivory'.[58] Sanders discovers that the culprits are the Ochori, a local tribe who until recently had been the weakest on the river. However, Bosambo, a runaway convict krooboy from Monrovia, has established himself as their chief and trained them in his criminal arts. Sanders accosts him in the Ochori village but, following a palaver, agrees to let Bosambo stay so long as the thieving and murder stops. Moreover, Sanders decides that the Ochori should keep that which they have stolen: 'For if you hand them back to the Akasava you will fill their stomachs with rage, and that would mean war.'[59]

In this story the background of predation on the Ochori by neighbouring, and even far-flung, tribes is displaced. In the first instance Sanders treats their plight as a result of spinelessness. However, rather than training them to defend themselves through warfare (as Bosambo later does) he gives them a fetish to protect them, which they are to plant at their boundary with ceremony and sacrifice (the sign, we discover in due course, reads 'Trespassers Beware'). Sanders operates knowingly here, even cynically, within the traditions of local culture, rather than applying colonial law to the perpetrators of the raids on the Ochori. His understanding of the native mind is used to create a solution that appears to support the customary rather than providing a 'civilised' solution to the problem. All well and good, we might say, an example of indirect rule in action. But the narrative of this resolution shifts our attention away from the genuine economic plight of the Ochori and on to their superstitious and gullible characteristics. The end of the story creates a similar distraction. Returning the plunder to the Akasava 'will fill their stomachs with rage', Sanders argues, and thus Wallace focuses our attention on their

---

[57] Mamdani, *Citizen and Subject*, p. 51.
[58] Wallace, *Sanders of the River*, p. 45.
[59] Ibid. p. 47.

propensity for revenge, taking our attention away from the fact that the goods stolen would have been crucial to the Akasava's ability to support the community over the year and to pay their taxes. The narrative thus upholds the colonial view of the time that it was not the demands of colonisation that led to inter-tribal strife but the uncivilised instincts that were a lamentable yet inherent trait of the native.

What is equally interesting for our purposes, however, is the way in which Wallace expands upon his justification of Sanders's system of taxation in *Bosambo of the River*:

> Sanders was a wise man. He was governed by certain hard and fast rules, and though he was well aware that failure in any respect to grapple with the situation would bring him a reprimand, either because he had not acted according to the strict letter of the law, or because he 'had not used his discretion' in going outside that same inflexible code, he took responsibility without fear.[60]

Wallace encapsulates the paradox of colonial administration here, which defines itself in terms of 'the strict letter of the law' and yet which permits 'going outside that ... code' according to individual discretion. As I suggested earlier, this 'discretion' is permitted because in the authority that the Commissioner embodies, such discretion is understood as synonymous with civilised judgement. If the law's enforcement or suspension is discretionary then the District Commissioner enters that uncertain zone, 'where fact and law seem to become undecidable'.[61] Furthermore, the paradox as Wallace presents it, whilst intended to demonstrate the exceptional qualities of Sanders and his innate capacity for wise rule, in fact emerges as systemic, that is to say that this 'uncertain zone' is built into the structures of colonial administration. This is why Sanders can take 'responsibility without fear'. As long as his actions are taken with 'discretion', as long as they are civilised, those actions are permitted the force of law. Thus, for all that Wallace reminds us of Sanders's scant attention to the letter of the law, his maverick methods, far from challenging the system, are in fact only the other side of the same coin. As the embodiment of the law *as* civilisation, Sanders enforces the colonial regime even when he flouts the legal codes, since both the letter of the law and the discretionary action that carries the force of law are instruments of civilisation.

---

[60] Wallace, *Bosambo of the River*, p. 29.
[61] See Agamben, *State of Exception*, p. 29.

'I Am the Law'[62]

Another way in which the District Commissioner's exceptionalism is demonstrated in the fiction is through careful contrasting between the Commissioner and those with whom he comes into contact. Whether Africans, Americans or Europeans, Sanders is invariably shown to be their superior in his understanding of the local populations and in judgement of tricky situations. By far the most uncomfortable representations of such encounters for the modern reader are those with 'educated Africans': 'the browny men of the Gold Coast, who talked English, wore European clothing, and called one another "Mr.," were Sanders' pet abomination,' Wallace tells us.[63] The first story in the first of the Sanders series, 'The Education of the King', is a case in point. In this story the educated men are not from the Gold Coast but 'two cultured American negroes of good address and refined conversation ... [who] spoke English faultlessly, and were in every sense perfect gentlemen'.[64] They fall foul of Sanders because they are members of 'the Reformed Ethiopian Church'.[65] These 'perfect gentlemen' are initially presented as attempting to educate the eponymous young king, who is a child at this point. This might itself have been problematic given the interdict against missionary education in the North at the time; however, this factor is glossed over and instead it is their 'creed of Equality' with which Sanders takes issue, accusing them of 'encroaching upon the borderland of political agitation'.[66] Their reproachful response, 'Would you have the heathen remain in darkness?', is dismissed and, despite the fact that we are told 'in consequence ... questions were asked in Parliament' about Sanders's treatment of the missionaries, we are invited to take Sanders's view of the matter that Ethiopianism, like the educated Negro, can only mean trouble to the colonial regime.[67] What we are asked to recognise about these missionaries, as we are of the educated Africans in District Commissioner fiction in general, is that they

---

[62] Wallace, *The People of the River*, p. 67.
[63] Wallace, *Sanders of the River*, p. 7.
[64] Ibid. p. 14.
[65] Ethiopianism began as a Christian movement in Southern Africa, when several ministers and evangelists from the Anglican and Methodist traditions split away from their churches, frustrated with segregation. The movement went through several instantiations and was influenced by African American Christian church movements. As a result the movement never adopted a single definitive doctrine but was motivated by a desire for equality within the church and an interest in pan-Africanism.
[66] Wallace, *Sanders of the River*, p. 14.
[67] Ibid. p. 15.

are untrustworthy: they say one thing and do something else. Just as the civilised clothes of the men from the Gold Coast are given the lie by their laziness, the fiction implies, so the universal message of Christian goodwill that the missionaries proclaim is undone by the seditious nationalism that their doctrine of equality conveys. From this perspective the civilised African is always wilfully deluding either himself or someone else.

The educated Briton, however, does not fare much better. Young Torrington, for instance, who 'was a Bachelor of Law, had read Science, and had acquired in a methodological fashion a working acquaintance with Swahili, bacteriology, and medicines', takes up a deputy commissionership under Sanders.[68] His efforts to educate the Isisi about 'how sulphuric acid applied to sugar produces $Su2$, $Su4$' mean he is 'worshipped as a Great and Clever Devil'.[69] When he attempts a vaccination programme, however, the first baby treated dies of croup and 'Torrington came flying down the river telling Sanders a rambling story of a populace infuriated and demanding his blood'.[70] Torrington's educated failings are pointedly contrasted with the intellectually average yet profoundly more effective capacities of Sanders. The latter, we are told, 'had forgotten all the chemistry he ever knew, and who as a student of Constitutional Law, was the rankest of failures' and yet is able to resolve the situation single-handedly.[71] The contrast set up between Torrington and Sanders reflects a common attitude in the colonial administration from the second half of the nineteenth century onwards, which valued a sturdy constitution and a sense of fair play over scholastic prowess. Hastings notes with careless pride that his generation within the 'Political Department' in the Northern Nigerian Protectorate 'underwent no painful examination to test the quality of our brains' and doubts whether the training later introduced 'in a string of subjects from law to logwood' could make 'a good political officer' any better than his own experience learning 'in the field'.[72] As J. A. Mangan has demonstrated, whilst recruitment to colonial administrative departments such as the Sudan Political Service was dominated by a preference for public school-educated Oxbridge graduates, a sturdy and sportsmanly constitution was nevertheless highly valued from within that potential cohort. Mangan explains that this was not only because physical fitness was essential to survival in what was considered

---

[68] Ibid. p. 48.
[69] Ibid. p. 49.
[70] Ibid. p. 50.
[71] Ibid. p. 49.
[72] Hastings, *Nigerian Days*, pp. 15–16.

an inhospitable geography and climate, but also because the job required bluff self-assurance given the isolation from support in which many of the administrators were understood to operate.[73] Cunninghame Graham's admiration for Hastings's ability to convince a tribe to relinquish their considerable armoury at the blast of a whistle bears witness to this argument.[74] By contrast Torrington's wilful refusal to take advice from his District Commissioner indicates his failure as a 'team-player', and subsequent events show him as one unable to stand his ground in the scrum of animosity caused by the death of the inoculated infant.

Of course, these figures provide useful hooks for the stories' plots and the Sanders series is consequently peppered throughout with similar feckless Europeans.[75] They also help us understand Sanders, however, by providing a clear indication of what he is not. In such stories, what characterises Sanders by dint of contrast is his relative humility, his common sense and his mundaneness. He is cautious where others are brash; he is practical where others are hoist on the petard of their own intellectualism; he is resolute and commands obedience, where Torrington, among others, is terrified. Moreover, Sanders, like all heroes of District Commissioner fiction, has the supreme privilege of being white and therefore of being naturally civilised, whilst the educated Africans and African Americans can only ever ape the customs of civility, and in doing so merely suppress their innate primitivism.

When we look more closely, however, Sanders in fact frequently embodies these traits that in others prove their downfall. While he may have failed miserably in his Constitutional Law exams he has, like many other District Commissioner heroes including Major Dane, a linguistic facility that exceeds that of language scholars like Torrington and yet which remains acceptable in a way that the perfect English of the Ethiopianists clearly is not.[76] Equally, Sanders's disregard for his formal training, which in others is presented as misplaced arrogance, is in

---

[73] Mangan, *The Games Ethic and Imperialism*, p. 82ff.
[74] Cunninghame Graham, 'Introduction', p. xv.
[75] In *Sanders of the River*, for example, we also encounter Miss Calbraith, the would-be governess, who, like the Ethiopianists, wants to be a teacher to the little king; Mr Niceman, whose rather obvious niceness leads to his swift demise and his 'head, stuck on a pole before the king [of Isisi]'s hut' (p. 11); and Professor Sir George Carsley, whose solipsistic scientific interests make him particularly susceptible to a fascination with witchcraft, causing his rapid descent into madness.
[76] In this he mirrors the new mental prowess of Newboltian heroes such as Nayland Smith, whose linguistic facility is commented on at various points in the Fu Manchu stories.

keeping with his Newboltian qualities of modesty and practicality. In several stories, moreover, this disregard for institutionalised knowledge also contributes to Sanders's affinity with the simplicity and superstitions of the natives.[77] However, once again, whilst these characteristics in the natives are used to primitivise them and demonstrate their mental limitations, in Sanders simplicity and superstition become additional weapons in his administrative armoury. On the one hand, simplicity gives him an innate sense of fairness; on the other hand, attunement to local superstitions allows him to understand the natives and to operate effectively within the customary.

Sanders's affinity with the natives reaches its apex in one of the final stories of *Sanders of the River*, 'The Lonely One'. Having lived so long with the native people, we are told, Sanders 'had acquired the uncanny power of knowing things which he would not and could not have known unless he were gifted with the prescience which is every aboriginal's birthright'.[78] In this story, Sanders's prescient suspicion that something is afoot amongst the Isisi sends him upriver undercover, disguised as a Nigerian prince. The bizarre audacity of imagining Sanders could pass, through several tribes no less, and could choose the moment of his self-revelation is frankly astonishing, and yet this is not the only example of a fictional District Commissioner blacking up and passing in order to foil a plot. We find a similar storyline, for example, in Arthur E. Southon's *A Yellow Napoleon*.[79] In both stories the willing suspension of disbelief, with which we started this chapter, is pushed to its limit in order to underwrite the romance of exception embodied in the fantastic mutability of the District Commissioner's very person. Wallace refers to Sanders's 'uncanny power' as a 'birthright' shared by 'every aboriginal' so that his mental assimilation mirrors his ensuing physical assimilation with the people over whom he rules. In assimilating his body and his mind Sanders becomes both hidden and visible: his private anonymity, facilitated by his visual passing, allows him to exercise his public powers all the more effectively.

What this storyline highlights for us is the way in which Sanders and other Commissioners who perform the same feat are able and permitted to do things that are otherwise forbidden. Sanders can do and be all the things that in other characters lead to their downfall, and in doing so he succeeds. As a result, whilst on the one hand he is utterly ordinary,

---

[77] This is a quality similarly attributed to Major Dane.
[78] Wallace, *Sanders of the River*, p. 154.
[79] Perham restrains herself from this particular popular trope in *Major Dane's Garden*.

by comparison with the other characters, he is also utterly exceptional. For insofar as Sanders issues the law it is issued from a figure of authority who places himself in a state of exception to it, enforcing the law in the process of breaking it. If Sanders is in Nigeria not simply to keep the peace but to assist in the civilising mission of the colonial project, as it understood itself in this period, transgressions of race and culture such as his passing become the exceptions that prove the rule against the cultural horror of educated and besuited Africans. Sanders enacts a wild fantasy of control through embodiment that is forbidden not only to the other characters but also, and equally importantly, to the readers of the book. Thus, in Sanders we see that elusive quality which drives all utopian visions: the law that is paradoxically absolute and absolutely benign. At a time when the practicalities of how the colonies should be governed were under considerable scrutiny and debate, Wallace creates a fabulous counterfactual reality in which the figure who breaks the law in order to enforce it is heroic, rather than (and, in certain instances, even if) the cause for questions in the House of Commons. To this extent the District Commissioner in his state of exception perfects the *homo newboltiensis* species of earlier colonial adventure fiction. For whereas earlier Newbolt Man failed to embody the full paradoxical power of the state of exception, since he began and remained outside the law, Sanders inscribes his becoming the law in the very process of stepping outside it.

'A Semblance of Truth'[80]

I noted earlier Cunninghame Graham's comment that 'in the multitude of negroes a solitary white man is just as much alone as on a desert island, exposed to frequent fevers in a climate hostile to North Europeans, and with no single ray of limelight turned upon any one throughout the colony'.[81] While his emphasis is on the isolated experience of the District Commissioner, he is also alert to how that isolation translates into media ignorance of colonial activity in Northern Nigeria. In 'Central Africa' he claims 'there were no Press-boomed Empire Builders; no manipulators of the money market; no gimcrack raids … no flag-wagging, no cant about the mission of the Anglo-Saxon race, and not a single word about the White Man's Burden'.[82] In each of the District Commissioner books discussed here the assumption that there is no 'story' in West Africa is

---

[80] Coleridge, *Biographia Literaria*, p. 174.
[81] Cunninghame Graham, 'Introduction', p. x.
[82] Ibid. p. ix.

challenged by a figure who is required to reflect the miraculous mundane that was understood to characterise British colonial service. Cunninghame Graham's description implicitly contrasts the media circus that attached to other colonial enterprises, not least Henry Morton Stanley's exploits in the Congo, with what he claims is a lack of media 'limelight' on Nigeria. Whilst the comparison holds true by and large, the fact that a steady stream of fictional and factual accounts of colonial service in West Africa, and particularly Nigeria, appeared from the start of the century onward indicates that there was an appetite amongst readers for this material and an interest in the subject. Moreover, the popularity of the Sanders novels, in particular, demonstrates that in fiction at least the public's appetite was sharp. Cunninghame Graham's claims, then, rebound back once again on to the character of the District Commissioner himself and the colonial service he represents. Just as Sanders must encompass both absolute normality and exceptionalism in order to reflect the dominant narrative that colonial rule in Nigeria was exceptional in its benevolent, civilising influence, so too the texts themselves must be both exceptional in what they recount and utterly normal in their manner of recounting, 'devoid of bombast', as Cunninghame Graham puts it.[83] The lack of media attention, the 'great sincerity and equal modesty' in Hastings's memoir and in Sanders's character, these are represented as, in and of themselves, exceptional qualities that justify the telling.

Returning to *Major Dane's Garden*, we can see how the genre must have appealed to Perham. Although her novel is set beyond the borders of Nigeria, in British Somaliland, the novel valorises the exceptionalism enshrined in Lugardian indirect rule, and this valorisation came to characterise her engagement with Britain's colonial activities in West Africa for many years after. Perham's text certainly differs in significant ways from the fiction of Wallace and Southon in its interest in affairs of the heart. Nevertheless, her embrace of the form indicates its capacity to communicate a sincerely felt ideal of service that came under increasing scrutiny and debate following the First World War. In the following chapter we will see how the administration's inventive relationship to the law, its preference for acting as the force of law in exception to the law, was critiqued by later memoirists and ironised by Joyce Cary. What these later texts demonstrate, however, alongside Perham's novel and those of Wallace and Southon, is the critical role played by the District

---

[83] Ibid. p. xi.

Commissioner as the embodiment of colonial law in the popular and administrative imagination.

I started this chapter by suggesting a parallel between the willing suspension of disbelief in the romance of early District Commissioner fiction and the suspension of disbelief that is required by the state of exception. When we examine contemporaneous accounts of colonial activity in Nigeria alongside District Commissioner fiction we can see how the fiction echoes, develops and feeds back into those factual accounts a narrative structure and rhetoric of exceptionalism that justifies the British colonial project. Major Dane's claim, for example, that 'every bit of honest work done … in fulfilment of our trust justifies our country and redeems our mission' might as easily be found in the pages of Hazzledine or Hastings, in its heartfelt defence of 'holding power *in trust* for the native people'.[84] Both fictional and factual accounts imaginatively erase the limits of the law through the romantic ideal that the law and civilisation are one and the same, and that both are congruent with the body of the District Commissioner. Thus, at the start of the twentieth century, adventure fiction and its Newboltian heroes provided the anomic space in which readers, including those in the colonial administration, might learn to suspend their disbelief and to imagine the colonies as non-places of legal exceptionalism.

---

[84] Perham, *Major Dane's Garden*, p. 262; emphasis added.

3

'Seeking a Legal Form': Joyce Cary's *Mister Johnson*

As we have seen in the previous chapter the District Commissioner novel developed out of the adventure romance tradition of the nineteenth century. The genre's innovation was to bring its hero into the professional sphere of the law from the unregulated province of independent adventure, which had been the domain of popular romance protagonists from Allan Quatermain to Sherlock Holmes. In its presentation of colonial administration the genre placed the law front and centre and, more specifically, the law's erasure in the state of exception. This was done without irony or critique. Consequently, the genre contributed to a larger justificatory discourse, found in memoirs and reports as much as fiction, that conflated the legal exception and civilised values with the person of the District Commissioner.

The popular taste for this sincere romance of early District Commissioner fiction (and colonial fiction more generally) persisted during the early decades of the twentieth century, evidenced by the continued international appeal of Wallace's Sanders series.[1] During this era, however, a second approach to representing the colonial enterprise emerged, which ironises this romance. Here, the key tropes of earlier romantic presentations were knowingly deflated, with suspense and heroism ironically replaced by bathos and banality. This approach reflected politically the evolving public debate and criticism of British colonialism in West Africa, and registered aesthetically the irony and ennui characteristic particularly of second-generation modernist literature. As early as 1932 Evelyn Waugh, in *Black Mischief*, took this approach to his representation of a newly independent African state, Azania, loosely based on his impressions of Ethiopia, which he visited in 1930 to cover

---

[1] Republished at the end of the war in 1919, *Sanders of the River* alone went on to be reprinted in 1933, 1945, 1963, 1972, 1986, 2001 and 2011, with the first American edition appearing in 1930. The novel was also translated into Danish (1925), German (1928), Swedish (1930) and Hebrew (1955), with many of these translations also going into reprint.

the coronation of Haile Selassie. In the same year that *Black Mischief* appeared, Joyce Cary, who was a generation older than Waugh, also experimented with ironic romance in his first novel, *Aissa Saved*. Like Waugh, Cary, who had served in the colonial administration in Nigeria during the First World War, drew on a combination of personal experience and the ironic humour of inter-war modernism in order to shape his colonial fiction. Cary's first experiment was followed up four years later with *The African Witch*.

The very titles of these two early novels by Cary make clear their contention with their Haggardian predecessors. In both *Aissa Saved* and *The African Witch* Cary sought to complicate the representations of cross-cultural colonial encounter found in earlier romance through a combination of satire and relativism that called into question the moral and civilising force of colonialism in general and of missionary activity in particular. His focus in both these novels on religion and magic as sites for exploring cross-cultural colonial encounter, however, inevitably reinforced the correlation between West Africa and primitivism that persisted in the contemporary popular imagination, not least through the still dominant paradigms of earlier District Commissioner fiction.

In *Mister Johnson* (1939) Cary moved away from these exoticised topics to the more mundane business of infrastructural planning and development, notably road-building. In doing so, he turned his critical and satirical attention to the practical rather than the spiritual arena in which British colonialism claimed to bring benefit. This focus allowed Cary to create a greater ironic distance between the romantic ideals of his protagonists and the romantic expectations of the genre, on the one hand, and, on the other, the banality of the novel's action. At the level of characterisation a hesitant and domesticated protagonist, Rudbeck, replaces the self-confident and heroic Sanders, while the primitive trickster, Bosambo, is replaced by the educated yet ludicrous Johnson. The fact that Rudbeck's favourite author is none other than Edgar Wallace, moreover, underlines the quixotic lack of self-awareness that typifies almost every character, and this quixotism forms, in large part, the basis for Cary's satire.[2] For rather than present the banality of his protagonists' activities in the high rhetorical register of earlier romance, he presents the romantic self-delusion of his protagonists in banal form, emphasising this banality even at the

---

[2] Cary, *Mister Johnson*, p. 103.

grammatical level through his insistent use of the present tense (something to which we will return).

In what follows I want to tease out not only how *Mister Johnson* reflects contemporaneous experiences of the legal machinations of colonial Nigeria, but also how the systematisation of the state of exception that we observed in Chapters 1 and 2 is imbricated in the very generic and rhetorical form in which Cary works. Cary attempts, like his more famous counterpart Waugh, to deflate the conventions of earlier romance that characterised the District Commissioner genre in the first three decades of the twentieth century, and that relied unquestioningly on the romantic appeal of the unexceptional exceptional hero, exemplified in the fiction of Wallace, Southon and Perham. Yet, for all his knowing satire of the paradox at the heart of the genre, Cary nevertheless is drawn inevitably to reinscribe the romance of civilisation and the state of exception as colonialism's redemptive keystone. To understand how and why Cary falls back on the state of exception in this way I start with an account of the historical context for the novel, including Cary's own experience of administration in Nigeria. This context is important to grasp if we are to make sense of the novel's detail, for it is through this detail that Cary reveals the discontinuities, gaps and ruptures in the colonial project that the state of exception enables and that the rhetoric of civilisation attempts to obscure.

Education and Indirect Rule

In 1914 the colonial office circulated a minute in which it was claimed that education in Southern Nigeria 'has gone far to help in producing the "trousered ape" with his European clothes, yellow buttoned boots, boiled shirt, resplendent tie and almost utter lack of industry, morals or manners'.[3] This stunningly offensive characterisation of those who had sought to benefit from the supposedly civilising influence of colonial education and opportunities is reflected clearly, as we have seen, in the attitude of fictional District Commissioners such as Sanders. What the stereotype of the 'trousered ape' also signposts is the broader shift at the turn of the century from an assimilative colonial policy to one that attempted to preserve cultural differences through indirect rule. In this context the educated African represents a transgression of custom, polluting the purity of native tradition through what amounts to cultural miscegenation. If one goal of

---

[3] CO 583/20 (1914), 'Education in the Colony …'. Minute by A. J. Harding, quoted in Mason, 'The History of Mr Johnson', p. 206.

indirect rule was to protect and perpetuate cultural distinctions within the colonies, the educated African disrupted that aim through his or her own aspirations to adopt British practices. Nevertheless, in contradiction to this purported disavowal, colonial Nigeria relied upon educated and trained Nigerians to assist in the administration of indirect rule, and their role as interpreters and assistants was commented upon in diaries and memoirs from the beginning of the century onwards.[4]

As in other aspects of colonial rule in Nigeria, the initial split between the Northern and Southern Protectorates enabled and compounded differences of policy in education at the turn of the century. Whereas in Lagos there was a well-established primary and secondary school system along British lines and an extensive Nigerian anglophone press, elsewhere, particularly in the Northern Protectorate, indirect rule kept education in the hands of local rulers. The justification for this was that, in Michael Mason's words, 'Northern Nigeria might follow a unique trajectory which would guarantee racial, or at least cultural, purity and assure loyalty to the British Crown.'[5] However, with the Northern Protectorate operating at a deficit in its early years and with mission schools banned, the result of this policy was that educational provision was woeful. The first primary school was not established until 1905, and by the start of the First World War Northern Nigeria still had only five primary schools to serve a population of close to one million. Post-primary education, moreover, was not introduced until 1922.[6]

This paucity of education in the North was hardly incidental but was in fact part and parcel of the larger policy behind indirect rule. As Mahmood Mamdani explains, the claim that indirect rule was a result of a lack of colonial administrative capacity was predicated on an assumption that such capacity was not available from the Nigerians themselves. In the past, colonial policy had been to engage West African administrators in senior positions. Mamdani notes that by the 1890s in Sierra Leone, for example, 'nearly half the senior posts were held by Africans' and points out that in Lagos 'Africans sat in the legislature and held senior offices from the 1850s on'.[7] However, by 1912 the

---

[4] For a larger discussion of indigenous employees in Europe's African colonies, see Lawrence, Osborn and Robert, *Intermediaries, Interpreters, and Clerks*.
[5] Mason, 'The History of Mr Johnson', pp. 205–6.
[6] Mason provides the contrasting statistics for the South, where by 1918 there were '44 government schools, 189 "assisted" schools, and probably more than 1,400 non-assisted schools'. 'The History of Mr Johnson', p. 206.
[7] Mamdani, *Citizen and Subject*, p. 75.

number of African senior officials in Sierra Leone had been reduced to one in six, and similar reductions were made throughout the rest of West Africa.[8] As the British expanded their colonial interests into the interior of Nigeria they sought to resolve resistance from the local population through the promotion of local leadership under indirect rule. Accordingly, the colonial administration attempted to keep as many of the local customs and systems as were thought necessary to maintaining safe access to the trade routes and markets opened up by the expansion into Northern Nigeria. One feature of this policy in the North was a restriction on anglicising educational programmes. Nominally this education policy preserved local custom for native Northerners, but it also effectively blocked their routes to senior administrative roles within the colonial administration.

Whilst disavowing the educated elite of the coast, the tandem systems of native and colonial administration that were yoked together under indirect rule in the North nonetheless required considerable clerical manpower. As a result they inevitably came to rely upon educated English speakers from the South as well as the local middle-class, who were brought in to staff the ever-expanding administrative complex of courts and councils. These men filled the need for clerks, translators, messengers, court orderlies and other roles required to support the bureaucracy of the colony. Clerks within the Nigerian colonial administration were generally sourced from the South and this placed them in an isolated position if they were posted North: separated, on the one hand, from the local population by education, regional background, culture and frequently by religion, on the other hand, they were separated by race and authority from the District Commissioners with whom they worked. Moreover, amongst administrators in the North particularly, the essentialising spirit of the colonial zeitgeist served to reinforce the kind of violent antipathy to educated West Africans that one finds in Harding's 1914 minute.

Twenty years later, when the colonial administration was finally beginning to encourage education in the North, the rhetorical tone might have changed but reservations about the efficacy of educating Nigerians remained. In April 1934, W. R. Crocker, a colonial officer in Misau Emirate, queried in his diary:

---

[8] Ibid. p. 76.

> What is the good of sending more boys to the schools? Many, if not the majority, cannot find jobs when they have finished, and, given the African's preoccupation with status, they are not likely to return, except by force, to hoeing and digging when they have been dressed in white gowns for five to ten years. It is not surprising that parents say that it is better not to lose the boy's character and services from the farm from the beginning: if we let him go to the Government school he cannot find a job, we are short of the labour of one producer for five to ten years, and after that he is a liability … The mere production of literates, or, rather, semi-literates, is as expensive as it is bad socially.[9]

Crocker's pessimistic assessment of the new education policy that he had been asked to administer recycles the rhetoric of Harding's minute: he assumes that without the opportunity to contribute clerical labour to the colonial administration, education will merely produce an unindustrious, shiftless and socially irresponsible male population. Crocker's complaint should be understood in its context of the financial constraints that the Great Depression had on the administration in the early 1930s. These constraints restricted the administrative expansion of a decade earlier meaning that there were fewer clerical jobs available than there had been previously. Nonetheless, a reasonable number of educated Nigerians continued to find employment throughout the 1920s and 1930s in both trade and administration, despite the continued prejudices against them.

'Large Debts and … Illegal Taxes'[10]

Joyce Cary's *Mister Johnson* fictionalises these conditions in Northern Nigeria in the 1930s, and places an educated Southerner centre stage as the eponymous protagonist. The setting of the story is biographically significant as Cary's service as a colonial officer had been in the North. Sent out in the summer of 1914, the same year as Harding's minute, he only retired from service at the end of the decade when his short fiction finally began to meet with success. Of the seventy admitted to the Nigerian service in Cary's cohort, sixty-four requested the North but only six – including Cary – were successful. Although highly competitive, the North was considered a tougher assignment than the South, having been colonised far more recently and comprising as it did challenging terrain and varying degrees of hostility from the local populations. Despite the recognised challenges, however, training had barely moved on since

---

[9] Crocker, *Nigeria: A Critique*, p. 150.
[10] Cary, *Mister Johnson*, p. 85.

A. C. G. Hastings's time a decade earlier. Cary's biographer, Malcolm Foster, notes that 'at the Imperial Institute there were a few lectures on medicine, some talks on Nigerian law, an introduction to surveying, and scarcely anything else'.[11] As had been the case for Hastings, the implicit assumption was that the colonial officer would possess the capacity for administrative rule as an inherent feature of his civilised British upbringing and education.

Cary's experience in Nigeria was mixed. The outbreak of the First World War meant he was initially deployed against Germany in Cameroon. Later, when he returned to political service, the war contributed to understaffing in the North. This latter issue led to delays to leave, for lack of anyone else to take over his post. Long postings in poor conditions – his quarters were roofless at times, and his clothes, papers and bedding frequently rotted away – aggravated Cary's asthma and frayed his nerves. Although he seems to have resisted sliding into alcoholism, a resort to which some of his colleagues took, his temper got the better of him both physically and verbally, as his letters attest. His attitude to his superiors was changeable and he could be by turns both paternal and vitriolic about the Nigerians with whom he worked. Foster notes that in this correspondence we can see Cary working out his own attitude towards the mission and methods of the service.

What Foster doesn't mention, however, is the way his letters draw upon the already familiar tropes of Nigeria that circulated in contemporaneous popular fiction and memoirs. Thus, for example, in a letter home in spring 1917 he describes his position in his new district of Borgu in a style that borrows directly from the romantic rhetoric used by Southon and Wallace: '*Lord* of some 10,000 square miles, *mostly deserted* bush, with a large population of liones [sic], snakes, crocodiles & mosquitoes – the administration is in confusion and the people backward. Hundreds of miles are swamp.'[12] Cary's account was no doubt true in essence but its neat yet sweeping rhetoric, 'some 10,000 square miles ... the administration is in confusion ... the people backward ... hundreds of miles', mimics the eager romanticism that we encountered in the previous chapter, not least in the way it emphasises Cary's isolation. Cary's own letters thus demonstrate the persistent influence of the generic form of District Commissioner fiction in structuring not only popular opinion but also administrative officers' own understanding of their role and circumstances.

---

[11] Foster, *Joyce Cary*, p. 83.
[12] Quoted in Foster, *Joyce Cary*, p. 142; emphases added.

Isolated as he may have been in Borgu, Cary's experience was, like that of Hastings, Crocker and others, shaped by the system he served. Like them he relied upon interpreters and clerks in his day-to-day work, and although at times separated from other British colonial officers he was nonetheless expected to remain in contact with his seniors through regular reports. Moreover, as for Hastings and Crocker, Cary's role was to put into practice new policies from the senior administration, 'confused' though it might be; and at times he experimented with his own ideas, with varying degrees of success. One such experiment occurred in 1917 when Cary appointed a 'Serakin Mata, or queen of the women' to police the wives left behind by native soldiers deployed to Tanganyika.[13] As Foster explains, 'soldiers, who were apt to be transferred anywhere, had to marry girls who would follow them' and such women were often those already cast out of their own villages for misdemeanours of one kind or another.[14] When the soldiers departed, trouble amongst their wives broke out. The Serakin Mata's job was to maintain order in the community and, with policewomen of her own appointing, to bring any criminal cases to Cary's court. This arrangement, irregular though it might have been, gives an indication of the way Cary sought to operate effectively if inventively within the administrative system by replicating its ad hoc approach to bureaucracy. In doing so, Cary exemplifies the legal expediency that Speed provides for in the 'indeterminate' limitations that apply to a District Commissioner's actions.[15]

His years of service in Nigeria's colonial administration contribute the kind of realist detail to Cary's African fiction that is lacking in that by Wallace and even by Southon, despite the latter's claims to personal experience. In *Mister Johnson* not only do we encounter the various clerks of the colonial administration but we also encounter members of the Islamic legal administration – the waziri (judge), the mallam (*malam* – scholar) and the dogarai (police). Moreover, whereas Wallace and Southon maintain their vision of Nigeria as one that remains in the earliest days and most extreme reaches of colonial influence – Sanders, it seems, is forever on the very edge of the map – in *Mister Johnson* we are aware that time has moved on, bringing with it, amongst other things, greater urbanisation and new political complexities. Publishing *Mister Johnson* two decades after his own time in Nigeria, Cary was careful to check his facts, at least

---

[13] Foster, *Joyce Cary*, p. 147.
[14] Ibid.
[15] Speed, *Richards's Table of Offences*, p. v.

with regard to the legal status of Rudbeck's killing of Johnson.[16] Thus, although the colonial environment of Cary's fiction is certainly simplified, it nonetheless dispenses with much of the romantic isolation and exoticism of earlier romance, exemplified in the Sanders series, in favour of increased detail that gives, at the very least, the *effect* of realism. This effect is key to Cary's ironic approach in that it is through the inclusion of detail that he can reveal the gap between ideal and reality. This gap occurs not only between a given protagonist's ideal self-image and the reality of their actions and standing within the community, but also between the idealising plot and style of earlier romance, and of District Commissioner fiction in particular, and the satirical impetus of Cary's ironic romance. Indeed, it is by means of this gap that, consciously and unconsciously, Cary draws our attention to the work of imagination, the suspension of disbelief, necessary to the states of exception by which the colonial administration operates.

A good deal of the detail that adds to the novel's impression of realism is located in Cary's attention to corruption and deceit. In earlier District Commissioner fiction, Nigerian corruption is presented as a cultural weakness that can be cured through subjection to the civilising force of the Commissioner as the embodiment of civilisation as/and the law. In *Mister Johnson*, these accounts instead draw attention to the failure of the colonial system to inculcate administrative transparency in both the British and native administrations alike. Moreover, in detailing the small as well as large instances of corruption and deceit that come to characterise all aspects of colonial society, Cary illustrates the comedy and the danger inherent in rendering such corruption banal. For, unlike the tricksterish exploits of Bosambo and Sanders, the misdemeanours of *Mister Johnson* exacerbate rather than resolve problems, failing to attain the heroic exceptionalism that characterises the actions of earlier protagonists in District Commissioner fiction. Thus, our earliest encounter with the Emir's representative, the Waziri, referred to only by his official title throughout, shows him attempting to persuade Mr Johnson, who is a clerk to the District Commissioner, to give him access to all the reports in the district office. Mr Johnson initially refuses Waziri but later, beleaguered by his creditors, Johnson accedes to Waziri, who keeps the creditors at bay in exchange for transcriptions of official correspondence and

---

[16] Foster, *Joyce Cary*, p. 328.

reports. When Johnson brings the reports to Waziri he translates them aloud from English to Hausa for him. Both reports on the Emir and Waziri are damning: the Emir 'has large debts and still levies illegal taxes ... his women and servants freely rob the market. He cannot be trusted to look after his own interests, as he is subject to violent fits of temper'; Waziri 'never stops plotting and he is a skilful liar ... he is surrounded by enemies who would try to destroy him if the Emir withdrew his protection ... [h]e himself is fully aware of his desperate position and ... is therefore a most dangerous man'.[17] Waziri's gravest concern on hearing the reports is that the Emir will learn of the District Commissioner's poor opinion of Waziri. Waziri's young lover, Saleh, suggests he will be whipped, but the reader recognises that the danger Waziri perceives for himself is that he will be thrown out of office, because he poses a danger to the security of the Emir's authority.

These initial scenes with Waziri dramatise the everyday corruption of the customary legislators, including the Emir himself, a corruption attested to in the memoirs and historical accounts of the period too. Mamdani refers to this state of affairs under indirect rule as 'decentralized despotism'.[18] In combining the powers of the 'petty legislator, administrator, judge, and policeman all in one' in the person of the Emir, explains Mamdani, Lugard's ideal of indirect rule in Northern Nigeria gave carte blanche to the Emirs to proceed with the same corruption that the colonial system claimed to be stamping out.[19] Moreover, in positioning the Emir as a proxy for colonial authority itself, the colonial administration could rarely permit the Emir's position to be undermined. Therefore despite regular and blatant abuses of power, such as those in the reports Johnson reads to Waziri, little was done to check the Emirs for fear that compromising their prestige would politically rebound upon the prestige of colonial authority and would practically encourage resentment and rebellion within the districts.[20] To this extent Waziri is right to be more concerned about what is said about him than about the Emir. The Emir's faults will be tolerated but an insubordinate yet powerful figure beneath the Emir, such as Waziri, has the potential to destabilise the district, something that the colonial administration *and* the Emir would wish to avoid. Given that this is the case, however, these scenes also demonstrate the pragmatism of

---

[17] Cary, *Mister Johnson*, pp. 85–6.
[18] Mamdani, *Citizen and Subject*, p. 61.
[19] Ibid. p. 54.
[20] Ibid.

Waziri's corruption, since he is not in fact seeking to overthrow the colonial regime but rather to keep his position of power within it.

It is the banality of Waziri's political corruption that distinguishes it from earlier District Commissioner fiction. His is a world apart from the megalomaniac intrigues and almost supernatural powers of secret leopard societies imagined in Southon and Wallace. In his first attempts to persuade Mr Johnson to supply the reports he points out that Johnson's predecessor, Bauli, had done the same and been rewarded handsomely. Their 'private conference' is overheard by all the guests at Mr Johnson's party, at which Waziri has arrived unannounced, but 'this [fact of being overheard] does not disconcert the Waziri or Johnson. The arrangement with clerk Bauli is well known and, moreover, it is a very common one. All the clerks, even Ajali at the store, receive presents from various native ministers.'[21] The deflatory mundaneness of this scene of corruption and the way it is accommodated within the colonial system is part of Cary's satire, as is the fact that Waziri's political corruption is mirrored by the massaging of reports and accounts by the British colonial officers themselves. Indeed, in presenting these early scenes at length, Cary encourages his reader to draw uncomplimentary comparisons between Waziri's corruption and the routine inventiveness towards the law displayed by the colonial administration. Cary does not allow this comparison to exonerate Waziri completely, however, and he is careful to distinguish Waziri from the colonial officers by signalling an innate moral turpitude through the string of very young male companions he keeps. The vanity, manipulation and petulance of these boys underscore Waziri's implicit weakness of character, willing as he is to be mocked, shamed and shunned by these young tyrants on account of their beauty. Waziri's implicit pederasty goes uncommented upon by anyone in the text, or by the text itself, but, using a stock orientalist trope of sexual deviance to do so, Cary's intention is clearly to show the Muslim official as morally subordinate to the British administrators, however much his *political* corruption might be excusable.[22]

If Waziri is used to satirise the pragmatic corruption of the native administration, Rudbeck, the District Officer, represents the idealistic corruption of the colonial administration. Much of the novel's drama revolves around the more and less legal financing of the road that Rudbeck

---

[21] Cary, *Mister Johnson*, pp. 37, 38.
[22] Of course, Waziri's penchant for young boys goes uncommented upon in part in order to avoid censorship. Whilst Waziri's Muslim and Nigerian identity no doubt allowed for greater flexibility in representing homosexual relations than could be countenanced in representing white Christian colonial characters, Cary, desperate at this stage in his career for literary success, would not have wanted to court any undue controversy arising from his subject matter.

is determined to build, and which he hopes will connect his district, Fada, to the larger trade routes and in so doing bring increased prosperity to the region. But in a period of financial austerity Rudbeck has to engage in some creative accounting in order to realise his dream. By all accounts Northern Nigeria was run on a shoestring budget, particularly in the early years of the twentieth century. During the First World War and later in the Great Depression budgets were cut back in the interests of the British domestic economy. For the officers on the spot these cuts were all the more frustrating when they witnessed on a day-to-day basis apparently pointless squandering of what budget there was on impossible schemes and administrative inefficiencies. Crocker's diary entry for 26 April 1934 notes:

> The man who was in charge of this Division for some years in the past, and who has been given accelerated promotion, seems to have devoted his activities here mainly to spending N.A. [Native Authority] money on white elephants. The Azare workshops are piled high with things bought at his instance: there is a motor road-roller which does three miles (I think three) to the gallon of petrol – a cost so fantastic that it will be many a year, if ever, before the N.A. can afford to use it. The roller is thus rusting unused in a shed. There is also a Guy motor in similar condition. And a mechanical saw. And a steel lathe. And, most remarkable of all, an entire Decauville Railway complete with locomotive, trucks, and rails – and nothing to use it for. The surprising thing is that the then Resident of Kano ... ever sanctioned so much expenditure of N.A. money, not to mention its expenditure on such objects. But those were the good old days.[23]

This surreal list of machinery bought with the revenues amassed by and allotted to the Native Authority demonstrates two things. Firstly, despite the Native Authority's nominal independence in managing its own finances, it was in fact subject to regular and extensive direction on expenditure from the District Commissioner and the Resident.[24] Secondly, the passions and policies of one Resident or Commissioner were all too frequently superseded by those of their replacement, resulting in inefficient short-term spending on projects that were doomed to remain incomplete or, as in the case of the

---

[23] Crocker, *Nigeria: A Critique*, p. 158.
[24] Crocker says as much elsewhere: 'To anyone with a knowledge of African mentality it is a foregone conclusion that, for the time being, non-corruption no less than ordinary competence necessitate a European control over N.A. Treasuries, so strict that at the best the autonomy must be the thinnest of façades.' *Nigeria: A Critique*, pp. 133–4.

Decauville Railway, never even started. One of Crocker's repeated complaints in his diary is that administrators are rarely returned to their former postings and therefore all their local knowledge and local reputation, as well as their long-term plans, are wasted and instead another new officer must go through exactly the same process of laborious fact-finding and familiarisation, meaning that the implementation of policies and local improvements are once more delayed. In October 1933 Crocker recorded in his diary that he was handing over Katsina Ala District to the same man who had previously taken over from him at Abinsi two months prior, when Crocker had been sent on to Katsina Ala. This constant and apparently irrational movement of personnel, in stark contrast to the romantic stasis of Sanders and 'his people', kept District Commissioners constantly on their toes, used up valuable finances in the cost of transport, and explains to some extent the inevitable obsolescence of plans such as the railway stored in the Azare shed.

These inefficiencies and the larger financial pressures of the Great Depression, which were familiar to the general public through memoirs, reportage and fiction, form the historical backdrop to Rudbeck's dream of the Fada road and to his finagling of the accounts to make that dream a reality. Indeed, once we recognise the disorganisation of the colonial administration as a key context for the novel, we can see how Cary intends for Rudbeck's corruption to be mitigated: Rudbeck is driven to inventiveness (as Cary himself had been with his female police force) by the failure of the administration to provide adequate systems through which to operate within the law. In this regard, Rudbeck echoes his fictional predecessors, such as Sanders, and, just as the unseen powers of the central administration permit Sanders to justify his means retrospectively with his ends, so Rudbeck finds his creative accounting is forgiven on the basis that 'all these regulations meant to keep a check on every penny of expenditure are a bit of an *anomaly*'.[25] In this telling phrase Cary sums up the way in which corruption could be recalibrated by presenting regulation as anomaly and transgression as the sanctioned norm – 'the legal form of what cannot have legal form'.[26] Indeed, these echoes of the privileging of exceptionalism noted in earlier fiction are key to the novel's final capitulation to the romantic lure of the state of exception, despite Cary's apparent satire of its systemic effects.

Rudbeck arrives in Fada already enthused with road-building fervour, which he has inherited from the first Resident under whom he served,

---

[25] Cary, *Mister Johnson*, p. 126; emphasis added.
[26] Agamben, *State of Exception*, p. 1.

'Old Sturdee'.²⁷ When Rudbeck runs out of money from his Roads and Bridges account he proceeds with Johnson's encouragement to borrow additional funds from other accounts, including his own treasury, making up spurious costs to cover the expense:

> It is a common enough practice to spend one vote on another purpose. No honest hardworking official likes to see good money disappearing into the hands of the treasury at the end of the year ... Rudbeck himself only the week before, has shown the native Treasurer how to spend his vote for *dogarai* uniforms ... on a mosque.²⁸

Johnson's finesse to this procedure is to borrow next year's allowance of £150 from the treasury cash tank and replace it in the new financial year when the allowance comes through, at the same time writing up costs in the new financial year to cover the £150 spent. Rudbeck's desire to complete his road overwhelms his concerns that if such a scheme were found out it would see him 'kicked out of the service with seven years' imprisonment' and he acquiesces to Johnson's plan.²⁹

The road continues until Rudbeck's leave comes round, at which point his ruse is uncovered by his over-eager replacement, Tring. However, whereas Johnson earlier in the novel has faced arrest, losing his job, and prison when it is discovered that he has embezzled some of the money that should have been paid to the station labourers, Rudbeck's misdemeanour is buried by the Resident, Bulteel, despite Tring's best attempts to report it:

> Thanks to a private note from Bulteel to the Chief Commissioner, and because Bulteel's wife's first cousin is in the Secretariat, Tring's report, having stuck for two months in the provincial office, and another in the secretariat, reaches the Secretary at last only in the form of a précis in which the words 'embezzlement' and 'forgery' are translated into overspending votes and unorthodox accounting.³⁰

Just as the Emir's prestige must be maintained for indirect rule to be effective, so the administrative system cannot be seen to acknowledge the financial misdemeanours of its own white officers, not least in an era when punitive customs levies were being used to bolster the British economy at the expense of colonial subjects, who were already overburdened by heavy taxation. Resistance to the financial demands made by the administration

---

[27] Cary, *Mister Johnson*, p. 52.
[28] Ibid. p. 88.
[29] Ibid. p. 90.
[30] Ibid. p. 128.

was strong in the period in which the novel is set (Crocker records repeated instances of villages hiding their livestock in order to decrease their tax liability), and so any indication of mismanagement of funds would be liable to set off unrest.

That these practical considerations are not mentioned in the novel, however, is worth noting. Their absence draws our attention to the ironic gap that Cary maintains between ideal and reality, and in particular the way in which the novel's protagonists repeatedly transmute practical considerations (such as local tax evasion) into conceptual or ideological ones. This conscious and unconscious slippage between ideal and reality, between practical and theoretical considerations, takes us to the heart of the paradox of colonial law. Thus instead of invoking the practical necessities of not pursuing Rudbeck through the courts over his embezzlement and forgery, Bulteel's explanation operates at an ideological level that recalls Hazzledine's invocation of special laws: Bulteel counsels Tring that 'we're meant to be trusted – that's why they give us *special conditions* ... we've got to be trusted or the whole thing would come to bits'.[31] Bulteel's explanation is telling. Residents and their District Commissioners do not have to find special conditions to justify their suspension of the application of the law; rather, they are *given* special conditions. The state of exception is, as it were, built into the whole administrative system as a gift to its officers. The very regulations which are intended to circumscribe the actions of the District Commissioner contain within them the sanction to operate beyond their bounds. Moreover, this sanction of irregular action stands for the trust upon which the system, which is to be exceeded, is grounded. The paradox of a system that operates on the basis of trust in its officers to defy that same system is immediately apparent. What is less clear at this point, however, is the extent to which Cary intends to satirise or sanction this state of affairs. In a parallel paradox, Cary's narrative seems at once to critique humorously and to endorse affectionately the gift of special conditions. Such a paradox of narration is made possible by the formal qualities of romance itself, whether sincere or ironic, which, like Bulteel's explanation to Tring, coalesce around the translation of the real into the ideal enabled by the heroic or anti-heroic state of exception. This translation, in the case of

---

[31] Ibid. p. 127; emphasis added. See Hazzledine: 'Special laws must also be made for the people themselves on the introduction of conditions not provided for by their own.' *The White Man in Nigeria*, p. 94. We might also recall Major Dane's exclamation that 'every bit of honest work done ... in fulfilment of our trust justifies our country and redeems our mission.' Perham, *Major Dane's Garden*, p. 262.

Mister Johnson, overwrites the jurisprudential issues at stake with farce so that the critical point is repeatedly deferred by the bathetic means of Cary's satirical form.

The Road

Before examining the significance of this paradox for Mr Johnson himself, we must first consider Rudbeck's road-building passion in a little more detail. Transport and security were key issues from the start in colonial Nigeria. The Northern and Southern Protectorates were formed in part because the Royal Niger Company was struggling to maintain the security of its trade routes through the interior of the region. The development of railways and roads was of primary concern at the inception of colonial rule, therefore, in order to improve the transport out of commodities and the transport in of military, administrative and commercial personnel. As with other aspects of colonial operations the practical demands for improved transport were often transfigured by the justificatory rhetoric of civilisation: roads and railways would bring peace where slave-raiding had been practised by facilitating the policing of those regions; would bring modernity to the pagan interior; and would transform the productivity and therefore wealth of previously subsistence communities. To this latter end seed was distributed to encourage the growth of cash crops as opposed to subsistence farming, on the grounds that cash crops would deplete the soil less, and would increase the circulation of currency, thereby providing the necessary cash revenue for the payment of taxes without having to resort to payment in kind. As noted in the previous chapter, taxation where communities did not have sufficient currency required District Commissioners to take payment in kind (livestock, produce and commodities), which then had to be auctioned off to raise the necessary surplus. Not only was this a laborious process but it excluded the poor from entering the currency system. Cash crops, it was argued, had the power to resolve both these problems. Moreover, better transportation routes were also necessary for more efficient and securer tax collection.

Despite these available arguments, both practical and ideological, Cary is emphatic about the arbitrary cause of Rudbeck's enthusiasm for road-building:

> Rudbeck, like other juniors, had no idea when he joined [the colonial service] of what would be expected of him. If he had come to Blore first, no doubt he would have ... considered census much the most important

duty of a political officer. But from Sturdee he has caught the belief that to build a road, any road anywhere, is the noblest work a man can do.[32]

Rudbeck does later justify the Fada road using the various common arguments noted above; nonetheless, his pleasure in the making of the road, the process itself, reflects his absorption of Sturdee's aphorism that 'when you make a road you know you've done something – you can see it'.[33] Of course, the actual making and doing of the road is not the labour of the District Commissioner but of those who labour at his command. But in Sturdee's phrase the reality of that labour is translated on to the Commissioner as proof of his idealised capacity.

Once Rudbeck decides to fall in with Johnson's suggestion of borrowing from the cash tank against the following year's vote he throws himself into the project, ignoring his office work and giving way completely to the romance of road-building.[34] Rudbeck encourages the labourers to imagine 'a kind of paradise' that will result when the road is built; indeed, he selects the labourers 'precisely for [their] quality of optimism, ambition, and imagination'.[35] These labourers stand in contrast to the unromantic 'poorer, more cut-off people' who 'do not want roads and have not enough energy or imagination to break out from their poverty'.[36] The road, Cary thus suggests, requires not only physical but also imaginative exertion for its benefits to be grasped. This emphasis on the importance of imagination is telling. Imagination it seems is essential not only to the colonial authorities but also to their subjects. Both require imagination to produce the 'paradise' of civilisation.

Rudbeck is caught up in the romantic ideal of the road, going out 'at night by moonlight to look at the long gulf stretching away through the

---

[32] Cary, *Mister Johnson*, p. 52. As an aside, Blore's penchant for census-making helps to explain his sharp disdain for Mr Johnson at the beginning of the novel. As Mamdani points out, the census was a key instrument in the colonial programme of preserving native custom. The census enabled and encouraged careful categorisation of tribal affiliation by which to define indigenous populations and thereby bind them to specific geographies and cultures. Mr Johnson's abandonment of his native custom through education and geographical movement goes against the ideological values of cultural stasis that census-making underpinned and reinforced. See Mamdani, *Define and Rule*, pp. 43–7.

[33] Cary, *Mister Johnson*, p. 52.

[34] Once again we find here Rudbeck's actions suggested by others when Cary explains: 'Rudbeck has always despised office work, because someone, probably his father, when he was young, has said something contemptuous about it.' *Mister Johnson*, p. 93.

[35] Ibid. p. 92.

[36] Ibid. p. 169.

forest' that gives him an 'unusual' emotion: 'keen and exciting'.[37] This emotion is addictive and 'he is on the road every day, simply to enjoy it'.[38] But Cary once again satirises Rudbeck's enthusiasm by characterising it as capricious, comparing it to that of 'thousands of Englishmen who every year, from some *accidental* source, get the idea to … build a summer house'.[39] The 'accidental' nature of Rudbeck's road-building enthusiasm undermines its practical justifications and proves its ideological justifications arbitrary.

Moreover, Rudbeck's faith in the transcendental value of the Fada road is challenged in time by its consequences. When the road is completed and the first lorries roll through, Waziri points out to Rudbeck that 'it is a most strange thing, but all the thieves and blackguards in the country have come to Fada, especially from the north. The Fada people, too, have never been so insolent.'[40] Waziri's disingenuous bemusement at the crime wave hitting Fada is met with threats from Rudbeck, who claims that spreading 'false reports' of the road's deleterious effect will displease the Governor and result in a pay cut.[41] Nevertheless, despite his rebuttal of Waziri, Rudbeck begins to doubt the benefit of the road. 'Could it be that dirty old savages like the Emir and Waziri were right in their detestation of motor roads?' he wonders. However, whereas the Emir and Waziri's concerns are practical – thanks to the policies of indirect rule they, more than Rudbeck, are responsible for the day-to-day policing and jurisdiction of Fada and must do so out of their own treasury – Rudbeck's doubts are once more expressed in characteristically conceptual terms: the road, he fears, has the power to bring 'confusion, revolution', 'the breakdown of civilization'.[42]

Rudbeck's concerns, and his conversation with Bulteel about them, reflect long-standing debates in the service about the relative values of tradition and change, and particularly the application of that debate to the civilising mission of colonial activity. This was a concern that was particularly felt in Nigeria at the time. Indirect rule was intended to answer this concern by binding together traditional and colonial systems to mutual benefit. However, the persistence of the debate demonstrated the failure of indirect rule to cut the Gordian knot and, indeed, indirect rule's

---

[37] Ibid. p. 92.
[38] Ibid. p. 93.
[39] Ibid.; emphasis added.
[40] Ibid. p. 181.
[41] Ibid. p. 182.
[42] Ibid. p. 184.

contribution to the perpetuation of the debate. Rudbeck's challenge to Bulteel – 'don't you believe in the native civilization?' – indicates the acceptable relativism that had entered into the debate by the 1930s, a hypothetical recognition that 'dirty old savages like the Emir and Waziri' might be noble as well.[43] Bulteel's response – 'how would you like it yourself?' – invites Rudbeck to pursue the logic of his claim to its conclusion and in doing so implies that to do so is a *reductio ad absurdum*.[44] Native civilisation, Bulteel suggests, is no civilisation any civilised white man would tolerate and as such is no civilisation at all (this, after all, is the significance of the repugnancy test). Rudbeck acknowledges Bulteel's point but declares that there still needs to be a justificatory idea, if not a plan, behind British colonialism (Bulteel warns that he'll be taken for a 'Bolshy' if he speaks of 'a plan').

Cary's dramatisation of this conversation consciously echoes an early passage in Joseph Conrad's own ironic romance, 'Heart of Darkness', in which the narrator, Marlow, reflects on the Roman conquest of Britain:

> The conquest of the earth, which mostly means the taking it away from those who have a different complexion or slightly flatter noses than ourselves, is not a pretty thing when you look into it too much. What redeems it is the idea only ... an unselfish belief in the idea – something you can set up, and bow down before, and offer a sacrifice to.[45]

Rudbeck's desire for an idea, 'something to work to', demonstrates the persistent need for a concept that can justify the colonial state of exception – in Conrad's words, 'something you can set up ... and offer a sacrifice to'.[46] At the same time, Cary's allusion to Conrad here invites the knowing reader to recall Marlow's pragmatic evaluation of colonisation, as 'robbery with violence, aggravated murder on a great scale, and men going at it blind', an evaluation which Marlow expresses immediately prior to his analysis of colonial idealism.[47] This pragmatic account inevitably undermines the rhetorical force of colonial idealism both for Marlow and, through Cary's allusion, for our reading of Rudbeck.

When Rudbeck returns to the road it 'seems to speak to him. "I am abolishing the old ways, the old ideas, the old law; ... I am the revolution ... I destroy and I make new. What are you going to do about it? I am

---

[43] Ibid. pp. 185, 184.
[44] Ibid. p. 185.
[45] Conrad, 'Heart of Darkness', in *Youth and Two Other Stories*, pp. 57–8.
[46] Cary, *Mister Johnson*, p. 185.
[47] Conrad, 'Heart of Darkness', in *Youth and Two Other Stories*, p. 57.

your idea.'"[48] In this declaration the road appears as the material manifestation of the colonial enterprise *as* the state of exception, not least in the final claim, 'I am your idea'. In Rudbeck's imagination the road becomes a symbol of revolution, the 'idea' he is seeking to articulate in his conversation with Bulteel. But in imagining the road as an independent force that can drive men and excite revolution, Rudbeck exculpates himself from responsibility. As before, Rudbeck's withdrawal into a conceptual realm displaces his responsibility for the road, including his responsibility for his arbitrary enthusiasm for it, on to something beyond himself – the idea.

For the reader, however, the road operates on two levels. We see the practical irony that the figure of the law embodied by Rudbeck, through his passion for the road, brings increased crime to the district over which he is supposed to extend his protective, paternalistic and civilising jurisdiction. At the same time the road also symbolises the colonial state of exception whereby the gift of special conditions permits the suspension of financial regulation (Rudbeck's finagling of the accounts) in order to enforce the arbitrary will of the District Commissioner, in the place of law. In both instances Rudbeck carries greater autonomous responsibility than he wants to believe. And just as the Marlovian 'idea' requires its sacrifice, Rudbeck's road claims its own in the extra-judicial killing of Johnson at the novel's end.

Mr Johnson

So far my discussion has focused primarily on those figures of the law whom the colonial administration endeavoured to protect in order to preserve the effective functioning of its system. What remains to be seen is the place of those who in serving the administration are exposed to its violence, those who, in Agamben's terms, become the administration's *homines sacres*. In doing so we turn to Mr Johnson himself, clerk both to the administration and also to Sergeant Gollup, who runs the Fada store. Cary makes Johnson a version of the administrative clerk stereotype: Southern, mission educated, and out of place within both the local communities of Northern Nigeria and the expatriate community of the senior colonial staff. For both the local and the expatriate population Mr Johnson is by turns a figure of fantasy, an object of ridicule, and a financial resource.

---

[48] Cary, *Mister Johnson*, p. 186.

Johnson's initial presentation introduces key qualities that shape his character and treatment throughout the novel. He is, first and foremost, 'a young clerk', but he is also almost immediately defined as a 'stranger'.[49] In his first interactions with his bride-to-be Johnson speaks Hausa, but she recognises him as a stranger not only because of his darker colour but also because of his accent. The distinction is immediately glossed in the following way: 'in Fada history all strangers have brought trouble; war, disease, or bad magic.'[50] Finally, he is presented as juvenile: 'He is young, perhaps seventeen ... half-grown ... loose-jointed like a boy ... he smiles with the delighted expression of a child.'[51] Each of these characteristics, his job, his strangeness, his youth, contribute to his liminal position within the town of Fada.

Taking his youthfulness first, it is immediately apparent that this feature allows Cary to literalise the common characterisation of the African as childlike. Whether singled out for praise or criticism this characteristic was part of colonial discourse boilerplate, in fiction, memoir and critical discussion. In whichever literary form, this trope built upon the false premise of a parallelism between an individual human life and the progress of civilisation as promulgated in European historiography of the period. The frequent claim of this historiography that sub-Saharan Africa lacked any civilisational history (ancient Egyptian civilisation was often explained as the product of a non-African, even Aryan, culture) implied across the parallel that the African had no life experience that could give them an adult/civilised understanding of the world.[52] Johnson is made to embody the innocence and irresponsibility that was read as inherent in the African mind. Moreover, Cary's more or less quiet insistence on Johnson's immaturity throughout the novel offsets, and enables him to play down, Johnson's considerable skill and value as a clerk. At 'perhaps seventeen' he is trilingual (his accented Hausa implies that, like his English, it is not his native tongue), has a perceptive grasp of the potential of financial credit, and, despite being a stranger to the region, has a far better sense than Rudbeck of how to enthuse and engage the local community in the road-building project. He is also a consummate craftsman

---

[49] Ibid. p. 13.
[50] Ibid.
[51] Ibid.
[52] For an account of the development of Southern Nigerian scholarship on Nigerian history through colonialism and into independence, see Zachernuk, 'Of Origins and Colonial Order'.

in constructing a latrine for Rudbeck's wife.[53] Nonetheless his linguistic, mathematical, managerial and engineering skills, essential though they are in fact to the plot of the novel, remain overshadowed in Cary's narrative by the attention given to his mental affect.

Ignoring Johnson's silenced yet implicit qualities, Cary's attention to his youth emphasises Johnson's capacity for optimistic fantasy. Johnson's responses to the events of his life are exaggerated in their physical and emotional tenor. When the threat of administrative approbation hangs over him Johnson fears he is dying; when he is confident of marriage to the beautiful Bamu his joy is expressed through singing, dancing and liberal spending. Moreover, Johnson's imaginative enthusiasm is made to parallel Rudbeck's not only in its exuberance but also in the relatively slight and arbitrary prompts that ignite it. In creating this parallel Cary seems, at least on one level, to imply that the two young men are equivalent to each other, but we must be alert to the subtle differences between their characteristics as much as the gross differences of their positions of privilege. Thus, at first glance, we might assume that Johnson's enthusiasm for Rudbeck's road is picked up as an arbitrary consequence of serving under Rudbeck, just as Rudbeck has picked it up from Sturdee. However, even though Johnson and Rudbeck offer similar justifications for the road to Waziri, their reasons for doing so are subtly different. The *idea* that the road will bring the benefits of civilisation is something Rudbeck has the power to enforce. If the Emir or Waziri criticises, Rudbeck can punish them for such criticism, as he explains in no uncertain terms. Moreover, insofar as the road is an idea dreamt up by the District Commissioner, as the living embodiment of the law and of civilisation, the road itself comes to represent civilisation and/as the law.

Johnson has no such recourse to power. Instead he starts in a position of negation. His existence as a stranger to both the European and Northern Nigerian communities in which he operates is predicated on a particular idea of the civilising mission of the colonial project. Johnson is neither 'civilised' European, nor pagan or Muslim Northerner. Instead he has been shaped by colonial influences that inform his aspirations to live as a Nigerian according to European codes of behaviour (in dress, custom, language and social practice). Johnson aspires to do so because the rhetoric of colonialism implied that success as an individual and as a nation required mastery of these European codes, and that the intention of colonialism was to assist in the acquirement of such mastery. However,

---

[53] Cary, *Mister Johnson*, p. 100.

as his treatment in the novel makes clear, in practice those like Johnson who ventured down this road of social re-education at best were treated with a patronising encouragement that simultaneously maintained their status as outsiders to European privilege, and at worst were treated with scorn as dangerous imposters and 'trousered apes'. That both arguments (for and against) Europeanisation could be made at the same time, and often by the same people, demonstrates another paradox within colonialism.[54] This paradox results from the rhetorical necessity for the simultaneous exposition of the educated-native ideal and of the failure of the native to embody that ideal adequately. In these terms the ethical value of the colonial project was justified: colonialism would civilise the native, but because the native does not respond to civilising influences appropriately, colonialism must persist in an ever deferred *until they do*. This 'until they do' is the *durée* of the state of exception.

For the Southern clerks in Northern Nigeria there was an additional layer of alienation, insofar as they also differed from the Northerners not only in their European trappings but in their Southern ones too. And just as their adoption of European practices was snubbed by the British colonisers, so it could be regarded with suspicion and disdain by the Northerners as well. In *Mister Johnson*, Cary emphasises this point through Waziri and Ajali's curiosity about and contempt for Johnson's behaviour. As a stranger, moreover, Johnson is beyond their bounds of empathy and exists primarily as a means to an end: for Waziri he is a source of information; for Ajali he is a source of emotional entertainment akin to Aristotelian drama, producing cathartic bouts of amusement, amazement, jealousy and ridicule by turns. Above all and to all he is a 'clerk', identified by an administrative role that sets him outside the local community and that, at the same time, excludes him from the authority of the administration by his colour. This role, emptied out by a failure of both Cary and his characters to acknowledge fully Johnson's humanity, and thus reduced to something like 'bare life', becomes a site for the projection of fantasies and fears.[55] As the product of colonialism's desires – for the civilisation of Africa – he presents the horror of the real. Johnson is the civilised African and, insofar as his existence as such is a challenge to the claim necessary to colonialism's perpetuation that no such thing

---

[54] See, for example, Margery Perham's claims throughout *Africans and British Rule*, not least that the continent 'must have foreign rulers, and for a long time to come' since the power of law and civil rights are no advantage to those who 'have not the ability to use' them; pp. 86, 64.

[55] See Agamben, *Homo Sacer*, p. 66ff.

exists, his presence disturbs the rhetorical surface of the colonial project. This is as much the case for the local Northern population as for the expatriate community and explains why they respond with ridicule and disdain, for these responses attempt to negate the challenge his embodiment throws up. This fact reflects in interesting ways on the shift between the acceptance of educated Nigerians in senior positions of the Lagos Colony while the presence of Britain was justified through a rhetoric of commerce, and the reduction in such posts once the ideological rhetoric of civilisation overtook that of trade at the turn of the century. Johnson's ostracisation from the fictional community thus represents on the one hand Cary's satire of the failure of the colonial enterprise's civilising mission, and on the other Cary's unconscious reflection of the colonialist's terror of its success. Therefore, when Johnson defends roads to Waziri as 'the most civilized thing' he is also seeking to justify his own existence.[56] If the products of colonialism equate to civilisation, and the value of the road as a product and thus symbol of civilisation is called into question, so too is Mr Johnson.

If the debates about the value of the road rebound upon Johnson to untether him from the system that gives his existence meaning, Cary finds other ways by which to communicate Johnson's precariousness too. In his preface to the novel, Cary justifies his choice of the present tense for his narration by claiming that it reflects Johnson himself who 'lives in the present, from hour to hour' and thus allows the reader the 'liberty to feel with' his protagonist.[57] Tellingly, Cary also acknowledges that the present tense 'can give to a reader that sudden feeling of insecurity ... which comes to a traveller ... when he feels all at once that not only has he utterly lost his way, but also his own identity'.[58] This metaphor is swiftly dismissed, but with the ambiguous inducement that 'as Johnson swims gaily on the surface of life, so I wanted the reader to swim, as all of us swim ... for our lives'.[59] Cary thus introduces the destabilising implications of the present tense for Johnson only to deflect them, returning us to the relative security of the bathos of his ironic romance. As the archetypical childlike African, with no individual or collective history to speak of, the present tense is intended to reflect a carefree existence for Johnson, unmarked by causal relations or depths of experience. However,

---

[56] Cary, *Mister Johnson*, p. 95.
[57] Ibid. pp. 9, 10.
[58] Ibid. p. 10.
[59] Ibid. p. 11.

as the unsought realisation of an ideal – detested and under threat of erasure exactly because he embodies an ideal whose use value must remain perpetually in the theoretical realm – Johnson is also the 'traveller', the stranger utterly lost, and as such is reduced in Cary's fiction to the threshold status of 'bare life'.

If Johnson is utterly lost, this state of being also provides a dangerous freedom. His alienation permits him exceptional behaviour that social convention would otherwise curb were he a part of the white administrative or local Nigerian communities. Indeed, exceptional behaviour is expected of him and serves to delight and appal his friends. Thus when Johnson, down and out at the end of the novel, starts to steal from the white store-keeper, Gollup, Ajali is first of all effervescent 'with delight and excitement' and later 'amazed, excited, sweating with the thrill of Johnson's deeds … astonished by Johnson's triumph'.[60] Similarly when Johnson, after a violent beating from Waziri, suggests he will become a trader like his fellow guests in the *zungo*, they laugh at him but continue to watch him 'waiting for amusement'.[61]

Johnson's status as stranger also explains the otherwise unlikely friendship that he strikes up with Gollup. Despite – indeed, perhaps because of – Nigeria's commercial heritage as a colony, there was in the administration a prejudice against European commercial representatives, whether individual or corporate. This prejudice is evident in the representation of traders in early District Commissioner fiction, including the Sanders series where traders are repeatedly portrayed avoiding the law and sowing dissension through illegal commerce (most frequently in gin or guns).[62] In *Mister Johnson* the critique is extreme but it is indicative of the broader attitude in British West Africa in the last decades of colonial rule, which saw trade as an inferior pursuit to administration. Gollup embodies precisely a set of characteristics that indicate his déclassé status within the European community and that allow him to contribute a distinctly Dickensian addition to Cary's novel. Gollup has been a sergeant of the British Army, presumably serving on one of the African fronts during the First World War. However, rather than retiring back to Europe, or

---

[60] Ibid. pp. 215, 216.
[61] Ibid. p. 210.
[62] The role of trader is nonetheless heroised in some adventure fiction novels, such as Edward Shirley's *Up the Creeks* (1900). For a broader sense of the low status of traders in popular colonial fiction, see also the dissolute South Pacific traders of Louis Becke's *By Reef and Palm* (1894). For discussion of fictional representations of low-class traders in West Africa, see Newell, 'Dirty Whites'.

entering the political ranks of the colonial administration, he has settled independently in Fada, building 'a fine store and a good trade'.[63] Gollup attempts to maintain his military air – 'he struts like a little king' and condescends to the world 'from the height of his military rank and native genius', regardless of the fact that his strutting is done 'in cotton drawers, a spotless singlet, a white linen coat, pale blue socks with green suspenders, and white canvas shoes'.[64] Cary's satirical presentation underscores Gollup's self-delusion: he scorns all headgear despite his susceptibility to sunstroke and fever, for example. This self-delusion has its darker side in his treatment of Nigerians. Cary notes, ironically, that 'he is precise and polite in all his dealings with clerks, labourers, and servants' before describing only a sentence or so later an instance of violence against Ajali, his store assistant, prompted by a minor misunderstanding.[65] Moreover, although Gollup has a wife back in Britain he lives with a local woman, Matumbi, whom he beats unconscious every Sunday, enraged by the self-pity of his alcohol-fuelled nostalgia for his British home. In his business practices, his African lover, his violence and lack of self-restraint, Gollup thus embodies in banal form the horror of Conrad's Kurtz, whose methods are famously characterised as 'unsound'.[66]

Gollup's pride, miscegenation, violence and unorthodox approach to business and attire mark him as an outsider to the self-restrained, ordered and racially exclusive society of the administration. And just as Cary's characterisation of him as excluded from the society of the administration creates a bond between him and Johnson within the plot of the novel, so too the comic banality with which Cary presents Gollup's shortcomings creates a stylistic parallel between the two that extends precisely between their pride, dress code, business practices and choice of local wife. Moreover, Gollup, like Johnson, represents the unpalatable reality of an ideal that formed a justificatory plank for colonialism, in this case trade. For, if colonialism justified itself back in Britain as necessary to the protection of valuable trade interests in West Africa (not least the new markets in the interior for cheaply manufactured fabrics such as those which Johnson buys for Bamu in Gollup's store), nonetheless the Gollups of West Africa, even more than the larger corporations, were figures of British trade from which the administration sought to distance itself. Like

[63] Cary, *Mister Johnson*, p. 135.
[64] Ibid. pp. 135–6.
[65] Ibid. p. 136.
[66] Conrad, 'Heart of Darkness', in *Youth and Two Other Stories*, p. 156.

the 'trousered ape' of the colony's civilising mission, the reality of British trade embodied in Gollup was disruptively at odds with its ideal form. Gollup, then, like Johnson, makes immanent a monstrous real that gives the lie to its ideal, and as such occupies a liminal position in relation to the two communities that he serves.

Something of the potency of that liminal position is exposed in the incident mentioned before, in which he kicks his store assistant 'with an unexpected power and dexterity which moves Ajali visibly into the air'.[67] Gollup explains to Johnson: 'you didn't see anything 'appen just then … you take bleeding good care not to see, neither, I know the law as well as you do, Mr Monkey-brand.'[68] Gollup's exhortation to deny the assault of Ajali *as* an application of the law, which Johnson willingly accepts, knowing that if he does not he in turn will be assaulted, makes a mockery of colonial law's intent to protect its colonial subjects. Moreover, we might go so far as to read in Gollup's assertion of their shared knowledge of the law a shared relationship to the law that allows both Gollup and Johnson as outsiders to sidestep or reinvent the law to their own ends. For Gollup this is borne out by the fact that in an era when physical violence against Nigerian clerks was officially discouraged, Gollup's regular violence against his employees and Matumbi is either accepted or ignored by both the local and the expatriate communities.[69] For Johnson, it is borne out by his own apparent immunity to the law, which amazes and frustrates his friends: 'it seems to [Ajali] that Johnson defies the very law of being; and still goes unpunished. It is most unjust.'[70]

However, the shared lawlessness that Gollup implies between himself and Johnson has its limits. Unlike those of the British store-owner, Johnson's crimes do not go unnoticed or unpunished, even if Johnson shares Gollup's optimism that he can evade the law because of his exceptional status. Ajali, jealous of Johnson's capacity to defy the law, alerts Gollup to the fact that someone is stealing from the safe. Lying in wait for the thief, Gollup startles Johnson, who stabs him with a kitchen knife just as Gollup attempts to shoot him. Ajali, 'trembling and sweating', betrays his friend by identifying the murder weapon as Johnson's.[71]

The ensuing investigation is telling:

---

[67] Cary, *Mister Johnson*, p. 136.
[68] Ibid.
[69] For an account of the shift in colonial attitudes to violence against clerks in the administration, see Mason, 'The History of Mr Johnson', pp. 202–5.
[70] Cary, *Mister Johnson*, p. 216.
[71] Ibid. p. 217.

> Rudbeck turns out the police, not with any expectation that they will catch anybody, but simply as a necessary official act ... He knows that if the murderer is caught, it will be by the native administration. He therefore sends a message to the Emir, saying that a white man has been murdered and that the murderer must be found. Also he would like to speak to Mr Johnson. The Emir sends for the Waziri and tells him to provide a murderer, either Johnson or another, within twelve hours or take the consequences, which will be severe, since the murdered man is white.[72]

Here towards the end of the novel the procedures of the law are emptied out of meaning, followed *as* procedure but without interest in their ethical effect. Rudbeck deploys his police fully but expects them to fail. His recognition that the native administration will be more effective is not because they have inherently better detective skills but because they will be less discriminating in identifying their target. Moreover, this indiscriminate success is a direct result of the racial significance attached to the crime. Rudbeck's decision to send for Johnson in person likewise undoes the law since it is clear that he desires to sidestep the law, in a way similar to his literary hero Sanders, by warning or finding a way to excuse Johnson in advance of his arraignment (as Sanders often finds a way to excuse Bosambo). Moreover, the Emir chooses to ignore Rudbeck's request and names Johnson as a suitable but arbitrary suspect, thereby throwing down a subtle challenge to the colonial official. Rudbeck and the Emir, then, both aggregate to themselves the force of law through the state of exception that the colonial system enables.

'I Tink You Hang Me Yourself'[73]

The novel ends with Rudbeck's extrajudicial killing of Johnson. Johnson is inevitably brought to trial, found guilty, and sentenced to death. On the morning of his execution Johnson pleads with Rudbeck to execute him personally: 'I don' 'gree for dem sergeant do it, too much. He no my frein'. But you my frien'. You my father and my mother. I tink you hang me yourself.'[74] Initially Rudbeck claims that it is 'out of the question', but while Johnson kneels to pray Rudbeck exits his cell, returns with the sentry's carbine, and shoots him in the back of the head before 'the whole population of the barracks and station'.[75] Despite the tangible

---

[72] Ibid.
[73] Ibid. p. 247.
[74] Ibid.
[75] Ibid. p. 249.

horror of the onlookers, who 'press away in panic' as he walks back across the yard, Rudbeck insists to himself 'with the whole force of his obstinate nature that he has done nothing unusual, that he has taken the obvious and reasonable course'.[76] He returns to his office to fill in 'the forms of a coroner's inquest, No. 5 in duplicate – one for himself, as sheriff, one for headquarters'.[77] Cary replicates the whole brief form on the page using underscoring to represent the blanks that Rudbeck must fill in, the last being cause of death:

> Rudbeck hesitates, *seeking a legal form*, and then writes, 'By hanging, duly executed according to the law,' and signs 'J. H. Rudbeck'. He fills in Johnson's name, and calls, 'Messenger'.
>
> Adamu comes in and makes his morning bow. Adamu shows no agitation. For him, an old-fashioned Moslem, men are always responsible before God, and there is nothing surprising in the fact that Rudbeck, as a ruler, should discharge that responsibility according to his own unique conscience.[78]

The legal form that Rudbeck finds for himself is the state of exception that enables him to act outside the law with the force of law. Rudbeck quite literally writes the legal status of his actions into existence on the form through the same revisioning of the truth that Gollup demands of Johnson when he claims they both 'know the law'. What is most disturbing about Cary's presentation of Rudbeck's actions is the way in which he frames them as prompted, understood and excused by Johnson himself and the ideal Northern subject embodied by Adamu. The final lines of the novel draw attention to the way in which Rudbeck aggregates the action to himself as his own idea (he grows 'ever more free in the *inspiration* which seems already his own idea'[79]). In doing so, however, these lines remind us with uncomfortable irony that in fact this was Johnson's will, something already and gratuitously emphasised in his dying words: 'Oh Lawd, I tank you for my frien' Mister Rudbeck – de bigges' heart in de worl'.'[80] Thus, despite the horror of the onlookers, Cary redirects our attention so that Rudbeck's ethical exculpation emerges from the mouths and thoughts of his Northern and Southern colonial subjects.

---

[76] Ibid.
[77] Ibid. p. 250.
[78] Ibid.; emphasis added.
[79] Ibid. p. 251; emphasis added.
[80] Ibid. p. 248.

Foster points out that Rudbeck would have been legally liable for the murder of Johnson, because he shoots him unofficially in public rather than hanging him officially, and that Cary was aware of that legal liability. This liability, however, is not communicated to Cary's reader. Instead, at the last, Rudbeck is allowed a Sanders-like moment of extra-judicial action, an action with the force of law outside the law. Framing it as he does with the apparent approbation of Johnson and Adamu (whose Southern and Northern origins allow them to stand metonymically for the whole colony), Cary suggests that this action is justified through a code of ethics that trumps the law and in doing so relinquishes his ironic critique of popular romance to reinscribe the narrative supremacy of the state of exception. Johnson's embodiment of bare life as the ideal and loving colonial subject thus structures Rudbeck's extra-judicial killing of him as the perfect resolution to the novel's rhetorical logic of exception.

Four years before the publication of *Mister Johnson*, the Korda brothers' film adaptation of the Wallace novel *Sanders of the River* found its resolution in the crowning of Bosambo and thereby, implicitly, the instigation of indirect rule. Wallace and the Korda brothers are able to permit Bosambo to persist because he remains visibly and culturally distinct as the idealised embodiment of indirect rule, shaped and reflected as it was by the romance of colonial adventure fiction (a romance we also noted in Cary's own letters home). By contrast, the educated Johnson, as the disruptive embodiment of the real of colonialism's justificatory ideal (civilisation), must be eliminated in order to restore the romantic equilibrium of colonial exceptionalism. In the penultimate scene of the Korda film, Bosambo declares to Sanders, 'Lord Sandi, I have learnt the secret of government from your lordship … it is this: a king ought not to be feared but loved by his people', to which Sanders replies, 'that is the secret of the British, Bosambo.'[81] In Cary's novel, love, too, is presented as justification for exceeding the law in the name of the law. Rudbeck is moved by the appeal of friendship from Johnson and at one level his response retrieves Johnson from bare life, making a sacrifice of him as he kneels to pray. Within the structure of the novel, however, Johnson's death *because* he is a friend is also the necessary killing of the impossible relationship between coloniser and colonised. Johnson's death reinscribes the exceptional right of the colonial officer as the law, and by expansion the exceptional right of the colonial administration to 'special conditions' by which the Nigerian subject, and in particular the educated Nigerian subject, is always under the erasure of

---

[81] Korda, *Sanders of the River*, 1:24:48–1:25:23.

bare life.[82] Through this sleight of hand Rudbeck's action is sanctioned exactly because it exceeds the failing legal system that Cary has satirised throughout the preceding pages, and because as such, in its freedom from that system, it finds the approbation of the subjected people the system claims, and fails, to serve. Thus, in a final capitulation to romance, Rudbeck's state of exception is endorsed by Cary as the only possible, the only desired, solution to the paradox of colonialism's civilising mission.

---

[82] In *Homo Sacer* Agamben writes that '*the sovereign sphere is the sphere in which it is permitted to kill without committing homicide and without celebrating a sacrifice, and sacred life – that is life that may be killed but not sacrificed – is the life that has been captured in this sphere*' (p. 83).

4

'Beast of No Nation': Bribery, Corruption and Late Colonial Administration in *No Longer at Ease*

In his analysis of Nigeria's Corrupt Practices and Other Related Offences Act (2000), Paul D. Ocheje points out that 'the corruption of public office has arguably existed in Nigeria since the establishment of modern structures of public administration in the country by the British colonial government'.[1] Ocheje cites the Storey Report (1954), which dealt with bribery in Lagos, as well as reports for Port Harcourt (1956) and the Eastern Region of Nigeria (1957).[2] What the previous two chapters have shown us is that, in fact, corruption was built into the administration of colonial Nigeria even before the post-war 'establishment of modern structures of public administration' to which Ocheje refers. This incorporation of corruption into colonial rule was enabled by the normalisation of the state of exception, summed up in Bulteel's explanation to Tring that 'regulations ... are a bit of an anomaly'.[3] In this context of an 'emptiness of law', where the rules are suspended and the will of the individual as the embodiment of civilisation acts instead with the force of law, there is technically no corruption because there is nothing to corrupt.[4] The District Commissioner must be, by virtue of his civility, incorruptible. For this to hold, however, requires an act of imagination, the willing suspension of disbelief that Cary attempts to satirise. But as Wallace and Cary's fiction highlights, this act of imagination is not colour-blind. Where 'special conditions' applied to the

---

[1] Ocheje, 'Law and Social Change', p. 174, fn. 9.
[2] Ibid. p. 174. See *Commission of Inquiry into the Administration of Lagos Town Council, 1953* (Storey Report, Lagos, 1954), *Report of the Commission of Enquiry into the Working of Port Harcourt Town Council, 1955* (Port Harcourt, 1956), and *Report of the Tribunal Appointed to Inquire into Allegations Reflecting on the Official Conduct of the Premier of, and Certain Persons Holding Ministerial and Other Public Offices in, the Eastern Region of Nigeria* (London, 1957).
[3] Cary, *Mister Johnson*, p. 126.
[4] Agamben, *State of Exception*, p. 6.

British, Nigerian subjects who imagined themselves outside the law had no such recourse. For them such actions were classified as either consciously criminal or naturally corrupt behaviour. Either way, this behaviour signalled an inability to conform to the norms of civilisation, and thereby reaffirmed the need for a continued colonial presence, the 'until they do' noted in Chapter 3. As Ocheje's commentary suggests, however, in the post-war era, when Nigerian representation in government increased and independence emerged on the horizon, the issue of corruption became more complex. In *No Longer at Ease*, Achebe examines this aspect of the late colonial Nigerian administration and in doing so invites his audience into critical engagement with the problems that emerge.

Achebe has written on various occasions of his desire for his fiction to provide an alternative vantage point to the racist representations of West Africa found not only in popular fiction, like Wallace's, but also in middle- and highbrow fiction, such as that of Cary and Conrad. In his first novel, *Things Fall Apart*, Achebe animates sympathetically the West African indigenous culture that Cary and Conrad had reduced to caricature and symbolic masque. In his version of the narrative of colonial incursion, the ignorance and arrogance of both missionaries and colonial officials is thrown into relief by the sophisticated polity of the Igbo society into which they blunder. Moreover, in both *Things Fall Apart* and *Arrow of God*, those Nigerians who do embrace the social changes brought by colonialism are not presented as semi-comic freaks, out of place in both their own society and that of the colonials, but as serious representatives of the varied and variously motivated responses of a community faced with a radically new political landscape. In particular, Achebe challenges both the normalisation of Nigerian kingship that Wallace presents in his narratives of life upriver and the natural corruption that Cary attributes to Nigerians through characters like Waziri and Mr Johnson. Thus, even as these two novels by Achebe focus on singular powerful male figures, Okonkwo and Ezeulu, within a given community, the communitarian nature of decision-making in Igbo society is repeatedly highlighted. Moreover, both Okonkwo and Ezeulu refuse to be manoeuvred into subservience to the colonial administration. Although the pride of both is hubristic, straining community relations and failing to stop colonial incursion, they nonetheless reflect the social complexity and political acumen of Igbo (and by extension Nigerian and West African) culture that Wallace, Conrad, Cary and others had so assiduously omitted from their fiction.⁵

Rather than trace what is by now a well-worn critical path outlining the 'writing back' of these two novels, however, I want to turn in this chapter to the novel which appeared in between their publication: *No Longer at Ease*. Less frequently discussed than the books that immediately preceded and followed it, *No Longer at Ease* is equally a challenge to the colonial fictions of the pre-war era. This challenge is staged not in the (pre)colonial polis of Igbo village culture, however, but in the heightened modernity of near-contemporary urban Lagos. In what follows I trace Achebe's exploration of corruption and its relation to ideas of exception in the novel. To do so I turn first to an examination of the literary and factual context of the novel's plot, before exploring the hubristic fall from grace of Obi, the novel's anti-heroic protagonist. This fall from grace is then considered in relation to Obi's own aspirations to exceptionalism on the one hand and his deracination on the other.

'An Untidy Spot'⁶

In *No Longer at Ease* Achebe turned his attention away from the period of pre-war colonisation and village life that had occupied his previous novel to focus instead on life in 1950s Lagos. Yet even here colonial and village forces are ever present, shaping the actions of the novel's young protagonist Obi, who, we learn, is the grandson of Okonkwo, the central character of *Things Fall Apart*. Whilst grandfather Okonkwo had resisted the incursion of Christianity and colonialism in Umuofia, the village of which he was an elder, Obi is the product of that incursion: missionary school educated and the beneficiary of a local scholarship which enables him to study abroad in Great Britain. Obi's scholarship is paid for by the Umuofia Progressive Union (UPU), a collective of Umuofians who have moved out into the burgeoning urban centres of Nigeria. They realise that to have an Umuofian voice in Nigerian politics and administration they must ensure that the brightest of the next generation receives a British education, thereby gaining access to the colonial civil service. That brightest is Obi, the first recipient of the UPU's educational scholarship.

The UPU had intended Obi to read law, 'so that when he returned he would handle all their land cases against their neighbors', but Obi instead

---

⁵ Although Cary presents the Emir and Waziri as political animals, their moral bankruptcy undercuts any implication of productive sophistication.

⁶ Achebe, *No Longer at Ease*, p. 46.

chooses to read English.⁷ Returning to Nigeria, Obi settles in Lagos and takes up a position on the civil service Scholarship Board following his examination by the Public Service Commission. He also takes up with a girl, Clara, with whom he falls in love but who is an Osu, an outcast. Obi is determined to marry her despite the fact that both the UPU and his family oppose the marriage because of her Osu status. Meanwhile Obi falls into debt as his costs mount up – tax returns, financial support for his family, running costs for his car and so on. When Clara becomes pregnant he pays for her abortion but the couple split up. At the same time his mother dies and soon after he begins to accept bribes from those wishing for their children to be considered by the board for scholarships.

The overt cause for Obi taking the bribes is his financial situation, which Achebe takes pains to enumerate throughout the novel, demonstrating how the high salary he earns comes with high expectations from his family and the UPU both for financial support (he is expected to pay back his scholarship in instalments) and with regard to his dress and deportment (for example owning a car). Clara too loans him £50, which is promptly stolen from the glove compartment of the car, leaving him in even greater debt. Eventually Obi is caught in a sting operation, tried and found guilty. The spiritual and political strength in which Okonkwo and Ezeulu hubristically trust in *Things Fall Apart* and *Arrow of God* is replaced in Obi by a misplaced hubristic trust in his own moral strength to resist the corruptions of administrative power. For throughout the novel Obi argues against accepting bribes of any kind, even reading a paper at the Nigerian Students' Union in London against corruption amongst the older generation of Nigerians in administrative power.⁸ Nonetheless it is bribery, rather than any of his other acts of legal or social transgression, that brings his downfall.

The Job-like structure of the narrative, which also contributes to the shape of *Things Fall Apart* and *Arrow of God*, invites comparisons with what is perhaps the most significant British colonial novel of law in West Africa, Graham Greene's *The Heart of the Matter*. Indeed, the novel is alluded to early on when in Obi's job interview he declares it to be the 'only sensible novel any European has written on West Africa and one of the best novels I have read'.⁹ True to Obi's critique of *The Heart of the Matter*, however, Achebe refuses his own protagonist the 'happy ending'

---

⁷ Ibid. p. 8.
⁸ Ibid. p. 44.
⁹ Ibid. p. 45.

that Greene provides Scobie.[10] Whereas Scobie evades having to live with giving up either God or his mistress by committing suicide, Obi's fate following his sentencing remains unclear.

The novel's frame narrative underwrites this inconclusiveness through its circularity. Following the opening trial scene the narration shifts to a meeting of the UPU in which the members are trying to decide whether they should pay his fine and thus save him from prison. This meeting is never concluded in the narrative, but is used instead as a device to loop back to the chronological start of the tale when Obi first won his scholarship.[11] Achebe ends the novel back in the courtroom again, and with a climactic statement of emphatic uncertainty: 'Everybody wondered why.'[12] By contrast, the neatness of Greene's ending and the strangely dissatisfying success of Scobie's plans for suicide (even if he is unsuccessful in making the cause of his death appear natural) have none of the qualities that Obi attributes to tragedy and which apply to his own life: 'Real tragedy is never resolved,' he argues, '[i]t goes on hopelessly forever ... real tragedy takes place in a corner, in an untidy spot ... [t]here is no purging of the emotions.'[13] To make his point Obi contrasts '[c]onventional tragedy' with the observation of a Christian convert from his village that 'life was like a bowl of wormwood which one sips a little at a time world without end'.[14]

The reference to Greene, however, is not simply a ruse by which to trump European philosophy with Igbo philosophy; the invocation of Scobie remains pertinent because of, as much as in spite of, Obi's critique. Firstly, Obi shares Scobie's lack of self-knowledge. Each prides himself on doing things by the book, on his incorruptibility, and on his duty to his post. Scobie's failure to understand his own romantic weaknesses, the vanity of his self-deprecating self-belief, is echoed in Obi's sense of righteousness in relation to government corruption. Secondly, as a police officer, Scobie represents a further step in the normalisation of the figure of the law in colonial narratives of West Africa. Greene draws attention to this lineage by repeatedly naming Edgar Wallace as the reading matter of other British colonials in the novel. Scobie's own distaste for reading and his practice of writing his diary with the least possible flourish ironically reinforce his inheritance from Sanders (himself a man of few words) even while

---

[10] Ibid.
[11] Ibid. p. 7.
[12] Ibid. p. 194.
[13] Ibid. pp. 45–6.
[14] Ibid.

it distinguishes him from those caught by the romantic allure of Wallace's fantasy of the colonial legal hero. Paring away at the romance of the figure of the law, Scobie doesn't even have the comic appeal of Rudbeck, but is presented by Greene, as Obi discerns, as a figure of tragedy. Through his reference to Greene, Achebe alludes to this lineage of legal colonial fiction and highlights its tragic conclusion in *The Heart of the Matter* as a particular literary context for the critique of colonialism that his own work articulates. Moreover, his critique aims at this very same lineage of fiction as a key contributing factor in the colonial culture of legal exceptionalism, which repeatedly thwarts his protagonists.

In *No Longer at Ease* we find an alternative narrative of the tragedy of the law in late colonial West Africa to that dramatised by Greene. Moreover, rather than presenting this tragedy as one occurring in the wake of first colonial encounter, as Achebe had done in *Things Fall Apart* and was to do again in *Arrow of God*, Achebe directs his readers' attention to the Nigerian middle-classes whose presence was belittled in *Mister Johnson* and whose Sierra Leonean counterparts were almost entirely erased in *The Heart of the Matter*. It is important to recognise the significance of this. Chinua Achebe and Cyprian Ekwensi, to whom we turn in the next chapter, were two of the first Nigerian authors to present in fiction for an international audience Nigerians living urban and Europeanised lives. Obi has a British university degree, he and his friends employ 'boys' as servants, and he works as a civil servant in a government department. In these regards, at least, his life is closer to that of his British colleagues than to that of his grandfather, Okonkwo. Whilst figures like Obi had been the subject of Nigerian fiction for local audiences for some time through a thriving local market literature scene, they had not been visible in the international literary scene. *No Longer at Ease* precisely undermines the primitivist stereotypes perpetuated by novels like *Mister Johnson* and the Korda brothers' roughly contemporaneous film adaptation of *Sanders of the River* before the war, and challenges Greene's post-war silence on the varied administrative roles filled by West Africans in government and industry even during the war-time period in which *The Heart of the Matter* is set.

In presenting the young Nigerian middle-class to a transnational audience that included both West African and European readers, Achebe is careful to construct a protagonist whose life's story is both plausible and yet not wholly conventional. Obi is different enough from the average Nigerian civil servant to engage our interest; his predicament with Clara's abortion is risky yet hardly unheard of; and Clara herself conforms to type as much as she goes beyond it. Moreover, within Achebe's typological construction of Obi, the ways his protagonist is made to typify and to deviate from the common backgrounds of Nigerians in post-war colonial administration are significant. As we shall see, Achebe's careful development of Obi's story stages a challenge to Cary and Greene not only in terms of his urban middle-class status but also, and more specifically, in rewriting the legal narrative of colonial corruption. In this new retelling of colonial corruption Achebe systematically unravels the neat solutions to which Cary and Greene's fictions cling by means of the conventions of satirical humour and tragedy respectively. Whilst each of these earlier novels places significant ironic pressure on the exceptionalism that the colonial figure of the law embodied, both in the end reinscribe it forcefully through their protagonists' extra-legal actions of murder and suicide.[15] By contrast, Obi's aspirations to exceptionalism are repeatedly curtailed by his own hubris and by the highly determined yet conflicting social expectations of his administrative context. Legal exceptionalism provides no resolution for Obi. Achebe's novel thus exposes the damage caused by the persistent incoherence that resulted from the underpinning fantasy of exceptionalism in the colonial administrative systems.

'Why Do You Want a Job in the Civil Service? So That You Can Take Bribes?'[16]

In his research into colonial and postcolonial Nigeria, the political scientist George D. Jenkins undertook a qualitative survey of civil servants working in Ibadan in 1963.[17] The survey invited respondents to list a variety of personal and professional information as well as to provide qualitative responses about the value of training opportunities available to them. All those surveyed were in the service prior to independence and their answers illustrate the common backgrounds, education, training and interests of civil servants at the time in which *No Longer at Ease* is set (i.e. 1956–7). What their answers show is that while Obi conforms to some of the norms of the civil service, Achebe ensures he is recognisably out of the ordinary as well – not that he is unrealistic or unbelievable, rather that he is shown to be of an unusual kind. For example, of the thirty-five men surveyed by Jenkins only one, like Obi, had a father in the church, although the overwhelming majority attended Christian schools and note Protestantism

---

[15] Indeed, even as Scobie's suicide resolves the irresolvable predicament of his mortal desires, its detection by Wilson permits the Catholic Greene to withhold his own authorial approval of Scobie's suicide, in this case reasserting not only civil but also doctrinal law.
[16] Achebe, *No Longer at Ease*, p. 46.
[17] George D. Jenkins Papers, formerly Box 11.

under faith (their choices are Protestant, Catholic or Muslim).[18] By contrast, by far the most common paternal profession given by the respondents is farming, with others in trade, and several in some form of administrative post (from Prison Warden to School Inspector).

All but one of the men surveyed who indicate what subjects they studied at university (and almost all of them do indicate their education) pursued vocational or at least vocationally relevant degrees of some kind, such as economics, law or agriculture. Even the one humanities scholar of the group, who studied history at Edinburgh following the war, followed this degree with a PGCE in London before returning to take up a position as an education officer in the Ministry of Education at Ibadan. Obi's choice to study English thus appears to be an unusual one.[19] However, despite these differences Obi emerges as an average civil servant: almost all of those surveyed by Jenkins took some form of further or higher education qualification overseas, many joined the Nigerian Union of Students or other associations overseas, and a good number were members of other local organisations back in Nigeria similar to the novel's UPU. The club memberships listed by the respondents are particularly interesting in that they demonstrate not only the social backgrounds that shaped these civil servants (for example, Boy Scouts) but also their practical and ideological commitments. Alongside local unions equivalent to the UPU are trade unions (including the Ibadan Association of Chartered Secretaries, and the Union of Agricultural Technology Workers), church groups, tennis clubs, dance classes, dining clubs, reading circles and the Nigerian Economic Society. Most respondents had held memberships across a whole range of organisations at different times and had often been involved as executive members of at least one. These memberships illustrate how Jenkins's respondents committed themselves not only to their professions (through training, unions and related societies like the Nigerian Economics Society) and to ethnic or religious organisations with ties to their familial communities, but also to leisure pursuits that were commonly associated with British colonial culture – ballroom dancing, tennis and cricket. Obi's own commitments, communitarian and colonial, are thus mirrored in those of Jenkins's respondents. What Achebe draws our attention to, however, but

---

[18] Interestingly the one respondent to list his father's occupation in the church is one of the few who have no written Yoruba or, in his case, any other written Nigerian language. His 'some written' French potentially indicates a Jesuit education; his mark for the religious affiliation question is unclear but seems to denote either Catholic or a rejection of all listed religions.

[19] Although this is not necessarily the case within the world of African fiction. We might recall both Mustafa and the narrator in Tayeb Salih's *Season of Migration to the North* (1966).

which the survey fails to capture, is the financial and emotional strain that these commitments could exert over ambitious young civil servants.

Achebe uses Obi as an exemplar of the challenges experienced by the young educated elite in late colonial Nigeria, for whom independence is in sight but whose success relies on their ability to position themselves within the framework of power established by the colonial administration. This success is sought not only for personal benefit but also for the benefit of family, community and an imminently independent nation state. Obi's challenge is to honour these varied and sometimes conflicting demands, whilst staying true to his principles.

Obi's car is a useful example of the pleasures and pressures experienced by young Nigerians in the colonial service. Immediately upon his appointment Obi acquires a Morris Oxford on credit with the car advance to which he is entitled as a senior civil servant: 'Nothing more was required. He walked into the shop and got a brand-new car.'[20] His car not only facilitates his ability to travel through the city but also provides opportunities to woo Clara. Thus, not knowing how to drive himself, when he first acquires the car he hires a driver 'at four pounds ten a month' who drives Clara and him 'twelve miles away, to have a special dinner in honor of the new car'.[21] The conspicuous consumption of this celebration is underlined by the precise figures given for the driver's salary and the distance covered. Moreoever, there is a comic elision between Obi's love interest and the car since the romantic dinner is taken 'in honor of the car' rather than Clara. Romantic affections become mediated by and interchangeable with material acquisitions here.

The prestige of his car is also important to the UPU, for whom it was 'a great occasion … when one of their sons arrived at their meeting in a pleasure car'.[22] Obi's friend, Joseph, purposefully delays their attendance at the meeting in order to ensure as many UPU members as possible are present for their arrival: 'The fine for lateness was one penny, but what was that beside the glory of stepping out of a pleasure car in the full gaze of Umuofia?'[23] The car, however, is also one of the earliest of Obi's financial woes. Despite a supercilious warning from his British colonial boss, Mr Green, Obi is taken aback when he receives the first insurance bill for his car. As well as the practical consideration of finding the money he also

[20] Achebe, *No Longer at Ease*, p. 76.
[21] Ibid. p. 79.
[22] Ibid. p. 89.
[23] Ibid.

feels the pressure of Umuofian expectations: 'Having made him a member of an exclusive club whose members greet one another with "How's the car behaving?" did they expect him to turn around and answer: "I'm sorry, but my car is off the road. You see I couldn't pay my insurance premium." That would be letting the side down in a way that was quite unthinkable.'[24] Nonetheless his car-related costs add up – licence, new tyres, insurance – and finally it is broken into and money that Clara has loaned him is stolen from the glove compartment. The car thus symbolises Obi's related commitments to his senior administrative post, to succeeding on behalf of the UPU, and to the leisured pursuits of colonial life to which the phrase 'pleasure car' alludes. But the car also represents the economic burden Obi takes up in pursuing unstintingly, and sometimes unthinkingly, these various commitments.

A second example of the pleasures and pressures of urban life for the youthful Nigerian elite is found in the trials of Obi's love life. Obi's girlfriend, Clara, tends to fare poorly at the hands of those critics who read the novel as a satirical critique of the immorality of Lagos life.[25] Certainly Achebe presents her as typically susceptible to the delights of Lagos. The typicality of Clara's interests is borne out by the evidence of the daily press in the period. The Lagos newspapers carried regular articles about women's dress, romance, home-making and women's careers. They also featured extensive cinema listings, clothing advertisements and promotions such as that for the 'Miss Ijebu' competition advertised in the *Daily Express* in 1962. This competition, held to coincide with a 'fabulous dance' at the opening of the Paramount Hotel, offered prizes of '£100 cash, Sewing Machines, Lady Bicycles, Trinkets, free trips and free Cinema tickets for a year'.[26] The combination of dancing, cinema tickets, cash and the means to make dresses was a potent one, clearly designed to appeal to the stereotypical urban girl of popular Nigerian literature and the local press. Achebe tightly aligns Clara's penchants with the tastes attributed to young urban women by popular print media, making her a recognisable type to his West African readers. Clara's honesty about her Osu status, however, her generosity, her willingness to persist with Obi despite their problems, and her clarity about these, create a more complex character than the stereotypical wily harlot of popular fiction with whom C. A. Babalola, among

---

[24] Ibid. p. 113.
[25] See, for example, Babalola, 'A Reconsideration of Achebe's *No Longer at Ease*', p. 141.
[26] *Daily Express*, 12 December 1962, p. 6.

others, aligns her.[27] Indeed, insofar as their tastes are formed by the popular media around them, Clara and Obi represent the consumers of popular literature as much as its protagonists.

The tipping point for Obi's financial and emotional state of affairs comes when, having broken off their engagement, Clara becomes pregnant and they agree she will have an abortion, for which Obi will pay. Since abortion was illegal the dangers as well as the costs were high. Newspapers in Nigeria regularly reported on abandoned babies and, with less frequency, criminal abortions. For example, in December 1962 the *Daily Express* carried the following story:

> The Lagos Police have detained a girl-nurse for questioning in connection with the death of 24-year-old Sadatu Ehimai of 200 Igbosere Road, Lagos.
>
> Sadatu, said to be expecting a baby, died at a private hospital in Yaba after some drugs had been allegedly administered to her by a nurse.
>
> The police stated yesterday that Sadatu's death was reported to them by her mother, Madam Moriamo Aliu.
>
> According to the Police, Madam Moriamo alleged that her daughter died as a result of abortifacient administered to her by one Bisi Thompson, a nurse of 67 Onototo Street, Surulere.
>
> Sadatu's father, Mr Aliu Ehimai, 55, told the 'Daily Express' that he heard that his daughter was expecting a baby 'just 72 hours before she died'.
>
> He claimed that when he heard this, he instructed his wife to take the girl to hospital for attention. He alleged that Sadatu had been divorced from her husband and that there was no 'marriage contract' between her and the man for whom she was expecting the baby.
>
> It was learned last night that the Police are also looking for the 'father-to-be' who is said to be an employee of a Federal Government Department.[28]

The article traces the net of connections that unwanted pregnancies could create: the father who sent Sadatu, the mother who took her, the nurse who administered the drugs illegally, the previous husband, the new lover, the government department, and Sadatu herself. Each is implicated in different ways in her accidental death and the illegalities of its causes. Thus with their plan for abortion Obi and Clara risk tangling with the law. This is spelled out

---

[27] Babalola, 'A Reconsideration of Achebe's *No Longer at Ease*', p. 141.
[28] 'Lagos Nurse Held for Questioning', *Daily Express*, 1 December 1962, p. 2.

to them very clearly by the first doctor whom they approach and who turns down their request for his assistance:

> I cannot help you. What you are asking me to do is a criminal offence for which I could go to jail and lose my license. But apart from that I have my reputation to safeguard – twenty years' practice without a single blot ... And in all those years I have not had anything to do with these shady dealings.[29]

A second, younger doctor is more pragmatic:

> he said he had no taste for the kind of job they were asking him to do. 'It is not medicine,' he said. 'I did not spend seven years in England to study *that*. However I shall do it for you if you are prepared to pay my fee. Thirty pounds. To be paid before I do anything. No checks. Raw cash.'[30]

The pride expressed here is of a different kind to that of the older doctor. The younger doctor believes his reputation is established by his English degree, not 'twenty years' practice without a single blot', and since, blot or no blot, the fact of his English degree cannot change, he appears to be more willing to take the risk for 'raw cash'. The second doctor's reference to his English training is striking in the way that it gives the lie to Obi's own confidence in overseas training as inuring young Nigerians against corruption. There is a sophistic distinction here: the doctor's English training, he implies, was not for procedures like abortion, but since this falls outside the purview of that refined training it can be done on the corrupt terms of 'raw cash', which Obi otherwise attributes to older, uneducated Nigerians.

Obi escapes the law in this instance but the danger to which he exposes Clara and himself physically, emotionally and legally still takes its toll, not least in the complications that Clara suffers when the procedure goes wrong. Moreover, the cost of the abortion leaves Obi in an even more parlous financial state than he had been in previously. This state of financial insecurity sets in motion Obi's downfall through the second and by far the most prevalent crime through which the law is invoked in the novel: bribery.

When Obi arrives back from England at the beginning of the book his very negotiation of entry into Nigeria is marked by an instance of attempted bribery, when a boyish customs official attempts to bargain with him over the customs due on his radio. Obi's response, having dismissed

---

[29] Achebe, *No Longer at Ease*, p. 165.
[30] Ibid. p. 166.

the lad without negotiation, is telling: 'Dear Old Nigeria.'[31] For Obi bribery is part of *old* Nigeria, a Nigeria that his generation will reform with the benefit of their (European) education. As readers, however, we are alerted to the naivety of Obi's attitudes to bribery early in the novel when he returns home to visit his family. His bus is stopped at an arbitrary police check designed to extort payments from bus drivers to avoid trumped-up charges against roadworthiness. Ever vigilant, Obi prevents the driver's mate from paying off the police, the result of which is that the police find fault with the driver's paperwork. Consequently, the driver stops the vehicle again some distance off and sends back his mate to pay off the police at a now much inflated rate, out of Obi's watchful gaze. While they wait for the mate's return the driver challenges Obi for interfering: 'Na him make I no de want carry you book people.'[32] While Obi goes on to contemplate in a thoroughly 'book people' fashion the best form of government to address the problem of 'so much corruption and ignorance', we are permitted a little narrative distance in which to sympathise with the driver and his other passengers who have been delayed as a result of Obi's pious but thoroughly ineffective interference. The fact that Obi's swiftly found answer to the problem of corruption and ignorance is 'an enlightened dictator' does not do anything to reassure the reader but does signal his susceptibility to the state of exception's appeals.[33] Humorous though this answer might be, it also demonstrates the trap of colonial rule: the normalisation of the exception under colonial rule prompts a desire for independence, but in its place the aspiring Nigerian administrator can only conjure another state of exception. Indeed, just as the colonial exception is justified through the rhetoric of civilisation, Obi likewise deploys benignity to justify his choice of 'dictator'.

Obi's attitudes to corruption are thoroughly formulated by the time he returns from his studies. While in London, we are told, Obi had presented a paper at the Nigerian Students' Union outlining his theory that 'the public service of Nigeria would remain corrupt until the old Africans at the top were replaced by young men from the universities'.[34] On his return to Nigeria he elaborates his theory to his friend, Christopher, an economics graduate from the London School of Economics:

---

[31] Ibid. p. 35.
[32] Ibid. p. 50.
[33] Ibid.
[34] Ibid. p. 44.

> take one of these old men. He probably left school thirty years ago in Standard Six. He has worked steadily to the top through bribery – an ordeal by bribery. To him the bribe is natural ... [whereas to the young men] bribery is no problem. They come straight to the top without bribing anyone. It's not that they're necessarily better than others, it's simply that they can afford to be virtuous. But even that kind of virtue can become a habit.[35]

Obi's argument is not that the older generation are wilfully corrupt but that their actions are naturally so in the context of the colonial administration. The younger generation, men such as Obi himself, are disconnected from the old indigenous systems by virtue of their university education and therefore will not, indeed cannot, make the same mistakes as their elders. Their rise to power has been through education and not through bribery and therefore they are already removed from the practice. Like Obi's preference for benign dictatorship, his argument here recalls the rhetoric of colonialism. First he naturalises the corruption of (the older generation of) indigenous rulers; then he predicates the incorruptibility of his own cadre on the inherent civility of their training. This narrative echoes Hazzledine's hazy explanation of colonial administrative fitness, where capacity is developed as if by osmosis.[36] In neither case, colonial or Nigerian, is the administrator imagined to attend to the law; instead his actions are made synonymous with it.

Obi's characterisation of these young men as able to '*afford* to be virtuous' is, with hindsight, not without irony. Not having to pay bribes themselves to gain or to retain their posts, these young men are not in need, Obi surmises, of the financial advantage that bribery offers. Little does Obi realise at this early stage in the novel that even without having to pay bribes for his post his handsome salary is not enough to cover the multiple financial demands under which he will sink.

Obi's naturalising arguments about older Nigerians also echo the racist opinions held by his boss, Mr Green. Green claims that '[t]he African is corrupt through and through', suggesting an essentially miasmic theory of moral corruption for this phenomenon: 'the African has been the victim of the worst climate in the world.'[37] However, it is clear from the start that Green's assured opinion is not a ubiquitous British colonial perspective. Unlike Green, Justice Galloway, the judge before whom Obi appears, claims he *cannot* understand why Obi accepted bribes. Furthermore, when

---

[35] Ibid. p. 23.
[36] See Hazzledine, *The White Man in Nigeria*, p. 40.
[37] Achebe, *No Longer at Ease*, pp. 3, 4.

Green makes this declaration at his tennis club his white British auditors look about anxiously in case any of the Nigerian staff are near enough to hear, indicating that even if they are in agreement with Green they recognise that his position is an inflammatory one. To complicate matters, Green's attitude is also reproduced by one of the Nigerians sitting on the committee that interviews Obi for the Public Service Commission. Having slept through most of the interview, in which Obi had been discussing the finer points of British and West African literature with the 'Chairman of the Commission, a jolly Englishman', the Nigerian committee member wakes up to ask, 'Why do you want a job in the civil service? So that you can take bribes?'[38] This question confirms Obi's view of the board member as one of the old generation of Nigerian officials, that is to say one for whom accepting bribes is natural. He fails to comprehend the real challenge it offers to his own integrity. What the question in fact points up is the assumption, shared by Obi, the Nigerian committee member and Mr Green, that bribery is something that the *other* does: the older generation, the younger generation, the African.

Obi's stance against bribery is made evident from the start, with his dismissal of the customs boy and his interference in the bus driver's transaction with the road police. It is reiterated through his debates on the topic with friends, and underscored by his paper to the Nigerian Students' Union. Obi initially congratulates himself on his capacity to withstand offers of bribes; he feels 'strangely elated' and even 'like a tiger'.[39] However, he notes, 'One should not … be unduly arrogant … the temptation was not really overwhelming.'[40] Obi presumes himself to be one of the young men he had theorised in his Nigerian Students' Union paper, one who can *afford* to refuse bribes. He fails to recognise fully the implications of this privilege, the fact that it is exactly when the financial need is overwhelming that one's morals are tested. Furthermore, Obi expresses the same incomprehension as Galloway when early in the novel he hears of another young civil servant sentenced for bribery. Even though this young Land Officer, 'straight from the university', appears to epitomise the incorruptible generation that Obi imagines for the nation, rather than modifying his position Obi dismisses the officer's example as anomalous, 'an exception' that proves his rule.[41]

[38] Ibid. p. 46.
[39] Ibid. p. 100.
[40] Ibid. p. 101.
[41] Ibid. p. 23.

It is worth noting that when Obi finally gives in to abuse of the administrative system, his first crime is not bribery but fraud. Having received a £25 travel allowance for leave to visit his family, he discovers on his return that he must account for his mileage and refund any difference. The mileage only amounts to £15, but Obi has already spent the full allowance and cannot afford to repay the £10 owing. He decides therefore 'to say that he spent his leave in the Cameroons'.[42] Obi's offhand reflection on his decision to lie in his paperwork, 'Pity, that', quietly underlines the disarming ease with which he slips into corruption. There is no examining of conscience, no deliberation; his decision is made almost absent-mindedly. Indeed, it is the naturalness with which Obi takes the decision that gives the lie to his ideal that the elite of his generation are immunised by their prized education against the opportunities for corruption that infect the older generation of Nigerians. His fraud is presented as barely distinguishable from the early creative accounting that Rudbeck uses before his larger finagling of the cash tank. Both men permit themselves this latitude under the 'special conditions' that adhere to their position.[43]

Between this brief instance of fraud and Obi's acceptance of bribes falls the death of his mother. He suffers the grief of his loss away from his family, choosing not to go home because, as he justifies it to himself, he would not arrive back in time for her burial in any case. Eventually his grief assuages and Obi is left with a new pragmatism that burns through his idealism: 'He no longer felt guilt. He, too, had died. Beyond death there are no ideals and no humbug, only reality.'[44] It is in this frame of mind that he is approached with bribes when the new season for scholarships begins. The first offer he accepts is for a boy whose name he knows is already on the shortlist. Unlike Obi's fiddling of his travel expenses, the bribe does not in fact cause Obi to do something he would otherwise not have done. Nevertheless, in clear distinction from his practical fraud, the immorality of accepting the bribe keeps him awake at night: '"This is terrible!" he muttered. "Terrible!"'[45] The next example Achebe gives is of a young girl who offers herself to Obi to secure a place on his recommendations list. Knowing she is already shortlisted, he sleeps with her anyway. Gradually Obi gains a reputation as a reliable accepter of bribes: 'He would take money, but he would do his stuff, which was

---

[42] Ibid. p. 177.
[43] Cary, *Mister Johnson*, p. 127.
[44] Achebe, *No Longer at Ease*, p. 190.
[45] Ibid. p. 192.

a big advertisement.'⁴⁶ Clinging to a semblance of decency, he 'stoutly refused … anyone who did not possess the minimum … requirements', and conscientiously pays off his debts.⁴⁷

Obi knows he is breaking the law, but creates for himself a new set of rules that he substitutes for the law – he will only take bribes from those who 'possess the minimum … requirements'. The outcome of these rules ensures that the result is the same for the briber as if they had not paid the bribe, and for Obi, at least, this seems to excuse the transgression: the scholarships are going to those qualified to receive them. The difference, of course, is that through the transaction of the bribe he is richer and his briber is poorer. Unlike with Sanders or Rudbeck, however, Obi's substitution of his will for the law is not justified through a rhetoric of a civilising mission. Imagining to himself that he can abandon his 'ideals' with impunity and embrace 'reality' as if it were the 'threshold where fact and law seem to become undecidable', Obi's corruption remains, nonetheless, just that.⁴⁸

'Art Is Important but So Is Education'⁴⁹

Achebe opens the final short paragraph of the novel with the blunt statement 'Everybody wondered why'.⁵⁰ The failure of the 'learned judge … [t]he British Council man … the men of Umuofia … [a]nd Mr Green' to understand why Obi accepted bribes challenges us, the reader, to do better. This implicit invitation to the reader aligns the novel with the aims of popular Nigerian literature, which already had an established tradition of dramatising the challenges of urban living when *No Longer at Ease* was first published. As I explain in more detail in the next chapter, these books were written and read with a lesson in mind, for example how to make money or how to avoid heartbreak. Authors often claim in their introductions that the story is their own and that their reason for telling it is to help others avoid their fate or learn their lessons for success. Common in these publications is the story of star-crossed lovers, in which the relationship between boy and girl is opposed by one or both families.⁵¹ Such stories either end happily with the families capitulating to true love

---

[46] Ibid.
[47] Ibid. p. 193.
[48] Agamben, *State of Exception*, p. 29.
[49] Achebe, 'The Novelist as Teacher', p. 162.
[50] Achebe, *No Longer at Ease*, p. 194.
[51] See, for example, Nwosu's *Miss Cordelia in the Romance of Destiny*.

or they end sadly with the lovers separating and ruing their fate.[52] These latter stories are often presented as warnings about the dangers of becoming involved with an unsuitable or unapproved suitor. The correlation between such stories and Obi's relationship with Clara is evident.

Achebe clearly understood his own work to be operating in a similar fashion to this popular 'market' literature. In an essay for the *New Statesman* in 1965 he wrote: 'most of my readers are young. They are either in school or college or have only recently left. And many of them look to me as a kind of teacher.'[53] He goes on to quote a letter received from a young reader thanking him for the 'advice' that his books contain. Another reader in Ghana, he recalls, had harangued him for not making Obi marry his true love because 'there were many women in [that] kind of situation … [and] I could have served them well if I had shown that it was possible to find one man with enough guts to go against custom'.[54] These examples make clear how Achebe's fiction was approached by readers with the same expectations that they brought to market literature. Likewise, his interactions with these readers are not different from those of market literature authors who often invited correspondence and, where they sold their own books, might interact personally with their readers. While Achebe defends his right to artistic independence in the article, he also expresses a willingness to be read in this way and a desire for his books to have practical influence on his readers' lives. He concludes that his aim is 'to help my society regain belief in itself and put away the complexes of the years of denigration and self-abasement': 'Art is important but so is education.'[55]

The correspondence of *No Longer at Ease* to the formula of market literature draws attention to the fact that the novel is not self-contained. It is written in such a way as to hail its reader into an active process of judgement. Achebe underlines this point elsewhere when he explains that literature should 'give us a second handle on reality so that when it becomes necessary to do so, we can turn to art and find a way out'.[56] The model of market literature makes apparent how we as readers become imbricated in the novel and in Obi's story. Achebe distinguishes his novel from market literature's common romance narratives, however, by complicating the set

---

[52] Representations of modern romance were also common in the parallel popular medium of newspapers in the same period. See Aderinto, 'Modernizing Love'.
[53] Achebe, 'The Novelist as Teacher', p. 161.
[54] Ibid.
[55] Ibid. p. 162.
[56] Rowell, 'An Interview With Chinua Achebe', p. 88.

of judgements that the novel elicits from its readers. The questions that we are left with in *No Longer at Ease* become not simply what we are to make of Obi, and therefore how we are to judge him, but also what we are to make of late colonialism and how we are to judge its legal efficacy.

Late in the novel when Obi visits the doctor who has performed the abortion, another patient accosts him for barging into the surgery without an appointment: 'Foolish man. He tink say because him get car so derefore he can do as he like. Beast of no nation!'[57] The deracination of this insult sums up Obi's predicament precisely. Obi has willingly embraced the role that the UPU scholarship originally bestowed upon him, one that catapults him out of the traditions of Umuofian life and into the contradictory structures of late colonial administration. As much as the Umuofians hope he will help promote and protect the needs of his community through his position within the administration, Obi himself aspires to promote his own ideal of administrative practice in the service of Nigeria's anticipated independence. But the Nigeria he envisions does not yet exist and the community he is supposed to represent is alienated from him by the education and position that their scholarship provides. Obi is not living in independent Nigeria, nor is he a British administrator, nor, however, is he any longer able to find home amongst the Umuofian community. What the novel suggests is that judgement of Obi is only possible if we choose to take as a given the impossible inconsistencies of his circumstances, including his own aspirations for himself and for his country. If we refuse to take these inconsistencies as a given, that is to say if we judge that these inconsistencies are ethically and politically intolerable, as Achebe encourages us to do, then we must attend to the way Obi is deracinated by the systems of privilege and exception introduced by colonialism.

The inevitable cost of those systems, Achebe suggests, is bribery, corruption and the concomitant deracination that befalls Obi, summed up in the insult 'beast of no nation'. Moreover, implicit in Achebe's indictment of the colonial administrative system is its failure to reform in the post-war period. Obi might imagine himself a revolutionary version of Rudbeck, committed to independence and imbued with inviolable civility, but his story, after all, is not that different from Mr Johnson's. Like Johnson,

---

[57] Achebe, *No Longer at Ease*, p. 173. Through the novel of the same name by Uzodinma Iweala (2005), this insult has more recently been associated with West African child soldiers. The phrase is much older and more widely applicable, though, used not only by Achebe here but by Soyinka, in *Season of Anomy* (1973), and most famously by Fela Kuti in his song (and 1989 album) of the same name, written following his release from jail in 1986.

Obi uses his education to take up a civil service job far from home. Both young men are optimistic about the opportunities available to them. The dissonant demands of their jobs, their ambitions and social expectations, however, mire both men in corruptions that are systemic and that ultimately demand of them something like a sacrificial role. Moreover, while Cary, like Wallace, is absent from the overt literary allusions of *No Longer at Ease*, nonetheless the colonial fantasy of the District Commissioner casts its long shadow across the decades into Obi's world. When Obi is finally caught in a sting operation, Achebe compares the arresting police officer's invocation of 'the name of the Queen' to 'a District Officer in the bush reading the Riot Act to an uncomprehending and delirious mob'.[58] Little in reality has changed since the days of Lugard, Achebe suggests here, except the topographical environments in which the legal structures of power operate.

Obi and Mr Johnson are released from family ties but also come to recognise their abandonment by the British colonial system to which they had dedicated their efforts in the hope of improving their own lot and that of their nation. For Mr Johnson, abandonment reduces him to the status of bare life. As a 'beast of no nation' this is precisely Obi's lot too. In this sense Obi echoes Clara's Osu status as well. As Taiwo Adetunji Osinubi explains, the Osu system cohered around a pattern of exclusion associated with religious practice:

> Among African forms of bondage, Osu belongs within so-called systems of cult, ritual, or shrine slavery. Cult slaves have no human masters, and they cannot be harmed or sold. Although Osu appears closer to caste discrimination than to slavery, Igbo communities consider the Osu slaves of the gods and human beings with liminal existence in the community.[59]

Osinubi argues that we should read *No Longer at Ease* as an Osu marriage novel, that is to say that we should resituate it within the minor genre of contemporaneous fiction that sought to respond to attempts by colonial legislation to eradicate the Osu system. Certainly the novel was read in that way at the time, as is made clear in Achebe's account of the reader who felt the novel could have better served women in Clara's predicament had it 'shown that it was possible to find one man with enough guts to go

---

[58] Achebe, *No Longer at Ease*, pp. 193–4.
[59] Osinubi, 'Abolition, Law and the Osu Marriage Novel', p. 54.

against custom'.⁶⁰ But in that account Achebe seems taken aback by his reader's comments, as if it had not struck him before that the book might be read as an Osu marriage novel. I would argue instead that Clara's Osu status is used typologically as much as it is used for social commentary. Indeed, as the 'beast of no nation' epithet suggests, the typological function of Clara's Osu status serves to highlight Obi's own reduction to bare life in the narrative. Moreover, this parallel between the Osu system and Obi's reduction to a 'beast of no nation' underlines the social function of his social exclusion. Like Johnson (and like Clara in a different context), Obi represents the embodiment of the real that disturbs the otherwise seamless narrative of the civilising efficacy of colonial rule.

Achebe's novel directs our criticism towards the predicament to which Obi, as a representative of his class, was reduced: the impossibility of idealism in the double bind that native administration and indirect rule imposed. This criticism is underlined by the fact that Achebe doesn't make Obi a martyr. His failings, his naivety, his pride are repeatedly emphasised and this emphasis operates in a Brechtian fashion to disrupt the temptation to romanticise the plot, a temptation that his earlier novel, *Things Fall Apart*, had offered. In that earlier novel Okonkwo's hubris verges on the mythic, so that his failure remains heroic.⁶¹ Obi, by contrast, is an anti-hero and the distance that Achebe leverages between reader and protagonist creates a space in which sympathy can be turned to critique.

Achebe's refusal to resolve the conundrum of 'why', with which the novel ends, throws responsibility for resolution back on to the reader. As I indicated above, this gesture is in keeping with the formula of market literature, a genre on which the novel clearly draws. At the same time, this open-ended gesture establishes an imagined community of readers charged with this responsibility. And in this suggestion of an imagined community we can detect a trace of Achebe's own ideas at this time about how the problems of corruption might be challenged: through the imagined community established by fiction, readers might begin to counter the deracinating force of colonialism and its recourse to the state of exception by imagining an alternative that improves upon Obi's suggestion of

---

⁶⁰ Achebe, 'The Novelist as Teacher', p. 161.
⁶¹ Hugh Hodges also invokes the phrase 'beast of no nation' to describe Okonkwo, arguing against Adéléké Adéékò's suggestion that he is a 'figure of law-making violence' to claim instead that he is a figure of necropower. This claim nonetheless does not negate the mythic quality of Okonkwo's actions. See Hodges, 'Beasts and Abominations', pp. 53–4.

benign dictatorship.⁶² The full force of this invitation from Achebe to his readers is apprehended when we remember that the novel was published in 1960, the year of Nigeria's independence. Challenging the narrative that had been imagined for Nigeria by colonialism, Achebe suggests fiction itself might be the place to begin imagining the community of the new Nigerian nation. In the following chapter we see how this suggestion is mirrored in the diverse publications of market literature and of Achebe's contemporary Cyprian Ekwensi.

---

⁶² The parallels with Anderson's thinking several decades later are evident. See *Imagined Communities*.

5

'Written in the Interest of the People': Representing the Law in Cyprian Ekwensi and Market Literature

Onitsha has been a major site of trade for centuries and became a key location for British palm oil trading from the mid-nineteenth century onwards. Following the Second World War, as Emmanuel Obiechina explains, the market also became home to a flourishing book industry that remains to this day. Obiechina accounts for the emergence of what has become known as 'market literature' by pointing to the combination of Onitsha's population expansion during the mid-century, a concomitant increase in a literate population, and the return of demobilised soldiers, some of whom invested their war bonuses in old printing presses that had fallen out of use during the war.[1] Press owners often published their own work but also that from a heterogeneous local authorship. Obiechina includes 'school-teachers ... newspaper reporters, railway men, clerks, traders, artisans, farmers and schoolboys' amongst the authors represented by the Onitsha presses.[2] This list makes evident the fact that authors were rarely professionalised or necessarily highly educated writers. Whether fictional or factual the content of their works is usually presented in simple language, and although fictional plots might be advertised as 'thrilling' (as with Speedy Eric's *Mabel the Sweet Honey That Poured Away*[3]) they tended to be straightforward and episodic rather than complex. The small print runs, often at the author's expense, were intended for a local readership reached through the Onitsha market stalls, local bookshops and even door-to-door sales. Poor production quality and frequent mistakes in typesetting speak of the publishers' priorities for quick sales and low costs. Indeed, although various popular titles were repeatedly reprinted over the years, far more disappeared rapidly following their first printing, as

---

[1] Obiechina, 'Market Literature in Nigeria', p. 109.
[2] Ibid. p. 110.
[3] See ibid. p. 112.

Donatus Nwoga notes: 'When the readers finished with a book they used it for toilet paper or rolled their tobacco in it to make cigarettes or just threw it away.'[4]

In the previous chapter I alluded to Achebe's borrowing from market literature in *No Longer at Ease*. Here I want to look at market literature's engagement with the law on its own terms before turning to two novels by Cyprian Ekwensi, a novelist who traversed the commercial and stylistic divide between market and international fiction with greater fluidity than Achebe. As we shall see, the law and its transgression permeated a whole range of publications in the years immediately preceding and after independence, and fiction and non-fiction alike repeatedly engaged with questions of crime and punishment. As well as attending to customary law and political disputes, this literature even invokes legal paradigms to explore sexual and emotional relationships. In this chapter, then, I turn to a broader range of legal indeterminacy, expanding my discussion beyond the state of exception per se, which has predominated in the previous chapters. This expansion is taken up in the following chapters to illustrate how legal indeterminacy and the state of exception were translated into Nigeria's postcolonial legal and literary imagination in a political context. Here, it allows me to demonstrate how market literature sought to generate through its own imagined communities discussion about and regulation of the apparent lawlessness of modern urban life. Ekwensi's novels take up this aim while remaining, like *No Longer at Ease*, more open ended in their response. In attending to the larger presence of the law in both high- and lowbrow literature of the period, I hope to show how the law was shaped in the popular imagination at independence.

'Good Novels Written in Simple English Languages'[5]

In her introduction to *Readings in African Popular Fiction*, Stephanie Newell notes that the 'authors' choice to write in English was not necessarily a sign of their metropolitan leanings or desire for accommodation in the Western academy'.[6] Newell doesn't provide any positive reasons; however, as Anderson suggests in a somewhat different context, at least one reason for market literature authors to adopt English was to work around linguistic diversity.[7] Certainly Onitsha, a major market city, was linguisti-

---

[4] Nwoga, 'Onitsha Market Literature', p. 26. For examples of titles that had a longer shelf life, see Newell, 'Introduction', in *Readings in African Popular Fiction*, p. 2.
[5] Egwuonwu, 'Foreword', in Okonkwo, *Never Trust All that Love You*, n.p.
[6] Newell, *Readings in African Popular Fiction*, p. 2.
[7] Anderson, *Imagined Communities*, p. 44ff.

cally diverse. English provided a common language amongst traders and visitors to Onitsha, and its use ensured the accessibility of publications across the differences of mother tongues. Moreover, writing in English can be seen as a mode of hailing the intended readers of much market literature insofar as the literature was frequently aimed at school-educated youngsters who were aspiring to new lives in the cities where the colonial language dominated.

Nwoga provides a useful explanation of this audience in the introduction to his study of Onitsha market literature in the 1960s:

> Sociological and economic factors have concentrated in certain centres a big collection of people who have left school after the minimum period of six to eight years with enough knowledge to be interested in reading novels, but not enough interest, or time, or even reading ability, to tackle the major novelists who were, in any case, in most of the novels available in the markets, talking of an environment that was most unfamiliar to the people under consideration.[8]

In such a context authors and publishers sought to provide material that was accessible to this burgeoning readership, and were keen to maintain their readers' trust and loyalty. Various elements of textual apparatus such as forewords and invitations to readers worked to gain their business. For example, J. O. Nnadozie, author and vendor of *Beware of Harlots and Many Friends*, offers to send greetings cards to regular readers on receipt of 'your name in full and postal address, with the list of our pamphlets or novels you have'. Furthermore, Nnadozie tantalises the reader with the lucrative, if vague, offer that he 'may as from December, 1962, start to share to his regular readers hundred guineas every December, in addition to other gifts already in existence'.[9] Halfway through *Beware of Harlots* Nnadozie turns his social advice to the value of reading his pamphlets themselves:

> Always read pamphlets published by Mr. Nnadozie Publications and acquire sense and wisdom. The author, Mr. J. O. Nnadozie is your famous author. He has been publishing wonderful books, novels and pamphlets which no family can afford to miss. His publications bring love and peace in the families.
>
> Do not borrow copies of our publications. Buy your own copies and have them in your house in order to help yourself and entertain your visitors.

---

[8] Nwoga, 'Onitsha Market Literature', p. 26.
[9] Nnadozie, front matter, *Beware of Harlots and Many Friends*, n.p.

> Whenever you have any family problem or any other problem concerning life, write to us for solution. We will give you best **advice** free of charge. We have been helping so many Readers with **advice**.
>
> Buy this pamphlet and send to someone you love. He will receive it with happiness.[10]

Alongside these specifically commercial appeals, whether in fiction or non-fiction publications, one distinct characteristic of the claims made by market literature authors and publishers is the urgency and immediacy of their material. Thus, for example, Okwudili Orizu's To Rule Is a Trouble gives accounts of several ongoing chieftaincy contests across Anambra state (the state in which Onitsha is located). Orizu presents these contests as wasteful and pointless, noting that 'the disputes seem to be long standing and elastic in their nature' whilst the 'internal strife' perpetuated by these contests results in 'open mischief and general hatred leading to loss of life, and injustice'.[11] Orizu lays the blame for these violent and protracted contests at the door of the 1958 Constitutional Conference, where it was agreed that the 'Eastern House of Chiefs should be created in order to make the chiefs in the regions have dignified status like their counterparts in the Western and Northern Regions'.[12] The ensuing race for appointment to the House of Assembly, spurred on by the prospect of title and privilege, led to bitter election rivalries with candidates mortgaging themselves to the hilt to pay for their campaigns.[13] Orizu's final chapter title, 'Hopeless Future', indicates his concern: '[s]ince many families are rendered hopeless in poverty and squalor through long protracted court cases over chieftaincy issue,' he writes, 'it is difficult to assume that the future is bright for the "Royal Families."'[14] He looks forward to the forthcoming 1964 elections with concern – 'anything can happen' – and leaves his readers with this challenge: 'Let our people think twice before it is too late. They must solve their problems or perish.'[15] To Rule Is a Trouble thus suggests that the ills caused by chieftaincy contests are a pressing concern that must be addressed by the populace at large and with some urgency. This claim is heartfelt but it is also commercially

---

[10] Nnadozie, *Beware of Harlots and Many Friends*, p. 21; emphasis in original. Throughout the pamphlet Nnadozie pauses at various moments to exhort his reader to buy the pamphlet for another who might benefit from his advice.
[11] Orizu, *To Rule Is a Trouble*, pp. 7, 8.
[12] Ibid. p. 5.
[13] Ibid. p. 7.
[14] Ibid. p. 29.
[15] Ibid. pp. 31, 32.

astute, since it promotes the idea that the book is worth buying because it addresses an important and immediate problem.

The authors' and editors' appeals in books addressing romance and friendship are pressed home in similar fashion. Would-be lovers must be warned because danger and betrayal lurk in every potential partner. In these volumes the dangers are often tied to 'modern' and urban living. Male readers are warned that women expect luxury goods as presents, that they become obsessed with dresses and dancing, and that the city offers opportunities for them to take many lovers undetected. Girls are advised to act chastely and refrain from demanding material trophies from their suitors. Authors often claim authority to speak to these dangers from personal experience, lending an apparent immediacy to their advice. Moreover, these books also respond to their wider contemporary zeitgeist, not least the social challenges of rapid urbanisation, whereby traditional networks of friendship and family are displaced by relationships based on personal choice and discernment. As in *No Longer at Ease*, 'high life' is repeatedly invoked as a source of contemporary social discord in market literature. Both the musical genre and the racy lifestyle associated with it, which the term 'high life' conjures, were symbols of the problematic displacement of moral values by materialistic ones. Thus, whether market literature publications assume a metropolitan or provincial context, for their contents and their readers, there is an implicit assumption in both pre- and post-independence volumes that the contemporary moment poses new and exceptional challenges to be navigated. On the one hand the liberties afforded by modern life – in choice of lover, friend and occupation – are valorised in contrast to the customary orthodoxies of arranged marriage and village life. On the other hand these same liberties are shown to increase the responsibility any individual must shoulder in making decisions for themselves, rather than sharing that responsibility with family and community, as had been the case for previous generations.

In response to the immediate needs that market literature sought to address, it frequently presented itself as overtly didactic even where education was mixed with entertainment. Authors and publishers, in their blurbs, prefaces and introductions, articulate their concern to inform the reader: whether to educate them on current affairs, as with those publications that covered contemporary politics, not only regional but also national and international; or to enable readers to learn from the authors' own mistakes in affairs of the heart, marriage or finance. In *To Rule Is a Trouble*, for example, page two is set out as a blank lined page with a note that '[t]he following lines below are for the reader's note making. The notes to be made are the indispensible facts that are contained in this book, eg. The dates on which the chiefs were crowned.'[16] Fictional stories of romance were frequently accompanied by proverbs and advice. Thus, for example, R. Okonkwo's *Never Trust All that Love You* (1961) opens with a variety of instructional chapters on such topics as 'love letters and how to write them' and 'how will you know that a friend loves you' before moving into a story of marital infidelity between a woman and her husband's best friend. The volume ends with twenty-two aphorisms under the title 'My important words to the public'. Moreover, a foreword by 'The Manager' of the press that published *Never Trust All that Love You* notes that 'this small booklet … teaches us the life of our modern girls and women' and that the 'writer believes, if given ears by the readers, that he will comment more in his next writing. He is also showing modern Nigerianisation. He is showing his capability of educating the illitrates [sic], who through the means of reading the good novels written in simple English languages [sic] learn greatly.'[17]

Nonetheless the morals and outcomes of market literature are sometimes hard to untangle, not least because those publications dealing with romance and family tend to perpetuate strongly patriarchal and even misogynist values even when they appear sympathetic towards, or are narrated in the voice of, a female protagonist. In some cases, authors even draw attention to this moral ambiguity in their narrative, inviting the reader to enter into judgement. Thus, in *Miss Cordelia in the Romance of Destiny*, following a doomed romance with her cousin, the eponymous narrator finds herself in a loveless marriage with an older wealthy man. The novel ends with a direct address from Cordelia: 'Now dear reader, I wish you to draw a moral for yourself from the stories of my life before you close this book. What is your opinion about me and what do you think will be my end?'[18] Although Achebe does not address his audience directly, this ending is not dissimilar to that of *No Longer at Ease*. Readers are invited to take up the narrative for themselves and, informed by the evidence presented so far, devise the 'end' to Cordelia's *Bildungsroman* beyond the pages of the novella.

Interestingly, legal models and points of reference are frequently used in market literature to dramatise moral dilemmas and to guide readers' judgements of them. In the instance of *Miss Cordelia*, Cordelia's first wedding is transformed into a public scene of customary investigation and

---

[16] Ibid. p. 2.
[17] Egwuonwu, 'Foreword', in Okonkwo, *Never Trust All that Love You*, n.p.
[18] Nwosu, *Miss Cordelia in the Romance of Destiny*, p. 42.

judgement when four old women 'religiously known as the messengers of the gods' appear with an objection to the marriage – the revelation of her consanguineous relationship to her fiancé.[19] This revelation ends with a ruling: 'you have no right to marry your cousin.'[20] What had started as a narrative of intimacy and romance thus reaches its denouement in a quasi-legal scene of public exposure in which the privacy and freedom claimed by the newly independent and educated youth, represented by Cordelia, is overruled by an alternative narrative of familial knowledge and communitarian regulation. Similarly, the story included at the end of *Never Trust All that Love You* concludes firstly with a financial settlement between the central protagonist, Tony, and his wife's paramour, Roland, and then with a court case in which Tony claims back from Roland the bride price he had paid to his wife's parents. Intriguingly, this case is presented in the manner of court reports, with the dialogue laid out like a play script on the page.[21] The reader is thus placed even more overtly than for *Miss Cordelia* in the position of judge and jury, 'listening' to the evidence presented in this final chapter. Lefebvre's model of creative response helps us to recognise the interpretative work in which readers are invited to participate by these legal allusions.[22] In these narratives the legal paradigms invoked enable the authors to indicate the necessity for their readers to reinstate moral order on the actions of the story by entering into creative judgement. In turn this paradigm implies that legal modes offer opportunities for readers to resolve similar issues in their own lives, and seeks to educate them about how such resolutions might be achieved.

Legal language also insinuates itself into the earlier materials of *Never Trust All that Love You*, where, in 'Love Letters and How to Write Them', Okonkwo presents a series of letters between a man, Gabriel, who lives in Okirikpo, and his girlfriend, Beatrice, who lives in Agbani. In the letters Gabriel accuses Beatrice of infidelity on the basis of a love letter shown to him by his friend and purportedly from Beatrice. In his first letter, Gabriel lists the 'agreement we entered before starting the love making'.[23] This enumerated and orderly list ('1. We agreed that … 2. We agreed that…' etc.) is followed by the assertion that 'I myself keep all the conditions of

---

[19] Ibid. p. 32.
[20] Ibid. p. 33.
[21] Okonkwo, *Never Trust All that Love You*, pp. 47–50. As we will see in Chapter 6, this was also a common format used in press coverage of court trials.
[22] See Lefebvre, *The Image of Law*.
[23] Okonkwo, *Never Trust All that Love You*, p. 13.

the agreement but you have contravened clause three of the agreement'.²⁴ The legalese of the letter is startling, and since Okonkwo provides no interpretative hints it is not clear if the letter is intended to demonstrate how relationships can go wrong if conducted in terms of legal contracts, or if the letter is meant to model the proper way to address a cheating girlfriend. Moreover, Beatrice's response fails to clarify this ambiguity and, although it is more moderate, her letter likewise deploys the law as a structure by which to understand their situation. She protests that '[t]he letter was a forgery. If I got [*sic*] hold of the forged letter I shall report the matter to the Police. It is a criminal offence.' In her valediction she reiterates, 'darling take no offence, as the letter was entirely forged.'²⁵ These final words tellingly elide the issues at stake here. Three 'offences' can be identified: the offence to Beatrice and Gabriel's enumerated agreement, which as Gabriel reminds her though 'verbal was traditionally made';²⁶ the offence of forgery; and the offence to both their sensitivities of (mis)trusting each other at a distance. The term's capacity to encompass these three different 'offences' highlights how legal language could be enlisted to structure the discourse of love and, more broadly, to provide a metaphoric framework by which to navigate the inherent deceptions and self-deceptions of affairs of the heart.

The emphasis throughout *Never Trust All that Love You* on male perspectives invites us to presume that the reader should identify with Gabriel. Given this, the reader is left with Gabriel to adjudicate between his friend and Beatrice on the evidence of the two letters. The forged status of the letter undoes Gabriel's earlier charges against Beatrice and reinstates the validity of the five-point agreement between the lovers; at the same time, however, it calls into question Gabriel's friendship with his colleague, who has produced the 'dated' letter from Beatrice. Either the friend or Beatrice is lying and this implicit fact underscores the book's exhortative title, *Never Trust All that Love You*. Furthermore, we should recognise the self-referentiality of the 'entirely forged' letter, coming as it does in a series of fictional letters. Readers are thus also implicitly invited to evaluate whether Okonkwo's fictional letters provide useful models for behaviour in their own interactions with friends and lovers. As Okonkwo explains in his introduction, the book is intended 'to meet the literary tests of serveral [*sic*] readers and all lovers of novels and stories. It is written in

---

²⁴ Ibid.
²⁵ Ibid. p. 14.
²⁶ Ibid. p. 13.

the interest of the people, both married and unmarried.'²⁷ Nonetheless, with Okonkwo's fictional letters, forgery as fiction is not subject to the strictures of the law that Beatrice invokes, and instead the made-up letters provide an imaginary space for working out the real challenges that readers are presumed to face in their own life.

The lively mixing of fact and fiction, entertainment and education, in which market literature so readily engaged, was underwritten by its paradoxical qualities of intimacy and anonymity. The small-scale nature of printing for market literature, and authors' claims to speak from personal experience, meant that their identity and their stories were potentially recognisable. In some instances authors capitalised on this as something that lent credibility, authority and authenticity to their advice. Nnadozie, for example, assures his readers of the veracity of his warnings: 'I have paid visits to some bars and hotels just to see the immoral activities of the prostitutes.'²⁸ He even goes so far as 'to offer the harlots an opportunity to defend themselves … The sum of £100 in cheque awaits any harlot who can clear the 24 charges [listed earlier in the pamphlet] made against them to the satisfaction of the public … [by writing] a letter to us.'²⁹ Once again the structure of trial and legal defence is invoked as Nnadozie continues, 'In the letter, you refer to the charges one by one, and say why each "is not true." You cannot just say that the 24 serious charges are not true then we believe you. We want points and clear facts from you.' He ends by requesting 'typed' letters to be sent to 'the Critic Writer, Nnadozie Publications'.³⁰ Were the invitation to harlots to end here the implicit structure of a trial would be striking enough, but on the following page Nnadozie sets out an extraordinary proposition:

> After six months of the publication of your letter [by Nnadozie], the Critic Writer shall invite some members of the public including five women to a meeting and consider your letter. After the conference of the members of the public, the Critic Writer who chairmans the meeting, shall write you a letter. In the letter you shall be informed whether you have defeated or knock out our charges, or whether the charges are still warming [*sic*] and holding the Harlots tightly. The decision of the meeting is final.³¹

---

[27] Ibid. n.p.
[28] Nnadozie, *Beware of Harlots and Many Friends*, p. 10.
[29] Ibid. p. 9.
[30] Ibid.
[31] Ibid. p. 10.

This proposal rests, of course, on the dubious assumptions not only that among his readers are self-identifying harlots, but also that these women would be willing to put themselves under public scrutiny in this way. Setting these issues of credulity to one side, what Nnadozie posits amounts to a sort of public trial *in absentia*. Whereas Nwosu and Okonkwo construct their trials within their fictions, even where they invite readers to enter into judgement, Nnadozie breaks down the conventional distance between author, fiction and reader by inviting his readers to enter into an apparently very real trial beyond the fictional realm. His readers will literally become the subjects of his publications, emerging named (and potentially shamed) from the usual anonymity afforded the reading public. The intimacy that Nnadozie invokes here is not like the confessional confidences to the reader which characterise Nwosu's Cordelia, but rather like the truth-telling demanded by the courtroom.

Unlikely though Nnadozie's invitation might seem as a source for future copy, he was drawing on a long publishing tradition in West Africa of presenting narratives of sexually voracious women. Stephanie Newell draws our attention to an early example in *Akede Eko* (the Yoruba language *Lagos Herald*), where 'Sẹgilọla of the Fascinating Eyes' maintained a tantalising weekly column, in fact written by the paper's editor, Isaac B. Thomas. Sẹgilọla's weekly letters to the editor 'all but named her wealthy, married lovers around town and gave details of the material goods she had extracted from them over the years'.[32] As both Karin Barber and Newell point out, Sẹgilọla is presented as 'coterminous with her readers, sharing the same public sphere as them'.[33] Sẹgilọla thus provided a thrilling voyeuristic entry into a world that readers presumed to know was true even though, and indeed exactly because, it was only partially visible to them. Sẹgilọla confirmed readers' fantasies of immoral indulgence, allowing them the comforting luxury of simultaneously aspiring to and disapproving of Sẹgilọla's lifestyle. Nnadozie draws on this tradition, but his challenge is paradoxical. Were a 'harlot' to respond, her letter would presumably fail to supply the titillating details of Sẹgilọla, since her evidence would be to show that she had *not* engaged in the nefarious activities, such as stealing, taking drugs and atheism, which Nnadozie lists. In the end, therefore, it is tempting to presume that Nnadozie's interest lies less in the harlot's story per se (in fact his pamphlet contains a good deal of material not pertaining to harlots) and more in the opportunity to engage with his readership that the character of the harlot afforded. As an anonymised

---

[32] Newell, *The Power to Name*, p. 141. See also Barber, *Print Culture and the First Yoruba Novel*.
[33] Newell, *The Power to Name*, p. 140; Barber, *Print Culture and the First Yoruba Novel*, p. 41.

figure of moral and legal transgression the harlot represented a social and personal threat that Nnadozie's pamphlet is designed to delineate and disarm.

The invocation of a public trial stages Nnadozie, as the 'Writer Critic', in the role of defender, and even embodiment, of the law. Providing assurance to his readership in an environment where the strength or will of the state's law to control harlotry was in doubt, Nnadozie presents himself as able to act in the place of the law as if he were the law. Indeed, the appeal on which so many market literature pamphlets are predicated is a sense that the laws of state, of social conduct and of morality have been abandoned, and that the reader is thus constantly at risk and otherwise defenceless without the lessons which their pages impart. Central to this perception is the fact of increased geographical and social mobility in the late colonial and early postcolonial period. Boys and girls might go away to school, while young adults moved to the cities to pursue their careers. Consequently, not only were the younger generations, in particular, crisscrossing regions between school, work and family, they also found themselves in environments bereft of the familiar bearings of home. Friends might be strangers, colleagues might be foreigners, and 'home' might be an alien city. Care is needed, advise the pamphlets, if you want to succeed at work; caution is required if you want to make true friends. In this environment Nnadozie, the 'Writer Critic', attributes to himself the same exceptional qualities that Wallace attributes to Sanders. Like the District Commissioner, the Writer Critic will apply his own judgement, as if it were law, to regulate the hostile world around him, on the basis that as a Writer Critic he has the innate capacity to do so.

In such environments the very size and therefore anonymity of the city itself creates dangers, market literature suggests. Indeed, the size and anonymity of the city is a staple feature of these works and is frequently characterised as enabling deception. Thus, for example, in *Never Trust All that Love You* Roland uses a hotel room to conduct his affair with Tony's wife, presuming that no one will recognise them in a big city hotel. More significantly, though, the size and anonymity of the city paradoxically provides the foundation on which market literature establishes its particular form of personal narrative. This narrative form maintains the intimacy of orality, and thus of the familial, through its direct addresses to readers and the confessional apparatus that regularly frames its contents. Yet it does so by transplanting orality into the isolation embodied by print format, something to be read privately, perhaps in silence. This transplanting of familiar orality into isolated print thus reflects, not only in its content but in its very form, the modern urban experience of market literature's primary audience, calling into being its imagined community of isolated readers who seek the lost comfort of orality.

'Person Who's Not Careful, the City Will Eat Him!'[34]

It is into this market that Cyprian Ekwensi launched his first publications in the late 1940s. Obiechina designates two of these early publications, *Ikolo the Wrestler and Other Ibo Tales* and *When Love Whispers*, as market literature.[35] Both appeared under the Tabansi imprint in Onitsha, in 1947 and 1948 respectively, and manifest the persistent twin interests of Ekwensi's work: the traditional oral narratives of his region and the modern, individualistic concerns of love. Ekwensi found a different market, however, with his ensuing fiction, reaching an international audience with *People of the City* (1954) and again with *Jagua Nana* (1961).[36] Nonetheless, the concerns of market literature persist in these later novels, which address the experiences of men and women living and loving in the deceptive and disorientating environs of Lagos. In the first, the hero is Sango, a young crime reporter for a Lagos newspaper and trumpet player in a nightclub band. The novel follows an episodic narrative in which Sango negotiates the seductions, demands and inequities of urban life, including encounters with a series of more or less suitable young women before finally finding his true match. The novel ends with Sango and his new wife taking off to Ghana, which, in both *People of the City* and *Jagua Nana*, represents a land of opportunity in contrast to the ubiquitous trials and tribulations of Lagos. In the latter novel, the heroine is Jagua Nana, a woman in her forties who, having abandoned her early career in dressmaking, has come to rely upon men to support her. Like *People of the City*, *Jagua Nana* is episodic and has even less of the *Bildungsroman* narrative arc that shapes *People of the City*. Although she is beautiful, Jagua's age and her taste for 'high life' mean that her hopes of marriage, particularly to her young lover Freddie, are unfulfilled. Moreover, her skills in oration and diplomacy, of which we learn through her actions in support of her lovers, provide little opportunity for economic independence in the patriarchal spheres of politics and chieftaincy disputes. Jagua's predicament places her forever on the fringes of (and sometimes in the thick of) lawlessness

---

[34] Ekwensi, *People of the City*, p. 11.
[35] Obiechina, 'Market Literature in Nigeria', p. 108.
[36] *People of the City* is sometimes cited as the first Nigerian novel to reach an international audience, although Amos Tutuola's *The Palm-Wine Drinkard*, published by Faber & Faber in 1952, is more accurately credited with that distinction.

whether in politics, prostitution or criminal gangs. In market literature Jagua Nana would be the exemplary harlot held up as a warning to young women and men of the dangers of 'high life' and promiscuity, just as Obi, in *No Longer at Ease*, would represent an erring young buck who values success over family. In Ekwensi's novel, however, she is treated with far greater complexity. For all her flaws and failings, which are many, she elicits sympathy, and Ekwensi, like Achebe, redirects the reader's judgement beyond his central protagonist and on to the broader malaise of Lagos society. Jagua thus provides an interesting parallel to her immediate contemporary, Obi, in *No Longer at Ease*.

Like market literature, Ekwensi's novels engage with the law in numerous ways. In practical terms his protagonists find themselves in a variety of legal relationships and subject to various more or less legal agreements. Ekwensi's choice of a career in crime reporting for Sango, in *People of the City*, provides opportunities for the inclusion of trials, crime scenes, investigations and police officers beyond the requirements of plot. Although some of these examples are woven into Sango's story itself, they also serve as an overtly legal backdrop against which the activities of his working and private life are set. In *Jagua Nana*, neither Jagua nor Freddie has such a direct relationship to the law but it nonetheless structures their world in various ways. Jagua must be bailed by Freddie early in the novel following her arrest for a catfight. Later Freddie engages in the lengthy legal process of applying to renew his passport after Jagua, who had obtained his first passport by bribery, tears it up. Thus in both novels, and in keeping with the features of market literature, civil law as much as criminal law emerges as a shaping influence on the lives of city dwellers. What differentiates these novels from market literature is the work to which they put these representations of the law. For whereas in market literature the law is invoked as a narrative structure or as discourse to be mastered (both uses exemplified in *Never Trust All that Love You*), in Ekwensi's fiction civil and criminal law embody a precariousness in modern life to which the novels offer little solution. Ekwensi's protagonists struggle either to avail themselves of the law or to act, like Nnadozie, with the force of law. Instead they are almost invariably subject to the law but without recourse to its protections, repeatedly at risk of being reduced to bare life.

Practically speaking, civil law exerts its influence on the lives of Ekwensi's protagonists in two key areas: tenancy and employment. In addition to this the demands of custom and customary law also retain their hold on the protagonists even as they seek to slough off the old ways of their familial cultures, as Obi had attempted in his commitment to

Clara despite her Osu status in *No Longer at Ease*. Turning to issues of tenancy first, it is striking that at the start of each novel Ekwensi carefully draws our attention to the domestic arrangements of his protagonists. Each lives in rented accommodation that consists of rooms let within a larger building. In *People of the City* these rooms are implicitly contrasted with the luxurious accommodations belonging to British colonial and foreign traders on the one hand, and, on the other, with the piteous squalor in which live the poorer migrants to Lagos. Although Freddie, Jagua and Sango all occupy rooms to themselves, they still share common space with other tenants and consequently are subject to the regulating gaze of their neighbours and, in the case of Sango, of his landlord. The shared space of the communal building creates a porousness that destabilises the apparent privacy of the rented room: neighbours watch, spread rumours and let in visitors; trouble comes knocking frequently and with consequences. *People of the City*, for example, opens with Sango's beautiful first lover, Aina, intruding into his room to demand from him a promise of love. As soon as she leaves she is attacked in the street, stripped and stoned, for stealing a 'worthless' piece of cloth.[37] This event does not go unobserved by Sango's villainous landlord, Lajide, who needles Sango about it. Later Sango's friend, Bayo, secretly uses his rooms to trade penicillin on the black market. When Bayo is caught Sango's rooms are raided by the CID. Lajide, furious at the possible damage to his reputation caused by these criminal associations, immediately throws Sango out. Nonetheless, the very next day Lajide offers accommodation to another of Sango's love interests, Beatrice, on the basis that she becomes Lajide's mistress, an offer she refuses. Landlords, we come to understand, are free to exercise their power in this way because affordable and secure accommodation is hard to come by. Rented accommodation thus exemplifies the precariousness of the protagonists' lives. Tenancy is a matter of appeasement, with the landlord's whim carrying the force of law, as opposed to any formalised legal agreement.

Employment is another area where legal (and quasi-legal) relations surface. Both Sango and Freddie employ houseboys and are themselves employed: Sango as a journalist and musician; Freddie, at least initially, as a teacher. When Sango loses his home and when Freddie takes up a scholarship to study law in London, their houseboys are dismissed. Nothing is made of this in the narratives, and we are left to assume that they take up work with other employers. Nonetheless these unwritten dismissals

---

[37] Ekwensi, *People of the City*, p. 9.

repeat larger patterns of expedient employment practices that reverberate through the novels.

Halfway through *People of the City*, for example, Sango is sent by his paper, the *West African Sensation*, to the 'Eastern Greens' to report on an incident in which the police have shot miners who are in dispute with their employer over 'an outstanding allowance, amounting to thousands of pounds'.[38] The abusive treatment of employees by overseas employers backed by the colonial government becomes a rallying point for the nation, with rival Nigerian political factions uniting momentarily to condemn the action and to find a resolution.[39] That resolution includes the establishment of a 'National Committee of Justice' and a 'Commission of Inquiry' into the shootings.[40] In this instance the breakdown of employment relations results in a positive outcome. Here, at the centre of the novel, exploitation and police violence are apparently challenged and curbed through media exposure, political cooperation and legal intervention. The visibility that Sango gives to the problem through his journalism contributes to its resolution. Moreover, and exemplifying Anderson's argument about the centrality of the press to nation formation, Sango's reportage seems to heal larger divisions between the nation's populace.[41]

Returning to Lagos from the Eastern Greens, Sango asks himself, '[w]hat catastrophe ... would crystallize for him the direction of his own life?'[42] The second half of the novel answers this question in a love plot that ends with another shooting. This time the victims are Sango's friend Bayo and Bayo's Lebanese lover, Suad. Thus, while the public divisions visible in the Eastern Greens may seem to be resolved, in the private realm new social divisions of class and race immediately open up. Having caught Suad eloping with Bayo, her wealthy brother, Muhamad, shoots both of them and then attempts to take his own life. Sango, who had assisted in the attempted elopement, writes up the story for the *Sensation*. The report, however, brings embarrassment to the paper, and his editor, whilst sympathetic, fires him. 'The *Sensation* does not stand for playing one section of the community against the other,' notes the editor, McMaster, explaining that '[t]he Board of Governors [had to employ] all tact and influence to avoid legal action'.[43] Here, catastrophe returns to 'crystallize'

---

[38] Ibid. pp. 56–7.
[39] Ibid. p. 57.
[40] Ibid. p. 59.
[41] See *Imagined Communities*.
[42] Ekwensi, *People of the City*, p. 59.
[43] Ibid. pp. 98, 99.

Sango's life, as he had imagined, but with very different consequences. Sango's reports from the Eastern Greens had led to national unity and a legal enquiry into the state of exception whereby police could shoot dead striking miners with impunity. His report on this private shooting, however, exacerbates community divisions and is suppressed not by the law itself but by the threat of 'legal action'.

The second shooting consciously echoes the first and in so doing draws attention to its variations from the first. Counterbalancing the national, political and legal successes to emerge from the Eastern Greens with the continued failures that beset the individual employee in the alienating environment of the city, Ekwensi demonstrates another side to Anderson's argument about the press. For the press's capacity to call into being the imagined community of the nation is predicated on a sense of something shared, whether that be ethnicity, geography, religion or simply, in the case of the Eastern Greens, outrage. Sango taps into this sense with his reporting from the Eastern Greens, but is excluded by it when his journalism exposes the limits of the community. Fired from his job, Sango is thus symbolically abandoned by the very medium through which the imagined community of the nation, to which he should belong, is invoked. This returns us to Sango's houseboy, Sam, whose job security was predicated on the financial and reputational stability of his employer. Sam's abrupt and silenced fate predicts and stands metonymically in the novel for the precariousness of employment for those who are subject, but without recourse, to the law.

Alongside the urban context of the law, reference is made at various points to customary law as a characteristic of the rural East whence Sango, Freddie and Jagua hail. Marriage agreements are one such example, with Sango promised by his family to a young girl from home and Jagua offered a bride price by Freddie's relation, Chief Ofubara, to obtain her hand in marriage for himself. Jagua takes the money but not the marriage offer, excusing herself later when she explains 'not so is de fashion. Person who want to marry from my place, he mus' go dere for himself.'[44] Jagua wins Chief Ofubara's admiration not only for her exotic urbanity but also because she contributes to the resolution of a long-running chieftaincy dispute between Ofubara and his brothers. This dispute resembles those lamented in the roughly contemporaneous *To Rule Is a Trouble*, mentioned earlier, where Okwudili Orizu catalogues the legal proceedings between rivals for titles and the accompanying violent clashes that

---

[44] Ekwensi, *Jagua Nana*, p. 134.

result between their rival supporters. Ekwensi's version emphasises the more romantic and exotic elements of such disputes (kidnap, murder, hubris) in order to underpin the alternative allure of the rural for Jagua at this moment in the novel. Nonetheless, the five years in which the dispute was pursued through the courts in the novel mirrors the 'years filing court actions, filing blank columns of subpoenas, contacting one legal expert or another' that Orizu records in his account of the 'Dispute at Ithiala'.[45] The customary constraints of marriage and chieftaincy are thus foregrounded as legal and cultural practices that parallel and contrast precisely with the comparatively and unnervingly deregulated worlds of love and politics in Lagos.

As we have seen, market literature suggests that modern (and urban) living is beset with opportunities for crime. *People of the City* and *Jagua Nana* elaborate on this proposition, incorporating criminal activity into their plots and their contextual background. Sango, as we have noted already, is thrown out of his accommodation following Bayo's use of his rooms to conduct illicit sales of penicillin; Jagua takes up with Dennis, the leader of a gang of cat burglars; domestic battery and murder also stalk the pages of both novels. Indeed, violence punctuates the two books throughout, and both open with incidents in which women are publicly attacked and shamed for 'stealing' and are consequently arrested. Jagua Nana is accused figuratively of stealing a wealthy lover from Mama Nancy, who is the mother of Jagua's rival for Freddie's affections. The fight that breaks out between Mama Nancy and Jagua in the Tropicana nightclub lands Jagua in the police cells. In *People of the City*, as noted above, Aina is accused of stealing fabric and is stripped in public by an angry mob of Sango's neighbours. When Aina is attacked, a nearby police officer, refusing to intervene, suggests that her lack of 'husband and family' are the cause of her stealing.[46] Aina's isolation in the city is made a sign of her guilt by the very legal authority whose responsibility it is to protect her from violence. Indeed, these violent scenes, like the shooting of Suad at the end of *People of the City*, illustrate the particular precariousness of women's lives in the city.

If crime provides one subject of the novels' plots, punishment provides its inevitable accompaniment. What is striking, though, is the extent to which punishment in both novels occurs outside the systems of criminal justice. Moreover, even where legal proceedings occur they are shown

---

[45] Orizu, *To Rule Is a Trouble*, p. 10.
[46] Ekwensi, *People of the City*, p. 10.

to be flawed in their motives and effects. Thus Aina is unreformed by her time in prison and is regarded with heightened suspicion by others because of her sentence. Following her release from jail, she attempts again to steal fabric and only stops because she is spotted by Lajide and thinks better of it. Her attitude to Sango is vindictive and grasping, demanding money to buy 'new clothes … glamour specs … a gold watch … all [she] had dreamed of at night in [her] cell'.[47] Elsewhere, the violence of the police in the Eastern Greens is presented as excessive and unjustified, while the treatment of the women at the police station, at the start of *Jagua Nana*, is 'lecherous'.[48] While on the run following his deadly attack on a police officer, Jagua's lover, Dennis, explains to her that '[a]ll policeman be thief … [i]f to say ah give am small money, he for lef' me', turning the accusation of criminality back on to the law's representatives.[49]

Dennis is caught, tried and sentenced to death for his murder of the officer, but his trial reveals that he has already been in prison five times for stealing, undermining any sense of the penal system's capacity to reform its inmates. Moreover, Dennis's sentence is made to appear all the more arbitrary coming as it does in the wake of the multiple other murders with which the novel ends. Dennis's girlfriend, Sabrina, holds the nagging wife of one of the other gang members responsible for Dennis's arrest and consequently turns up at a family funeral, where she shoots and kills the wife and then turns the gun on herself. When Freddie returns to contest an election against Uncle Taiwo, Jagua's new lover, Taiwo's area boys (hired thugs) attack him and he dies of his injuries. In turn, following Taiwo's failure to win the election, he too is murdered at the behest of his party and his body is abandoned in the centre of a major intersection in the city. Each of these murders represents a form of extra-judicial punishment that the law cannot contain. Indeed, in the case of Freddie, the police are implicated in his death, since they forcibly remove him from the hospital in which he is being treated for his wounds.

---

[47] Ibid. p. 70. Here Aina embodies the avarice attributed by market literature to loose women whose heads have been turned by 'high life'. Her list of desires reads like a shopping list drawn up from the many advertisements for the Kingsway department store that regularly padded the columns of Lagos's daily papers.

[48] Ekwensi, *Jagua Nana*, p. 22.

[49] Ibid. p. 127. Indeed, the fact that Dennis, like the other men whom Freddie recruits to be his area boys when he begins political campaigning, is a veteran of the Burma campaign gestures briefly but effectively to the traumatic back story of a whole generation of veterans, whose reintegration into West African civilian life following the Second World War was often troubled and wholly unsupported by the colonial government.

People of the City offers similar deadly forms of extra-judicial punishment in the police violence in the Eastern Greens, the murder of Suad and Bayo by Suad's brother, a dubious, apparently politically motivated, 'suicide' (on which Sango reports at the start of the novel), and the sad story of a body found in the lagoon. Sango discovers this is the body of a man who has joined a secret society that supports its members to get on in life. After joining, 'the unexplained portion of the pact' with the secret society is revealed to him: '[t]hey asked him ... to give them his first born son.' When he refuses and threatens to leave the society, they explain that no one can leave the society 'except through death'. Sango reflects that in this man's story 'he had discovered where all the depressed people of the city went for sustenance. They literally sold their souls to the devil.'[50] As in *Jagua Nana*, what these various instances of extra-judicial violence demonstrate is that society is policed not by the law itself, but by fierce and unforgiving forces that fill the vacuum created by the absence of the law.

'You've Left Nothing, Not a Mark'[51]

In this respect Ekwensi's presentation of city life differs from Achebe's in *No Longer at Ease* insofar as it is not driven by an epistemological urge to uncover the causal relations between events and their consequences. Characters' paths cross and diverge but their trajectories are unpredictable, underpinned by the episodic quality of the narrative arc of *Jagua Nana* and of *People of the City*. This episodic, almost disjointed style borrows from the heterogeneous techniques of market literature, which often brought together multiple genres – letters, proverbs, stories, historical accounts, and occasionally illustrations – to provoke its readers' critical faculties and to entertain their sensibilities. Ekwensi embraces the contingency of market literature's style, not least its capacity to reflect stylistically the chaos of urban life. In an Auerbachian sense, Ekwensi adopts a foregrounding narrative mode that can seem simplistic. The lack of telling detail, of readily given back story, and of a sense of narrative purpose reflect the experience of the protagonists for whom the disorientation of city life is often felt as a lack of understanding.

---

[50] Ekwensi, *People of the City*, p. 55.
[51] Ekwensi, *Jagua Nana*, p. 12.

To combat this lack of understanding and the anxiety it causes, market literature exerts a strong sense of authorial control over its material. Rather than adopting a naturalist style in which the author's presence is erased by verisimilitude, the presence of the author is made sensible through direct addresses to the reader and through the selection and arrangement imposed upon the varied material gathered in a single publication. In some instances weak writing skills and poor copy-editing unwittingly make this presence even more clearly felt. The author's presence assures readers of the aim to guide and to inform them even when the narratives are ambiguous. In this sense the author of market literature becomes a force of law who can reinscribe order on to the disorder, lawlessness and ethical turmoil that modern life is presumed to engender. This exertion of control in market literature, as something that stands in for the law in the apparent absence of the law, is frequently encoded and framed by traditional forms such as proverbs. The incorporation of these traditional references underpins the authors' claims to authority, demonstrating their alignment with a community of values and assuring the reader that familiar wisdom is capable of unpicking the tangle of modern life. Thus, in a volume like *Never Trust All that Love You* the author explicitly and allusively invokes colonial and customary systems of law (their language and their procedures) to control a story of illicit love and to teach his readers how to avoid a similar fate. The trial at the end of the story of Tony and his unfaithful wife, in particular, allows Okonkwo to exert a fantasy of exact and resolving justice over the messy problem of infidelity. Ekwensi, by contrast, stands back from his fiction and, for all its episodic qualities, his presence as an authorial voice is not obviously felt.

Nonetheless, writing and narrative still emerge as crucial modes of challenging, invoking and aping the law for Ekwensi, most explicitly in Sango's work as a crime reporter. Sango's various reports are designed to put pressure on official legal accounts and to expose criminal activity. What we read of his first article in the novel implies that a cover-up has been executed to hide the truth of a murder by making it look like a suicide. His report on the Eastern Greens exposes police brutality and leads to a national outcry and cross-party promises of reform. His investigation of the body found in the lagoon exposes the deadly extortion that secret societies exacted from their members, and his final article attempts to ensure justice is done for the murders of Suad and Bayo. Between them these events represent key areas of social anxiety and unrest frequently reflected in the press and in market literature: love, politics, race, labour, resources, and the power of secret societies. Sango's attempt to understand them and to reveal their truth to the general public through his journalism echoes in another form the desire for control that market literature expresses in response to anxiety about an absent or unreliable legal body. Sango's reports may not have the over-determining force of the trial scene in Okonkwo's story, but they nonetheless attempt a kind of extra-legal regulation that counters the perceived failures of the law. Indeed, we can detect the same instinct to establish an imagined community through readership that might challenge the law's failures in both Sango's reporting and market literature's direct address.

In *Jagua Nana*, however, this capacity to make sense of and regulate the criminal chaos of modern life is limited further. Freddie, it is true, goes to study law in Britain but on his return, rather than taking up legal practice, he turns to politics. When Jagua attempts to persuade him that politics is too corrupt an occupation for him ('Politics be game for dog'), he replies, 'I wan' money quick-quick; an' politics is de only hope.'[52] Breaking the causal connection that Achebe posits between ideals, ambition and corruption in *No Longer at Ease*, Freddie's desire to work towards justice is matter-of-factly overtaken by the hunger for power and money that governs the city and its inhabitants in both of Ekwensi's novels. Jagua's misguided hope that Freddie and his legal friends might help Dennis evade punishment in the courts is likewise abruptly extinguished. And whereas in *People of the City* Sango's reporting attempts to provide at least an ethical if not a judicial replacement for the failed processes of the law, in *Jagua Nana* the political activities of Freddie or Uncle Taiwo remain wholly self-interested. The nihilism of this state of affairs is summed up in Jagua's early statement of philosophy: 'You die, you're dead … It's over. You've left nothing, not a mark.'[53]

If Jagua sums up the urban experience of legal abandonment early in the novel, in its final pages there is at least the suggestion that she is able to create a new community from this extremity. At the novel's end Jagua miscarries and returns to live with her mother and a female companion, Rosa, back in her familial village. This community reflects the particular precariousness of women's lives, noted earlier, but in the

---

[52] Ibid. p. 137.
[53] Ibid. p. 12.

alternative it offers to the lawless patriarchal world that she escapes, it also gestures to Jagua's latent political talents. These talents are first evident in her reconciliation of the chieftaincy dispute between Chief Ofubara and his brothers, which she conducts with expertly calculated diplomacy. Her political potential is shown again in the second half of the novel, when she speaks powerfully on behalf of Taiwo at a political rally of market women. Both incidents provide an important commentary on the problematic exclusion of women from political life that the patriarchal ideals of indirect rule imposed. Jagua's skills in diplomacy and political rhetoric, demonstrated concretely in the reunion she effects between the warring clans of Freddie's family and in her speech to the market women at the rally for Uncle Taiwo, far exceed those of the men around her. Yet these capacities go untapped in a society in which Jagua remains bound to the regulatory laws of a gendered economics, whereby women's roles are circumscribed as prostitutes, as wives bought for a bride price, and as lovers kept through the provision of rooms and financial allowances.

Taiwo's women's rally invokes briefly the latent political power of women in Nigeria, most potently expressed in the inter-war years by the Ògù Umùnwaàyi ('Igbo Women's War'). In the years leading up to independence, groups such as the Nigerian Women's Union, led by Funmilayo Ransome-Kuti (FRK), spoke up vociferously for suffrage and equality on behalf of women regionally and nationally.[54] It is such politically active women's groups, often associated with market trading, that Ekwensi invokes in his depiction of the women's rally. The rally Jagua addresses is important to Taiwo because the women 'voted en bloc'.[55] He advises Jagua: 'Tell dem all de lie. When Uncle Taiwo win, dem will never remember anythin' about all dis promise. Tell dem ah'm against women paying tax … tell dem ah'm fighting for quality of women … dem mus' have status. Dem mus' have class.'[56] Taiwo parrots back to Jagua the key arguments of FRK and other post-war feminist political activists in Nigeria whilst brazenly admitting his support for them is an expedient lie. Jagua's political skills are thus coerced against her own interests here, in support not of women's rights but of the continuation of patriarchal political ambition.

---

[54] See Odim and Mba, *For Women and the Nation*. For a useful brief account of the Ògù Umùnwaàyi see Thomas, *Violence and Colonial Order*, pp. 285–91.
[55] Ekwensi, *Jagua Nana*, p. 144.
[56] Ibid. p. 142.

At the very end of the novel, however, following the final debasement of her miscarriage, the tiny community established between Jagua, her mother and her friend, Rosa, suggests an alternative source of security to the patronage of men. Jagua dreams of financial independence as a market princess, a career that will allow her to enter the political and economic fellowship represented by the market traders who joined organisations like FRK's Nigerian Women's Union. This emphatically gynosocial conclusion imagines a form of female companionship and familial solidarity that challenges the economies of colonial and postcolonial sexual normativities governing Lagos life. Jagua's community at the end of the novel, defined by sanguine and non-sanguine solidarity, when read alongside her ambition to become a market princess, thus gestures to the political potential of Nigeria's women's movements at independence. Moreover, in its creation of a gynocentric civility, this imagined potency emerges beyond the reach of the city and beyond the reach of the law.[57]

In strikingly heterogeneous ways market literature and the two novels by Ekwensi discussed here mobilise the law as both form and content. In particular, they repeatedly dramatise the risk of abandonment by and before the law. Countering this risk is the work of writing and of the imagination. Whether in Sango's journalism, Nnadozie's Writer Critic or the new independence Jagua establishes for herself, writing and the imagination are deployed to call into being new communities of understanding that can resist injustice and regulate lawlessness. Orizu's blank page is telling in this regard. Here the reader is invited literally to join Orizu's community of writing by making his or her own notes in response to the 'indispensible facts that are contained in this book'.[58] In the next chapter I demonstrate how a similar model of community formation is produced in the press coverage of the treason trial of the politician Awolowo. In that coverage we find the highly public arena of national politics intermingled with the kind of personal and direct appeals that characterise market literature. Each form – journalism, popular literature or the international fiction of Ekwensi and Achebe – draws our attention to the centrality of the law to thinking about the community of the nation in the years immediately preceding and following independence.

---

[57] In this it recalls the world that Benjamin imagines, whose goodness 'absolutely cannot be appropriated or made juridical'. See Agamben, *State of Exception*, p. 64 (citing Walter Benjamin's 'Notizen zu einer Arbeit über die Katagorie der Gerechtigkeit', *Frankfurter Adorno Blätter* 4 (1992), p. 41).
[58] Orizu, *To Rule Is a Trouble*, p. 2.

6

'Sensational Coverage of a Sensational Trial': Treason, Journalism and the State

In November 1962 Obafemi Awolowo and twenty-six other members of the Action Group political party were charged with treasonable felony in Nigeria.[1] The final verdicts in the ensuing trials were not reached until Saturday 7 and Wednesday 11 September 1963, only a few days before Nigeria formally declared itself a republic, on 1 October 1963. The trials are significant not only as historical events but also for how they encapsulated and became enmeshed in the key political, social and legal issues that Nigeria faced following independence in 1960.

As we shall see, the government and the defendants framed the trials as being of crucial significance for Nigeria's self-identity as an independent nation. If the nation state comes into being through the identification of who is, and what it means to be, inside the state, the traitor brings into being a definition of the nation state by figuring what is absolutely external to it. The traitor, as the figure of someone who violates the state, in doing so enables the state to define itself by pointing to what has been and must not be transgressed: the legally constituted boundary of the nation as such. This boundary may be geographical but it is also imaginative. In this sense the treason trial is a forum where nation formation can occur. This drama of national self-construction thus first took place in the courtroom three years before it was to erupt again in the civil war of the later 1960s. Indeed, the failure of the courtroom to resolve the political and legal conflicts at stake in these trials was an indicator of the troubles to come.

Throughout the trials the Nigerian press reported daily on the evidence presented in the courtroom, frequently quoting at length from witnesses on the stand. This press coverage was extensive and richly varied. Such variety stemmed in part from the political allegiances of the various newspapers but also from a desire to consider the trials from all angles.

---

[1] In the end, Awolowo and twenty-four others were tried and sentenced in the same case.

Moreover, what this keen interest demonstrates is that the newspapers believed both that their readers wanted to know about the trials and/or that those readers ought to know about them. In this chapter I want to explore the significance of the treasonable felony trials and in particular to attend to the ways in which they were translated into and narrated by the Nigerian popular national press.[2] How the Nigerian press covered the trials illuminates the ways in which legal process as a mode of nation formation was woven into the daily lives of newspaper readers. Moreover, attending to that press coverage reminds us of the importance of narrative and literary form in the process of national self-construction, to which Anderson draws our attention.[3] In what follows, therefore, I begin by outlining the relationship of politics and press in Nigeria before looking at the defining features of the trial itself. I then turn to examine how the trial was presented in the press and the readerly engagement that the press sought to foster. I conclude by reflecting on the larger significance of the trial and its coverage in the media at the dawn of Nigeria's first Republic.

Nigerian Politics and the Press

In the years following the Second World War the landscape of Nigerian politics began to cohere. Political organisations had existed throughout the twentieth century in Nigeria. Richard Sklar points to the founding of the People's Union in 1908 as the first Nigerian political party, but it was not until the Second World War that large national, rather than simply nationalist, parties started to emerge.[4] The first such national party was the National Council of Nigeria and the Cameroons, founded originally as the National Council of Nigeria in August 1944, incorporating 'the Cameroons' in the following year. The NCNC emerged from the Nigerian Union of Students and acted initially as a council of affiliated unions, whose aim was 'to coordinate the political endeavors of existing associations including political parties, trade unions, professional organizations,

---

[2] My discussion draws primarily on the extensive collection of clippings covering the trial in the George D. Jenkins papers, held in Hoover Institution Archives. During the process of my research this collection was recatalogued and significantly reorganised; originally held in Box 6, these clippings are now found in Boxes 32–5. These are supplemented by the microfilm holdings of the British Library's newspaper collections. Because both holdings are incomplete and the material in the Jenkins papers is held as clippings rather than full copies, it is not always possible to indicate page references. Where these are not available this is indicated by 'n.p.'.
[3] See Anderson, *Imagined Communities*.
[4] Sklar, *Nigerian Political Parties*, p. 41.

and tribal unions'.[5] In the 1950s, under Nnamdi Azikiwe's leadership, the NCNC transformed its identity from a coordinating council into the most influential of the three major political parties to emerge prior to independence. In doing so, it consolidated its identification with the Eastern Region of Southern Nigeria, although it was also a significant political presence in the North, the West and, later, the Middle Belt Regions.

Rivalling the NCNC in the South was the Action Group. Founded in 1950 by Obafemi Awolowo, the party drew together the radical political ambition of the Nigerian Youth Movement, whose influence was essentially limited to Lagos, and the larger national, ethnic affiliation of the Yoruba cultural organisation Egbe Omo Oduduwa, which had been established at the end of the Second World War but whose political stance was both limited and conservative. The Action Group aimed to provide a credible alternative to NCNC domination in the Western Region when regional elections were held following constitutional reforms undertaken by the colonial authorities at the end of the 1940s.

In the North, the main political party was the Northern People's Congress. Like the Action Group, the NPC provided a middle ground between the earlier Northern Elements Progressive Association (whose radicalism led to it being dismantled by the colonial administration) and a more conservative movement for regional and ethnic cultural representation. Anxious, like those in the West, to avoid domination from outside the region, but equally anxious to avoid the fate of the NEPA, the NPC embraced a conservative position and in 1949 expelled those with radical affiliations. Established as a formal political party in 1951, it incorporated into its membership prominent figures of authority in the North, notably Ahmadu Bello, the Sardauna of Sokoto, and Abubakar Tafawa Balewa, who had been elected Vice-President of the Northern Teachers' Association in 1948.

Each party emerged from, and frequently professed, ambitious intellectual and nationalist agendas, and each built on inter-war youth movements whose outlook was decidedly international. Indeed, both the youth movements and the political parties which emerged from them had a presence in London amongst the growing number of students, like Achebe's Obi and Ekwensi's Freddie, who studied overseas on government, industrial and ethnic-union sponsored scholarships. At the same

---

[5] Ibid. p. 57.

time, the NCNC and the Action Group, in particular, accommodated a range of political positions from radical to conservative, and commitments to either social or liberal economics were fluid. What distinguished the parties primarily was their ethnic affiliation: the NCNC represented primarily Igbo communities, the Action Group represented the Yoruba, and the NPC represented the Hausa. These affiliations, however, were not cut and dry, and all parties attempted in various ways to present themselves as something other than simply the political organ of a single ethnic group. Each had some measure of success in this regard, at least in terms of attracting non-Yoruba, non-Igbo and non-Hausa ethnic groups to their party. Nevertheless, there was a Gordian knot at the heart of pre-independence Nigerian politics, which was that all parties (and their respective regions) were resistant to the possibility of domination by another ethnic group, despite the fact that, particularly in the South, they sought shared nationalist goals via very similar means. Thus in the North, the NPC mobilised resistance to the perceived radical nationalism and modernism of the NCNC and the Action Group, whilst these in turn challenged each other along ethnic lines and challenged the NPC for its conservatism *and* its ethnic difference. This conundrum created a tension between a desire for unitary government on the one hand and federalism on the other.

Nonetheless, the constitutional reforms instituted by the colonial government in the late 1940s and early 1950s established a federal structure that remained largely in place at independence. Within this structure the Action Group dominated the Western Assembly for the final decade of colonial rule, the NPC dominated the Northern Assembly, and the NCNC dominated the East. When independence came in 1960 the Federation of Nigeria was established as a Commonwealth realm, with Azikiwe assuming the position of Governor-General and Alhaji Sir Abubakar Tafawa Balewa becoming his Prime Minister. This created a relatively conservative coalition government between the NCNC and NPC, against which the Action Group positioned itself as a more radical opposition.

The relationship between the press and the political parties in Nigeria at independence was tightly knit. This was because many of the early nationalist and political leaders in Nigeria, not least Azikiwe himself, had been journalists. In the inter-war years journalism was a crucial tool for the nationalist movement. In *Path to Nigerian Freedom*, a pamphlet published by Faber & Faber in 1947 with a foreword by none other than Margery Perham, Awolowo expressed his frustration with the colonial government's resistance to allowing or encouraging the development of an independent press in Northern Nigeria, and put this resistance down to an anxiety on the part of the colonial administration that a vigorous press would lead to nationalist agitation.[6] Newspapers were often founded by political groups to support their particular agendas. The *African Messenger*, for example, was founded by a journalist, Ernest Ikoli, to support his party, the Union of Young Democrats. Ikoli went on to found the *Daily Service* in 1938 as the official organ of the Nigerian Youth Movement, of which he had become the Vice-President.[7] Azikiwe began his professional career as editor of the *African Morning Post* in Accra, before returning to Nigeria in 1937 to establish the *West African Pilot*.[8] In the following years he continued to develop the Zik Group, which included five other local papers published across all three regions (in Port Harcourt, Enugu, Onitsha, Ibadan and Kano). Although he eventually gave up his holdings in the Zik Group, giving them to the Eastern Regional Government 'without compensation', the relationship between the Zik Group and the NCNC remained one in which the former constituted 'the main arm of publicity' for the latter.[9] Motivated not least by rivalry with the NCNC, the Action Group also ran a chain of papers, the Amalgamated Press of Nigeria, which was taken over in 1960 by Allied Newspapers Limited, a new company with close ties to the Action Group. Awolowo had been a founder of the Amalgamated Press's precursor, the African Press, and was an honorary director of the Amalgamated Press until 1955. Among the Action Group's titles were the *Nigerian Tribune* and the *Daily Express*, both of which regularly covered the treasonable felony trial, alongside the Zik Group's *West African Pilot* and the state-run *Morning Post*.

Although both Awolowo and Azikiwe eventually gave up their respective financial interests in these press syndicates, in both instances the syndicates were closely tied to (and sometimes majority-owned by) financial corporations that were controlled by leading NCNC and Action Group members. The newspapers were thus not simply additional or external wings of the political parties to which they were affiliated – supportive,

---

[6] See Awolowo, *Path to Nigerian Freedom*, pp. 51–2. For further discussion of the colonial government sponsorship of the press in Northern Nigeria, see Furniss, 'On Engendering Liberal Values in the Nigerian Colonial State'.
[7] See Sklar, *Nigerian Political Parties*, p. 53.
[8] The *Pilot*'s title is echoed in the *West African Sensation*, for which Ekwensi's Sango writes. Interestingly, Ekwensi's novel later featured as a cartoon strip in the *Daily Express* during the period of the Awolowo trial.
[9] Sklar, *Nigerian Political Parties*, p. 453, fn. 42.

but independent. Rather, the press was especially vulnerable to the legal machinations of the political parties and their financial organs. It is important to understand this financial as well as ideological imbrication of the press in the political fabric of newly independent Nigeria if we are to be fully alert to the implications of their coverage of the treasonable felony case.[10] This relationship is only underscored by the fact that several journalists were among those originally charged.

The treasonable felony with which Awolowo and others were charged was purported to have taken place in the first years of independence, a period marked by increasing political disorder within the Action Group and within the Western Region more generally. For whilst the Action Group dominated Lagos, its position was less secure in other areas of the Western Region such as Ibadan, where the NCNC was strong. A power struggle emerged between the socialist-leaning Awolowo, as leader of the opposition in the post-independence Federal House of Assembly, and the economically liberal Samuel Ladoke Akintola, who led the Action Group as Premier of the Western Region and who was more amenable to alliance with the NCNC. Inter- and intra-party tensions in the region became inflamed when those loyal to Awolowo sought to oust Akintola, resulting in physical violence in the House of Assembly. A state of emergency was declared in the Western Region by the federal government on 29 May 1962 and an administrator, the senator Chief M. A. Majekodunmi, was appointed in place of Akintola.

Majekodunmi's administration during the emergency was clearly partisan. Charged with bringing order to the region, initially Majekodunmi placed political activists on both sides of the Awolowo-Akintola divide under restriction and, in certain circumstances, removed them to remote areas. As John P. Mackintosh explains, however, '[b]y the end of two months virtually all the Akintola group and NCNC men were freed, but the office-holders and many of the principal organizers of the Action Group remained restricted.'[11] Under the Emergency Powers Act, Majekodunmi censored publications. Public meetings were banned and Action Group journalists were punished for criticism of the government. Majekodunmi also instigated a series of investigations into the management of the region's Marketing Board, Development Corporation,

---

[10] This imbrication complicates the more apolitical economics of the print market that Anderson attributes to the press in *Imagined Communities*, in which the communitarian function of the newspaper operates through shared language and chronotopical immediacy (p. 61ff).

[11] Mackintosh, 'Politics in Nigeria', p. 146.

Finance Corporation, Housing Corporation, Printing Corporation and Broadcasting Corporation. Although these investigations responded to the accusations and counter-accusations of corruption across the Awolowo-Akintola divide, as Mackintosh points out, there was 'no evident connexion between such an examination and the task of the emergency administration'.[12] Of these inquiries, the Coker Commission was the most extensive, invoked to investigate the relationship between the Action Group, the National Bank of Nigeria, which had been the majority shareholder of the Amalgamated Press, and the Nigerian Investment and Properties Company, which became the majority owner of Allied Newspapers Limited. Originally implicating both Awolowo and Akintola, the Coker Inquiry was still under way when Awolowo's own trial began. It was against this backdrop of emergency, political dissent and partisanship that the arrests, charges and trials of Awolowo and his colleagues took place.

Treasonable Felony

On the eve of the second anniversary of Nigerian independence the nation's governor, Azikiwe, addressed the people through a public broadcast in which he alluded to the discovery of a cache of illegally imported arms. At dawn the following morning, before the celebrations and military parades began, the Prime Minister, Balewa, gave more information in an additional broadcast. He reported that 'young men were being sent abroad for militant political training preparatory to an attempt to destroy our constitution completely and overthrow the government'.[13] The plot, he alleged, 'included a plan to seize arms and explosives, abduct members of the government and stage a coup d'etat [sic]'.[14] In his announcement he confirmed that three had been charged with unlawful possession of firearms or explosives and twelve others had been detained under the regulations provided by the emergency, but the three ringleaders had absconded abroad. As Charles J. Patterson noted in his report to the Institute of Current World Affairs, written a fortnight after the broadcast, '[h]ere Sir Abubakar had for the first time publicly joined the suspected coup d'etat [sic] with the suspension of the Western Region. For though he named no

---

[12] Ibid. p. 147.
[13] Quoted in 'Fifteen Men in Arms Plot', *Morning Post*, 1 October 1962, pp. 1, 2 (p. 1).
[14] Ibid.

names it was common knowledge that the three fugitives were top leaders in the Action Group.'[15]

In fact, for much of the second half of September the newspapers had been reporting on the police investigation that led to the announcements by Azikiwe and Balewa, and these reports left no doubt that the focus of police efforts was on the Action Group. On 21 September the *Morning Post* reported that police 'swooped on the federal office of the Action Group' in Lagos and that a 'round-the-clock vigil was being kept on the premises'.[16] This information was used to open an article on 'new developments in the arms plot' whose multiple headline ran as follows: 'Police swoop on AG offices / Chike Obi Arrested / Enahoro now on the run?' The article ends with a summary of the alleged plot:

> It is understood that doomsday – the day on which the coup d'etat [*sic*] should have been staged, was fixed for September 27.
>
> On that day a number of buildings should have been blown up.
>
> They include the Federal Parliament, the Central Bank, the Government Printing Press along Broad Street, the National Press at Apapa and the Senate Building.
>
> The explosions were timed to go off between 7–9pm.
>
> ... the seven top names billed for 'special treatment' were the Premier of Northern Nigeria, Alhaji Sir Ahmadu Bello; the Federal Minister of Defence, Alhaji Muhammadu Ribadu; the Federal Minister of Finance, Chief Festus Okotie-Eboh; the Federal Minister of Mines and Power, Alhaji Maitama Sule; the Administrator of Western Nigeria, Dr. M. A. Majekodunmi, and two other top names not unconnected with the Coker Inquiry.

As the police investigations continued over the following weeks, arrests, detainments and restrictions continued. On 2 November twenty-seven men were called to hear the charges against them in Lagos High Court, while a further four had their cases deferred because they had fled the country. The charge against them was first and foremost 'treasonable felony', by which it was alleged that

> the 31 accused between December, 1960 and September, 1962, in Lagos and in various other places in Nigeria 'formed an intention to levy war against our Sovereign Lady the Queen within Nigeria in order by force

---

[15] Patterson, 'Anniversaries, Emergencies and Teething Troubles', p. 3.
[16] 'Enahoro Now on the Run?', *Morning Post*, 21 September 1962, n.p.

or constraint to compel our Sovereign Lady the Queen to change her measures or counsels and manifested such intention by overt acts'.[17]

These overt acts included inciting others to 'levy war against our Sovereign Lady the Queen', attempting to arrange, and undertaking, overseas training in the unlawful use of weapons in preparation for this levying of war, illegal possession and importation of arms, and spying on various strategic locations including a power station, Lagos airport's control tower, the government magazine in Lagos, and the Royal Nigerian Naval Base at Apapa. Further charges included additional conspiracy to commit felony, and conspiracy to effect an unlawful purpose, that purpose being illegal possession and importation of arms. These two latter charges, as the defendants lost no time in pointing out, were essentially covered by the first charge through the overt acts alleged. Their inclusion implies that the Director of Public Prosecution was keen to ensure that even if any one of the counts were thrown out, the others would still cover the alleged offences.

Accusations of crying wolf were not slow in coming. Long before the trial, the *Daily Express* reported that the Nigerian Youth Congress intended to conduct its own investigation into the affair, believing it to be a hoax. To that end the NYC wrote an open letter declaring that 'any intention to use this arms allegation (which may well be a hoax from members of the governing party) to keep socialists out of existence will be fought with all the might of the Nigerian Youth Congress'.[18] Patterson, too, prior to the trial, seems to have been unconvinced, at least of the involvement of Awolowo. In his report he comments, 'a degree of gullibility is required to believe a politician as astute as Awolowo, with a mass following of thousands of Yorubas, would be involved in such an inept, fruitless endeavor.'[19]

The trial got under way on 12 November and continued almost daily until 27 June 1963, when the judge, Justice George Sowemimo (sitting without a jury), adjourned proceedings in order to deliberate on his verdict. It was another two and a half months before that verdict was delivered, on 11 September. In the intervening period, Chief Anthony Enahoro, one of those who had originally fled Nigeria and thereby avoided standing trial with Awolowo, had been tried and convicted on the same charges following a protracted extradition process from the UK. The twin trials of Enahoro and of Awolowo and his

---

[17] 'Awo Charged. Treason: 27 in Court', *Daily Express*, 3 November 1962, p. 1.
[18] 'NYC begins its own arms hunt', *Daily Express*, 22 September 1962, p. 1.
[19] Patterson, 'Anniversaries, Emergencies and Teething Troubles', p. 4.

colleagues provided a constant stream of copy for the major newspapers in Nigeria, whose reportage included daily courtroom accounts, investigative journalism, editorials and even occasional pieces by the defendants themselves, notably Awolowo. The trials and their protagonists offered any number of angles for discussion, not least since some of the defendants and witnesses were also entangled in other newsworthy events such as the Coker Inquiry, which ran concurrently for some time with Awolowo's trial. While the trials themselves were in session, key reforms to the legal system were debated in parliament and in the press. These included attempts to introduce a Preventative Detention Act and to give politicians more control over judicial appointments. Such reforms were aimed at negotiating the threshold between law and sovereign power, and clearly echo the colonial aggregation of emergency powers and the legal exception to the body of sovereign authority. As such the reforms were not unassociated with the stakes of the trials. Moreover, the trials offered opportunities to reflect on crucial issues for the postcolonial nation in terms of both its legal statehood and the relationship between law and state. These issues included the rights of Nigerians to British legal counsel and conversely the rights of British barristers to act in Nigeria; the legitimacy of the Nigerian legal system; questions of race and racism in the police force; Nigeria's relationship to its neighbour and rival, Ghana; and relationships between the press, the court and the political parties. Each of these issues raised fundamental questions about the legal limit of the state.

Why were the newspapers so eager to cover this trial? What larger significance did the trial embody for the readers of the daily press? There is more to this than simply a persistent partisanship, in which newspapers across the political spectrum were obliged to report on matters of political relevance. In order to understand the trial's importance, we need to take stock of its timing in relation to Nigeria's developing statehood. Looking back on the trial over fifty years later, what strikes one almost immediately is the way in which the investigations and trials were bookended by the second anniversary of independence in 1962 and the declaration of the Republic in 1963. The trial thus coincides with a key transformation in Nigeria's political identity.

At independence, Nigeria had remained subject to the Crown as a Commonwealth realm. Therefore the phrasing of the full charges against Awolowo and his colleagues included conspiracy 'to levy war against our Sovereign Lady the Queen within Nigeria in order by force or constraint to compel our Sovereign Lady the Queen to change her measures or counsels'.[20] So it was that while Awolowo stood accused of a crime whose victim was the foreign yet sovereign body of the Queen, inherited at independence, the federal state was undertaking in a sanctioned and ritualised format the very same action in absolute, namely compelling the sovereign to relinquish her legal relationship to Nigeria as head of state. The trial thus was made to carry a significant symbolic burden. The accusations against Awolowo and his colleagues performed two roles in the process of state formation. Firstly they defined the limits of Nigerian statehood, and secondly they served to define the legitimacy of the Republic.

Taking this second role first, in order for the declaration of the Republic to appear legitimate, a process that was natural and civil rather than a rebellion against its sovereign power (as well as a key partner in trade and investment), the government defined its declaration against the illegitimate, unnatural and uncivil act of treasonable felony against the sovereign. The treasonable felony of which Awolowo was accused stood for a rebellious act against the Crown, from which the declaration of republican independence could distinguish itself. At the same time the treason trial also helped to bring the Republic into being by identifying its limits at the moment of its birth. If treason is the transgression of the legal boundaries of the state – its aim being the destruction of the state itself, rather than a crime against something contained within the state, as with other kinds of (political) violence – then the verdict of treason, which the trial could deliver, reinscribed those boundaries by naming and making visible the treasonable act or acts.

In the case of Awolowo's treasonable felony trial the conceptual boundaries of the state, which the charges of treason made tangible both legally and politically, were reinforced by reference to the geographical boundaries of the state in several distinct ways. Firstly, and most obviously, the charges included accusations that arrangements had been made and carried out for the military training of selected Action Group supporters in Ghana. This training, it was asserted, was in service to the conspiracy to undertake a coup. Moreover, it was to Ghana that several of the accused fled when the investigations began in late summer 1962. Ghana was, of course, Nigeria's near neighbour and it was also Nigeria's rival in many ways. They had been the largest two British colonies in West Africa, and the staff of both colonial administration

---

[20] 'The Charges: Treasonable Felony', *Daily Times*, 3 November 1962, p. 5.

and business interests (such as the United Africa Company) frequently shuttled between the two, undertaking periods of service in one colony before transferring to the other. Consequently, the infrastructures and economies of Ghana and Nigeria were roughly similar in size, significance and organisation. Ghana had been the first of Britain's African colonies to attain independence in 1957, with Kwame Nkrumah and his Convention People's Party (CPP) at the helm. Nkrumah's political outlook was distinctly socialist and following independence he pursued alliances with the European Eastern bloc. For some Nigerians, he therefore represented a compelling voice for the Africanisation of national economies in order to escape the controlling forces of Western markets and corporations; for others, his nationalising of the press and troubled relationship with Togo reflected an alarming dictatorial bent.[21] Thus while Ghana did not share a physical border with Nigeria, it was in many ways Nigeria's most significant 'neighbour'.

This significance was made immediately apparent in the testimony of the first witness. Oladipo Maja had been the first of the accused to be named in the trial but charges were quickly dropped against him and against another, Richard Babalola, and both took the stand as witnesses for the prosecution. Before Maja was called upon to give evidence the Acting Director of Public Prosecutions, B. A. Adadipe, outlined his case for prosecution, promising to 'produce a man whom you may call a contact man between Chief Awolowo and a very poweful [sic] man in Ghana [and] [t]hat this contact man negotiated the unlawful importation of arms and ammunition into this country'.[22] Maja was duly brought forth on the second day and gave a detailed account of how he had provided introductions for Awolowo to Nkrumah, following which Awolowo had assured Maja that 'Dr. Nkrumah's views were identical with his own Pan Africanism' and that 'the CPP was going to help the Action Group'.[23] Maja continued to relate how he was entrusted with arranging to bring explosives back from Ghana, as well as acquiring training and equipment for Action Group supporters, alleging that he was instructed to request

---

[21] Nkrumah had sought to incorporate Togo into Ghana following its independence from France but was rebuffed by the country's first president, Sylvanus Olympio. Following two years of increasing animosity between the two presidents, Olympio was assassinated in a coup d'état on 13 January 1963, in which Nkrumah was expressly implicated.
[22] '20 steps to power', *Daily Express*, 14 November 1962, p. 3.
[23] '"Bloodless Coup by Awolowo" – as told by Oladipo Maja, accused No. 1 now freed and appearing as witness No. 1', *Daily Express*, 14 November 1962, p. 1.

this military support from Nkrumah himself, who duly provided it.[24] From the start, therefore, the trial not only sought to define the state through the actions of those within it who must be excluded as treasonable to ensure the security of the conceptual borders of the nation; it also literalised those borders by invoking the involvement of Ghana, whose recent interests in absorbing Togo had led to multiple accusations and counter-accusations of assassination attempts between Nkrumah and Olympio. Ghana was thus made to model what was deemed both geographically and politically beyond the pale. Its invocation in the trial demonstrated from the outset that what was at stake was sovereignty, even if the very sovereign body under threat (the Queen) was at the very same time also being excluded through the parallel legal process of declaring the Republic.

Foreign Lawyers and Nigerian Law

The question of the relationship between the sovereign, the state and the law was further complicated by the recourse of Awolowo, Enahoro and others to English law and lawyers. Just days before the trial started the British QC E. F. N. Gratiaen, an expert in colonial and criminal law who had seen long and distinguished service in Ceylon, was refused entry by the Nigerian immigration authorities. Gratiaen had been due to act on behalf of Awolowo, Chief G. Ekwejunor-Etchie and Alfred Rewane but was turned back despite having his papers in order. Gratiaen and his clerk had their passports confiscated until they returned to a London-bound plane.[25] Several days later R. A. Ghory, QC, who was briefed to defend several others in the trial, was also refused entry. The following year, Dingle Foot, QC, who had represented Enahoro in Britain during his battle against deportation, was likewise barred from entry to Nigeria. Foot had been 'ordered out of Nigeria' in the previous year following his representation of D. S. Adegbenro, who had replaced Akintola as Western Premier in the power struggle that led to the Western Emergency.[26] In anticipation of protest from Enahoro, the federal government put out a statement indicating that 'any British lawyer other than Mr. Dingle Foot and Mr. E. F. N. Gratiaen would be allowed to enter Nigeria for the

---

[24] Ibid. p. 3.
[25] See 'British QC deported', *Morning Post*, 10 November 1962, pp. 1, 2; 'Three Motions Filed', *Daily Times*, 10 November 1962, p. 4.
[26] 'Barred from Entering Nigeria', *Morning Post*, 18 May 1963, p. 1.

purpose of defending Chief Anthony Enahoro ... in accordance with a previous undertaking given by the Federal Government'.[27]

This statement alluded to the failed action brought by Awolowo, Ekwejunor-Etchie and Rewane against the Minister for Internal Affairs and the Attorney-General in November–December 1962 following Gratiaen's refused entry. Like the main treason trial, this case was covered by newspapers of all political affiliations with careful attention paid to the legal arguments presented in court, and with a range of opinion columns commenting on the rights and wrongs of the debate. The argument made against the ministers was that their actions obstructed the rights of Awolowo, Ekwejunor-Etchie and Rewane to their choice of lawyer – rights guaranteed, under the Nigerian constitution, to defendants in a criminal case. The plaintiffs argued that the constitution's guarantee stipulated no limitation on the nationality or residency of the lawyer chosen and that therefore the ban on Gratiaen was motivated by ill will rather than constitutional procedure. The ministers' defence argued to the contrary that the right was not absolute and that the lawyer 'must be someone who is able ... or ... who has a right to practise in the country'.[28] They went on to argue that the Minister for Internal Affairs had 'absolute discretion to prevent the entry of anybody into Nigeria, with or without a valid visiting or transit pass', and that this was also provided for within the constitution.[29] The minister's discretionary power was challenged in turn by the counsel for the plaintiffs, who argued that this discretionary power was nonetheless limited, and could not be used to exclude someone like Gratiaen who, as a British subject, was not an alien and who, as a member of the Nigerian Bar, might normally expect to be able to enter and to practise in Nigeria.

Because the defence relied on the right of absolute discretion, the decision to exclude Gratiaen went unexplained; the minister's decision was assumed to be reason enough. It fell to the judge to provide a rationale that could counter the attribution of ill will to the minister's exclusion. He observed, 'The constitution is a Nigerian constitution meant for Nigerians ... The natural consequence of this is that the legal representation contemplated [in the constitution] ought to be someone in Nigeria and not outside it.'[30] He went on to reiterate the circular argument made

---

[27] Ibid.
[28] '"No Absolute Right for Accused": Court Told', *Daily Times*, 4 December 1962, n.p.
[29] 'Gratiaen: Ruling on Monday', *Morning Post*, 4 December 1962, p. 7.
[30] '"Gratiaen" Motion Out!', *Daily Express*, 11 December 1962, p. 1.

by the defence that counsel can only be given if the lawyer is physically present to do so and that in the instance of Gratiaen his discretionary exclusion meant he was not an available choice for the plaintiffs. The case thus turned on two issues: firstly the extent of liberty permitted under the constitutional right to one's choice of defence in a criminal trial, and secondly the extent of the discretion that might be exercised by the minister in controlling the movement of people across the nation's borders. The complicating factor in both issues was Nigeria's postcolonial and federal relationship to Britain. In both instances, the geographical and political extent of the state was in question. For Awolowo and his fellow plaintiffs Nigeria's continued recognition of British sovereignty following independence meant that 'a Nigerian constitution meant for Nigerians' might still be interpreted as extending as far as Britain. For the defence and the judge, the nation state was, in this instance at least, coterminous with the politically monitored geographical borders of the country.[31]

This factor was picked up in the opinion pieces carried by the press. The Action Group-affiliated *Nigerian Tribune* ran a piece entitled 'A Naked Hypocrisy', calling the Minister for Internal Affairs' decision 'not only ludicrous but … palpably ignorant of the position which Nigeria has bargained for by accepting a status – whatever it is – within the Commonwealth'. Pointing out that Nigerian law 'has been erected on the British legal base' and that 'British Common Law, to a very large extent, is administered in all our courts', the editor also noted recent cases whose appeals had been passed up to the 'British' courts. The editor summed up his criticism in the central question of the piece: 'What wisdom is in people being accused of wanting to wage war against "our Sovereign Lady, the Queen" and yet denying the "Queen's Counsel" a right to pursue

---

[31] Despite the judge's ruling, the fraught subject of the relationship between Nigerian and British law was perpetuated by the extradition battle to return Enahoro from Britain to stand trial. Enahoro challenged the extradition process on the grounds that the charges were politically motivated and he would therefore not receive a fair trial. Enahoro was initially arrested in London on 27 November 1962 on suspicion of treason in Nigeria and was not deported until 16 May the following year. Enahoro's case was supported by politicians across the Commons, including John Lowe MP, who was the estranged husband of Enahoro's lover, Josephine Lowe, in whose house he was originally arrested. Josephine Lowe took custody of Enahoro's children in Britain following his sentencing (see 'Englishwoman Shares "Secret" with Chief's Sons', *Jet*, 31 October 1963, p. 26; 'British Beauty Quits M.P.', *Jet*, 7 November 1963, p. 26). The fact that the arresting officer alleged Enahoro had entered Britain 'by unorthodox means' and without a passport coincidentally placed him at variance with Gratiaen, whose papers were reportedly in order, and gave rise to the suggestion that he had in fact been arrested for illegal entry into Britain ('Enahoro is held', *Daily Express*, 29 November 1962, p. 1).

his lawful business in Her Majesty's Court?'[32] A day earlier the NCNC-affiliated *Sunday Post* had commented on the issue obliquely in a short piece that claimed to be prompted by 'the recruitment of an expatriate lawyer as legal advisor to an indigenous Nigerian bank'. The *Post* offered its support to the ensuing 'outcry in favour of "our home made stuff", legal version', underlining its case by suggesting that of the '1,213 Nigerian lawyers' currently practising, 'half of them [are] under-employed'.[33]

In both pieces we can detect a clear intention to shape readers' judgements of the issues at stake. The *Post* argued that it was unpatriotic to employ foreign lawyers and thus to leave Nigerians out of work. This focus on patriotism suggested an equivalence between the use of foreign lawyers and the treason with which Awolowo and his fellow defendants were charged: both acts were unpatriotic and demonstrated a willingness to undermine the wellbeing of the nation state. By contrast, the *Tribune*'s piece used the complexity of the legal relations between Nigeria and the Queen's sovereignty to suggest, through a diction that focused on intellect ('ludicrous', 'ignorant', 'wisdom'), that the Minister for Internal Affairs was inadequate to his post. Most telling of all, however, was the *Tribune*'s phrase 'whatever it is' to describe Nigeria's status within the Commonwealth. For all the *Tribune*'s display of legal knowledge, this phrase admitted that Nigeria's status as an independent nation whose head of state was nonetheless its former colonial monarch remained, in an elemental way, indefinite.

Courtroom Drama

The press had already been covering the arrests and investigations into possible treasonable felony before the announcements made by Azikiwe and Balewa on the anniversary of independence. Excited coverage followed as the number of those wanted and charged in relation to the investigation grew. Headlines presented the case with gripping language: 'Arms Drama in Ekiti,' read the *Nigerian Tribune* on both front and back pages (25 September 1962); 'Police Swoop on 500,' reported the *Morning Post* the following day. 'War Plot!' was the explosive front-page headline in the

---

[32] [Editor], 'A Naked Hypocrisy', *Nigerian Tribune*, 12 November 1962, n.p.
[33] 'Lawyers, Made in Nigeria', *Sunday Post*, 11 November 1962, p. 4. 'Our Home Made Stuff' was a comic retooling of the acronym OHMS (On Her Majesty's Service). Originally used to refer to palm wine, differentiating it from (often illegally) imported gin, the term was used by British colonials and Nigerians alike to refer to Nigerian-made products.

West African Pilot on the day after the hearing for the trial (3 November 1962).

These reports were augmented by CID 'Wanted' announcements in the newspapers, which included photographs of the wanted men and statements to the effect that they were sought 'in connection with the recent seizures of arms, ammunition and explosives'.[34] A few weeks later the most prominent of those to have absconded from the police, Chief Anthony Enahoro, mailed a document to the *Daily Times* from Ghana. As well as providing an account of its contents, the editors included careful authenticating details in the article, noting, for example, the postmark, the cost of the stamp ('bearing the photograph of Dr. Nkrumah'), the fact that the statement, which purported to be the result of an Action Group meeting at the end of September, was signed by Enahoro, and that it was a 'six page cyclostyled document' without accompanying correspondence.[35] These details not only established the credibility of this new piece of information, they also encouraged their readers to interpret the evidence presented, as if they too were investigative police officers or journalists, trying to get the story straight. Indeed, the press were at pains to find ways to maintain their readers' curiosity and interest and used a range of rhetorical techniques to attract, to hold and to direct that interest over the following months. In doing so they contributed to the larger work of the treason trial by engaging their community of readers in the project of identifying the legal limit of the state.

When the trial opened the front pages were full of pictures of the key figures involved. Coverage of the initial hearings included headshots of the accused with a full list of names. More significant political figures were given larger photos than lesser-known defendants. Also featured was the judge, Mr Justice Sowemimo, whose prior career and credentials were detailed alongside information about several of the defence and prosecution lawyers. The *Daily Express* also provided photographs of their own reporters in an inset article entitled '… "Express" Team'. The brief item read:

> The 'Daily Express' – the pace-setter in News Coverage – will be represented at the BIG TRIAL by a three-man team.
>
> Alhaji Lateef Teniola, News Editor; Victor Folivi, top newsman; and Miss Ebun Oshunkoya, 'Express' Woman Editor.

---

[34] See 'Wanted by the Police' advertisement, featuring James Olubunmi Aluko, published in the *Morning Post* on 13 October 1962.

[35] See 'Enahoro Writes from Ghana', *Daily Times*, 18 October 1962.

For their sensational coverage of a sensational trial. Book your copy of the 'Daily Express' today.

Footnote: Comment from the 'Express' Team: 'It's an exciting assignment.'[36]

This overt presentation of the reporters provided yet another way for the paper to hail its readers into the conversation promised by the trial. The inclusion of a woman, like the regular inclusion of women's pages in most of the major papers generally, was clearly intended to make an appeal to a female readership. Thus, as an 'exciting assignment' for both male and female reporters, the trial was framed as deserving the attention of the broadest range of readers. As we noted in the previous chapter, women, particularly those in Nigeria's urban centres, demonstrated keen interest and engagement in politics both before and after independence. It was a large group of female political activists, for example, who first gathered to protest against the refusal of bail for Awolowo and his colleagues.[37] Thus while the *Express* may have been trying to encourage the readership of women who might otherwise have assumed the trial was not relevant to them, it was also ensuring that members of (political) women's groups realised that it intended to include a female viewpoint in its coverage. More broadly, the introduction of named journalists covering the trial underlined the uniqueness of the trial as a news feature and an assignment. Generally speaking, outside of editorials and guest columns written by significant political figures, news articles were unattributed. Journalists were only named if they were undertaking a very unusual report.[38] In fact, in the ensuing coverage of the trial these three journalists disappeared from view. Whether they were responsible for the *Daily Express*'s reports, or whether their work was picked up by others in due course, is unclear. Certainly, it would have been hard for any of the papers to predict what a drawn-out process the trial would be when the initial hearings were held, and therefore their ambitions for tight coverage provided by a handful of key reporters may well have been revised as the proceedings wore on. The majority of the

---

[36] '... "Express" Team', *Daily Express*, 12 November 1962, p. 1.
[37] See 'Riot Police at Lagos Prison ...', *Daily Express*, 8 November 1962: 'Police riot squads with guns and batons went into action around Lagos Prison, Broad Street, yesterday against scores of women who had travelled to see Chief Obafemi Awolowo and others now remanded in custody there ... Yesterday's action followed the "siege" at the prison by people – mostly market women and relatives – who had turned up to visit the Action Group leader and others (as previously allowed by the prison authorities)' (n.p.).
[38] For example, the *Daily Express* featured Olusola Olukoya, a young reporter who set off with John Daly (an 'ex-officer of the British Royal Navy') to circumnavigate the globe, from time to time sending back reports on their travels.

day-to-day articles on the trial were anonymous in all the major newspapers, and there was in fact little distinctly female perspective represented in any of the coverage.[39]

With little to report in the first day or so, the press filled their pages with facts and figures. As well as listing and illustrating the defendants, they also enumerated the charges in detail once more, often repeating exactly the same copy they had used for coverage of the hearing a week or so earlier. With twenty-seven of the thirty-one accused present when the trial started, the papers generated considerable column inches by listing the multiple defence teams that were to act on behalf of the accused, as well as the team for the prosecution. Nonetheless, whatever their political affiliation, from the start the headlines of every newspaper made clear that Awolowo was the central figure of the trial, and although other actors in the proceedings took on significant roles in the press coverage it was he who attracted and commanded the media's attention most completely.[40]

As leader of the federal opposition party, Awolowo was, of course, the biggest name amongst the thirty-one accused. Practically, moreover, the refusal of the federal government to permit him representation by a British barrister led to Awolowo defending himself, meaning that as well as undergoing lengthy examination by the prosecution, he undertook his own cross-examination of witnesses as well. At various stages through the trial Awolowo wrote directly to and for the press, leading to additional media coverage; at the culmination of the trial he delivered a marathon summing-up (ten days long), which was reported at length in the papers. In addition, because the Coker Inquiry was still proceeding when the trial started, and because he also appeared in the later trial of Enahoro when it began in May 1963, Awolowo was, for much of the twelve months between September 1962 and September 1963, a central subject of the multiple political scandals that excited the press. A further and unsought pathos was given to Awolowo's presence in the public eye when his son, also a lawyer, was killed in a car crash in July 1963 while Awolowo was still detained in prison awaiting the verdict.

---

[39] The *Daily Express* did run a feature by 'Expressgirl Ebun Oshunkoya' covering the first day, with the headline 'The Queen vs Awolowo: Only Two Wives Saw It All …', in which Oshunkoya reported on the day's events inside and outside the court with particular attention to the wives of two of the accused (M. A. Omisade and L. K. Jakande), the only two wives who were permitted into the courtroom (13 November 1962, p. 8).

[40] The *Morning Post*'s front-page headline on the day following the hearing makes this focus abundantly clear: 'AWOLOWO (*and thirty others*) CHARGED WITH TREASON' (3 November 1962).

Awolowo's stature and his decision to defend himself in the absence of his barrister of choice certainly placed him at the heart of the story, but it also lifted him above the fray in many ways. He presented himself, and was usually represented in the press on all sides, as wise, articulate, at home in the courtroom, well versed in matters of procedure, and magnanimous in his bearing. While he, and other counsel from both sides, challenged the judge at various points over procedural issues (e.g. permissible evidence), the reports of his exchanges with the judge cultivated the impression of a shared demeanour of professional respect that elevated Awolowo above the cut and thrust of the courtroom drama as it was otherwise depicted. Awolowo crafted a singular role for himself in the trial and in the press, distinguishing him from the others in the courtroom, whether from the accused or the prosecution and its ever-expanding roster of more or less credible witnesses.

Alongside this distinctive presentation of Awolowo, the press characterised many of the other actors in the trial through a variety of tropes that helped to shape their readers' perspectives on the evidence presented. Unsurprisingly, newspapers tended to focus their attentions on characteristics and evidence that supported their own political affiliations. Those characteristics and evidence were presented in such a way as to direct readers' responses, through the use of emotions, affect and caricature. Thus, from the start, the Action Group organ, the *Daily Express*, developed a critical response to the police. In its early reports the *Express* particularly targeted John Lynn, the Irish Assistant Commissioner who led the police investigation, and Assistant Superintendent (Special Branch) Edward Ceulemans, who assisted him (he was identified as South African in several of the papers). The *Express* reports focused repeatedly on allegations of police intimidation made by the defendants and various witnesses called. Thus, under the headline 'Police promised me death', the front-page report for 1 December 1962 recounts how 'Mr. Lynn, the moustached Irish boss of the Nigerian CID', denied accusations that he 'put cartridges on his table and loaded a pistol in [the defendant's] presence and further threatened to shoot him'.

The same edition of the *Express* included, in its letters to the editor, an item criticising policing in Nigeria generally:

A Friend or Foe?
  I wish to call the attention of the Federal Minister in charge of the Police to the disappointing way our Nigeria Police execute their duty to the public.

> These police officers are always hated by millions of Nigerians because of irrational and inhumane treatments they give to people who fall into their trap.
>
> That the public respect the emblem of their uniform should not give them the licence to use it as an abuse of office.
>
> The reckless use of baton by these police officers on culprits is deplorable.[41]

Five days later the *Express* ran a story with the headline 'My 11-hour Ordeal in Police Hands – BY AN ACCUSED', recounting the evidence given by founding Action Group member Ayo Akinsanya. Akinsanya's ordeal, we are told, took place

> in the Police Headquarters, Obalende, in the hands of a hunch-backed expatriate Police officer who claimed to have dealt with German war criminals before.
>
> The hunch backed—Police Officer, Ceulman [*sic*], he said, assaulted and kicked him when he picked up courage to fight back, he drew out a revolver and a flick knife with which he promised to blow up his head because he had got the authority of the Prime Minister and Commissioner of Police to kill anybody who did not co-operate.[42]

In each of these instances, whether in the reportage or in the letter to the editor, police violence or its threat is strongly foregrounded. This focus is given additional dramatic colouring by the physical details provided for Ceulemans and Lynn. Ceulemans is defined by his 'hunch back', Lynn by his moustache and typewriter, and these characteristics were repeatedly applied throughout early reporting. The deployment of these characteristics reflects in part the persistent influence of oral traditions in Nigerian reporting, noted by Louise Bourgault. Bougault points up the ways in which traditions in oral narratives continued in post-independence reportage, shaping the choice and presentation of details.[43] In this case the repeated, epithetical descriptions of Lynn and Ceulemans' physical appearances invoked an association of physical deformity with moral corruption. This association directed the readers' judgement as they navigated through the evidence presented in the reportage. In such ways the *Express* encouraged a strong critique of the police from the start, whilst appearing to maintain an objective relationship to the trial: the letter is presumed to be sent in rather than written by the editors; the

---

[41] *Daily Express*, 1 December 1962, p. 4.
[42] *Daily Express*, 6 December 1962, p. 2.
[43] See Bourgault, *Mass Media in Sub-Saharan Africa*, and in particular the chapter 'Discourse Style, Oral Tradition, and the Question of Freedom in the Press'.

accounts of police intimidation likewise come from witnesses and defendants on the stand whose words appear to be simply recorded rather than shaped by editorial bias. These articles and features developed an image of the police as not only untrustworthy but, in their substitution of force for legal procedure, as claiming for themselves the state of exception that had previously characterised the colonial administration. This impression was underlined by the fact that both Lynn and Ceulemans were white officers. The persistence of these white officers in the service of Nigeria following independence, and the high-handed exceptionalism that they claimed for themselves, subtly implied that the federal NCNC-NPC alliance had not brought transformation to the political and legal structures that were inherited from British colonialism at independence.[44]

Interestingly, the government-supporting *Morning Post* drew on some of the same characterisations used by the *Express* (particularly of Lynn and Ceulemans) that lent drama and pathos to their accounts. For Lynn and Ceulemans, the *Post*'s hostility can be explained by the same concern about colonial revenants that colours the *Express*'s coverage. What is striking, however, is the way in which drama and pathos were augmented by relatively frequent moments of comedy in the courtroom in the *Post*'s reporting. In an exemplary article, describing the examination of a prosecution witness, the *Morning Post* repeatedly pointed to the laughter that his evidence provokes. The article opened:

> The Lagos Special Criminal Assizes rocked with laughter yesterday when a prosecution witness in the treason trial said that if there were contradictions between his statement to the police and his evidence-in-chief before the court, then the fault lay with the manipulation of the 'English Grammar' by the policeman who took down the statement.[45]

A second, larger article in the same edition likewise repeated how 'the court rocked with laughter' and that the witness, Ebido, 'threw the court into laughter'.[46] Ebido had been an Action Group area boy but left and joined the NPC, he said, because he was not adequately paid. His evidence was called because he claimed to be one of several men sent for military training in Ghana by the Action Group. Cross-examination by the defence clearly attempted to demonstrate that his motivation in giving evidence was a

---

[44] Ceulemans, at least, stayed on in the force as late as 1968, and in the *London Gazette*'s listing of his OBE in 1970 he is recorded as 'lately Acting Chief Superintendent, Nigeria Police Force', supplement to the *London Gazette*, 13 June 1970, p. 6384.
[45] 'Ebido Raises a Laugh', *Morning Post*, 22 January 1962, p. 7.
[46] 'Ghana Trains Rhodesians', *Morning Post*, 22 January 1962, pp. 7, 10.

persistent animosity towards the Action Group but, although its coverage reported this, the *Morning Post*'s headlines directed readers' attention to the treasonable training on the one hand and the comedy of Ebido's evidence on the other. By contrast the *Express*'s coverage of the same evidence was presented without any indication of this courtroom hilarity.

Nonetheless, the *Express* did pick up on laughter elsewhere in its reportage, where it was often directed at the police. Lynn and his typewriter, for example, became a stock theme, with Lynn typing up 'statements' which the witnesses then rejected, either at the time or later in the courtroom. Thus in early December one of the defendants, Chike Obi, objected to the admissibility of his police statement. To justify his request for its striking from the record, he described his experience of having his statement typed up by Lynn and his assistant, Chukuma: 'When Chukuma came in, Lynn brought out his inevitable typewriter. (laughter).'[47] Strikingly, Lynn's typed statements were not rejected simply because they failed to represent the witnesses' accounts of a given event; they were also often rejected on the grounds of the quality of his 'horrible English'. Thus Chike Obi recalled, 'I told him the English was not mine and that as a politician I would not like a statement credited to me to be read with such English.'[48] In another edition, the *Express* carried an article in which the evidence given by Detective Sergeant Joseph Ohaegbula was ridiculed with laughter in the courtroom during his cross-examination: 'There was constant laughter in the courtroom ... Almost every answer to Mr Odesanya's question by Sergeant Ohaegbula was greeted with laughter. And at one stage Mr Odesanya remarked "And you say you are a police Sergeant!"'[49] This report of laughter was included in an article about the search of Awolowo's house without a warrant, and followed immediately in the article after a statement from Ohaegbula that a government chemist had tampered with bullet shells seized at Awolowo's home. As a result of this focus on Odesanya's comic performance at the expense of Ohaegbula, the *Express*'s report succeeded in implying that not only were the police nefarious, they were also incompetent.[50]

---

[47] 'Enahoro's dramatic border escape as told the police by Dr. Chike Obi', *Daily Express*, 6 December 1962, p. 2.
[48] Ibid.
[49] 'No warrant to search Awo's House – Witness', *Daily Express*, 29 January 1963, p. 2.
[50] A month earlier the *Morning Post* had reported laughter directed at the Action Group, described by one of the witnesses as a 'milkless cow' because it was unable to pay its activists: 'the court once again roared with laughter'. 'Milkless Cow', *Morning Post*, 29 December 1962, p. 7.

The *Daily Express* invited its readers to use laughter against the white police officers, revenants of the colonial regime, whose actions on behalf of the Zikist government drew attention to that government's failure to throw off the shackles of the former colonial administration, not least its willingness to substitute violence for legal procedure. Lynn and his typewriter, moreover, reflected the insufficiencies of the old colonial regime; his comic inability to write in an English of the standard used by the Nigerians he was questioning underlined their intellectual and cosmopolitan prowess by comparison with him. Meanwhile, the Nigerian officers, such as Ohaegbula, were reduced to figures of fun whose incompetence stood metonymically for the incompetence of the case against those on trial. On the other hand, the *Morning Post* directed readers' laughter against the implausible excuses provided for contradictory evidence by Action Group members. The defendants were presented as self-important, loquacious and bathetic, and thus likewise not to be trusted. Thus, whether in the *Daily Express* or the *Morning Post*, laughter was used to share and communicate knowledge and judgement. Further, this apparently most genial of affects encouraged readers to identify that which needed to be excluded in order to define the conceptual boundaries of the nation state.

Permission to enter into a position of judgement was proffered to the readers of the various newspapers by the frequent use of apparently verbatim reporting, taken from the court records.[51] This verbatim reporting worked rhetorically to convince the reader that the information presented was simply an objective account of what had happened rather than a reporter's own political perspective. However, particularly where the newspapers recorded the to and fro of cross-examination, as happened a good deal in the first few months of the trial, the reports began to read like scripts, heightening the dramatic quality of the account. Indeed, readers were primed to expect this drama by the frequently purple prose of the headlines that accompanied the reports. The dramatising use of verbatim reports extended to the very layout of the page, with speakers' names represented in bold on the page and interjections, most commonly laughter, appearing like stage directions: 'Lynn brought out his inevitable typewriter. (laughter).' The presentation of events, brought to life in this way, encouraged the reader to enter imaginatively into the trial itself: to listen carefully, to consider the responses, and to assess the evidence. Caught up in this apparently minute-by-minute account, the readers were essentially coached by the newspapers, as if they were members of a jury who could shape the contours of their nation

---

[51] In Chapter 5 we noted this same mode of engagement with the reader in Okonkwo's *Never Trust All that Love You* (pp. 47–50).

through their imaginative judgement of the treason charges against Awolowo and his colleagues.[52]

To that end newspapers often chose different passages of the court records to reproduce according to their dramatic qualities and their usefulness in priming readers to particular political sympathies. Consequently, it is not unusual to find newspapers leading with very different headlines and content despite reporting on the same day's events in court. Nonetheless, whether readers remained loyal to a particular imprint or read across the diverse available press coverage, the effect of the verbatim reportage was to create a sense of immediacy that brought the trial to life (and kept it alive) for the reader. This creation of a popular and collective juridical body from the readers of the press is particularly striking given the absence of a jury from the trial. Instead, in fact, Sowemimo and Mr Justice Sigismund Olanrewaju Lambo, the latter sitting for Enahoro's trial, deliberated alone in their judgements. This lack of a jury, however, cleared an imaginative space for the newspaper readers. Had a jury been present, the press would no doubt have reported on the ways in which the actors in the trial appealed to that jury, and how that jury in turn responded to the trial's revelations and accusations. Instead, the requisite impassivity of the judges enabled the press to redirect the appeals made by prosecution, defence and witnesses out to the newspaper readers.

'Whatever It Is'[53]

I noted earlier in this chapter the *Nigerian Tribune*'s qualification of Nigeria's 'status ... within the Commonwealth' with the phrase 'whatever it is'. This qualification highlighted the tension inherent in Nigeria's independence from Britain whilst maintaining the Queen as head of state. As the *Tribune*'s editor argued, there was a paradox in accusing the defendants of waging war against the sovereign whilst refusing them access to her counsel on the basis of nationalism.[54] The indefiniteness of 'whatever it is' brings us back to the narrative and symbolic weight that the treason trial carried, in the year in which Nigeria prepared to become a republic. As I suggested at the outset, the precise way in which the case was announced to the nation on the anniversary of independence in 1962 cannot be read as coincidental. Likewise, the proximity of the double verdicts (Enahoro on

---

[52] We might compare this with Anderson's account of the power of newspapers to create a 'remarkable confidence of community in anonymity' in the modern nation (*Imagined Communities*, p. 36).

[53] [Editor], 'A Naked Hypocrisy', *Nigerian Tribune*, 12 November 1962, n.p.

[54] Ibid.

7 and Awolowo on 11 September 1963) to the declaration of the Republic (1 October) underlined the trial's dramatisation of the legal boundaries of the new sovereignty of the nation state. The trial provided a crucial site for defining the nation state; indeed, it was in many ways the only possible site for that definition. The divisions of region, religion, politics and ethnicity that emerged in the post-war federalisation of Nigeria, and that were the direct consequence of the innate incoherence and inconsistencies of indirect rule, excluded other potential ideological structures by which national identity might be confirmed. By contrast, the shared inheritance of English common law within the modern legal system of the federation provided a unifying ideal from which to deliver the new nation.

I say 'from which' not only because the trial constructed and defined the threat *from which* the government of Azikiwe and Balewa sought to save the nation, but also because the trial's temporal alignment with the Republic made it a chrysalis from which the nation state would emerge. Awolowo and his fellow defendants' crime of treasonable felony was made to stand in for the severing of the Queen's sovereignty enacted by the Republic. Their punishment symbolically freed the state to circumvent the elision of the law with the body of the sovereign. In the case of the treasonable felony, whilst the trial revealed no plot against the physical body of Queen Elizabeth II herself, it emphasised the threat that had been posed to those who embodied her sovereign power, such as Balewa and Azikiwe. The treasonable felony of conspiracy was thus against the Queen's legal body rather than her actual person. Reconstituting the legal body of the sovereign within and coterminous with the racial and geographical bounds of Nigeria moved the national government one step closer to severing the Queen's own claims to that sovereignty. Moreover, in this desire to remove the Queen from sovereign power and to aggregate that power to the Republic, the Nigerian government enacted the very same 'treason' against the sovereign body of the Queen for which Awolowo and his fellow defendants were convicted just three weeks before the declaration of the Republic.

This process of delivering the Republic through the trial operated not only in the symbolic realm but also in the realm of imagination and narrative. The media coverage of the trial in court reports, opinion pieces, letters, photo features and pieces by the actors themselves filled the pages of the papers for a year, often with multiple items in the same edition. The unfolding of the trial thus wove the nation together through the shared reading of its narrative of investigation, arrests, charges, examination and cross-examination, summing-up and verdict. Certainly, other narratives competed with that of the trial, not least those of national progress exemplified by industry, construction, education and the inspirational lives of the nation's leaders which appeared regularly as centrefold features in the *Morning Post*. Nonetheless, the overwhelming public narrative of the twelve months prior to the declaration of the Republic was that of the political limits of the nation state and the power of the law to delineate and to defend them.

Awolowo's trial was divisive and it is tempting to assume that the charges were trumped up as a way of ensuring the dominance of the NCNC, and the incapacity of the Action Group, after the declaration of the Republic. If, however, Azikiwe had hoped that the trial (orchestrated or not) might bring the nation together through a shared recognition of that which stood outside its limits in the form of treasonable felony, he was to be disappointed. The factionalism that had led to the Western Emergency persisted, and ethnic rivalries were exacerbated by moves to establish the Middle Belt Region and by contested census data on which political constituencies were based. Thus, barely two years after Awolowo's conviction, Akintola, Balewa and Bello (Governor of the Northern Region) were assassinated. The ensuing coup, counter-coup and massacres of Igbo in the North over the following twelve months led inexorably to devastating civil war.

The symbolic and narrative dominance of Awolowo's trial helps us to recognise the fundamental significance that the law had for Nigeria at independence, not only as a practical feature of life, as we saw in the previous two chapters, but also as a structural framework for thinking about – indeed, for bringing into being – the nation state. Indeed, whilst their ideological and generic modes for engaging with the law may have been quite different, all the writers, newspapers and politicians discussed so far were clearly invested in thinking through the law in relation to the state and, in particular, in exploring the limits of the law as the founding threshold of statehood. In the following, final chapter we return to Achebe to examine how he engages with the structures of the law in a novel composed in the wake of the Awolowo trial and which uncannily prefigured much of the political turmoil to come. Reading the novel in the light of the treasonable felony trial illuminates this fundamental imbrication of the law in fiction that sought to respond to the challenges of postcolonial Nigerian nationhood.

7

Violence and the Law in *A Man of the People*

On the night of 15 January 1966, Chinua Achebe met fellow members of the Society of Nigerian Authors in their office on Kingsway Road in Ikoyi, Lagos. At that time, Achebe was awaiting the publication of his latest novel, *A Man of the People*, and a few days earlier had sent an advance copy to another member of the Society, John Pepper Clark-Bekederemo. In his memoir of Biafra, *There Was a Country*, Achebe recalls: 'When J. P. arrived at the meeting his voice rang out from several hundred feet away. "Chinua, you know, you are a prophet. Everything in this book has happened except a coup!"'[1] It was only later the following day that news began to emerge of the Nzeogwu coup, in which the Northern and Western Premiers in Nigeria were killed and which was to lead inexorably to civil war. The general suspicion that the coup was an Igbo plot, and the particular suspicion that his novel's denouement demonstrated prior knowledge, meant that Achebe and his family were pursued in military reprisals in the following days. Achebe was forced to smuggle his family out of Lagos and followed them some time later to the Igbo-majority Eastern Region. Achebe comments that '[d]espite my fictional warning I never expected or wanted the form of violent intervention that became the military coup of January 15, 1966. I had hoped that the politicians would sort things out for our new nation.'[2] Indeed, *A Man of the People* studiously avoids locating itself within any real geography, instead relying on imagined place names generically suggestive of West Africa, as if the novel might be set anywhere. Nonetheless, the novel makes clear the trajectory of corruption, emergency and political violence that Nigeria itself tracked towards civil war in the years following independence. In this chapter I trace the novel's parallel trajectory of mob rule, martial law and assassination as forms of social and political violence that are substituted for legal process.

Told in the first person, *A Man of the People* recounts the short-lived political career of its narrator, Odili. At the start of the novel Odili is a small-town schoolteacher but he is soon taken up by a charismatic and

---

[1] Achebe, *There Was a Country*, p. 63.
[2] Ibid. p. 65.

corrupt politician, Chief Nanga. Moving to the city to stay with Nanga, Odili is rapidly disaffected, not by Nanga's power and politics (to which he is drawn) but by his usurpation of Odili's girlfriend, Elsie. Leaving Nanga's household, Odili joins another political party, which has been newly established by his school friend, Max, and Max's girlfriend, Eunice. Max and Eunice's socialist intellectualism inspires Odili and, although the party stands little hope of winning, he throws in his lot and agrees to stand against Nanga in their home region. His political challenge to Nanga on home turf sends shock waves through the community. Nanga uses bribery, corruption and violence to try to put pressure on Odili, who refuses to back down. The climax of the novel comes at one of Nanga's rallies, which Odili attends in disguise. He is recognised, hauled on stage, publicly humiliated by Nanga, violently beaten by Nanga's gang of area boys, and consequently hospitalised. The national vote goes ahead but Max is assassinated on the night of the election and Eunice shoots his opponent, Chief Koko, in revenge. Disorder breaks out across the country and despite the government declaring victory they are rapidly deposed in a military coup that takes advantage of the civil unrest and abolishes all political parties 'until the situation became stabilized once again'.[3] The novel ends in this period of martial law, a state of exception in which, Odili tells us, 'you died a good death if your life had inspired someone to come forward and shoot your murderer in the chest – without asking to be paid'.[4]

Read in the context of Nigerian politics the novel clearly draws upon a variety of recent events and concerns. As we saw in the previous two chapters contemporary political rivalries were often violently divisive and were reported not only in the press but also in popular publications such as Orizu's *To Rule Is a Trouble*. As Taiwo Adetunji Osinubi reminds us, however, it is important to recognise the novel's international contexts as well.[5] These include the assassination of Congolese independence leader and the nation's first prime minister Patrice Lumumba in January 1961, the political and military ramifications of which continued to be reported in the Nigerian press in the years that followed. Two years later the assassination of Togolese president Sylvanus Olympio was the first coup d'état in the former French and British West African colonies and was similarly widely discussed in the press. Meanwhile, Ghana's national and inter-

---

[3] Achebe, *A Man of the People*, p. 148.
[4] Ibid. p. 150.
[5] See Osinubi, 'Cold War Sponsorships'.

national politics under Nkrumah led to disturbances not only within its territories but also for its neighbours, exemplified by the destabilising fallout over Togo with Olympio in the early 1960s. This context of extreme political unrest in the wake of decolonisation was further influenced by the power play of the cold war, and while Olympio, Lumumba and Nkrumah, like Togo, Congo and Ghana, appear only as implicit allusions in the novel, the Western and Soviet blocs are not only referenced but characterised through minor protagonists. Indeed, Osinubi goes so far as to suggest that 'Achebe's reference to the Common People's Convention, and the figure of its only female founding member, Eunice, recall the politician Funmilayo Ransome Kuti (FRK) who founded the Commoners' People's Party in 1960'.[6]

As Osinubi demonstrates, with reference to the cold war specifically, the novel illustrates the closely knit relations between political corruption, foreign influence and political in-fighting. It also picks up on the anxieties we observed in the previous chapters about intellectualism (particularly the figure of the 'been-to'[7]) and the relationship of the media to politics and the law. Achebe treats this material in a deceptively realist mode that initially deflects our attention from the moments of symbolism and satire that shape the narrative. Closer attention, however, reveals a precise structure of repetitions and reversals that ironise the novel's events and protagonists, including its narrator.

In what follows, I examine Achebe's presentation of political disorder through scenes in which the law is suspended or displaced. These scenes include riots and mobs where the law becomes dispersed into the crowd, who act extra-judicially with a violent force that stands in for legal process. Underpinning these scenes we also find examples of corruption, criminality and the inevitable tension between urban and rural customs and ownership inherited from indirect rule. My argument is that through these scenes Achebe points up the incoherence of the inheritance of colonialism, not least indirect rule, and the inevitability of the imposition of new states of exception as a response to this incoherence. The structural permission that the state of exception provides for the suspension of certain claims to protection by and from the law enables politicians to cut through anachronism and to bypass the process of law, reaching

---

[6] Ibid. p. 411. FRK travelled extensively in the Soviet bloc in the 1950s and was perceived by the Nigerian government as a communist. As noted in Chapter 5, FRK is also indirectly invoked by Ekwensi in *Jagua Nana*.

[7] 'Been-to' is the common term used in anglophone West Africa to describe someone who has 'been to' Europe and comes back influenced by, and often demonstrative of, that experience.

instead for the violent force that the exception sanctions. This point is underlined by Achebe's omission of any courtroom scenes in this novel. The plot provides multiple opportunities for such scenes yet they do not appear, a fact all the more striking given their appearance in his earlier fiction, such as *No Longer at Ease*. Instead, in a paradoxical echo of District Commissioner fiction, through this absence of formal trial scenes, Achebe directs our attention to the various ways in which the law and legal processes are sidestepped, dissipated and conflated in an era of political corruption through scenes of violence that stand in for, but are markedly not, the legal process of the trial.

'Loss of Life and Property'[8]

Mahmood Mamdani argues that one of the fundamental inheritances of British colonialism in Africa has been the legislative divide incurred through indirect rule.[9] The split between town and country was shaped in part by the assumption that a form of British law might be appropriate in the 'civilised' environment of cities such as Lagos but that customary law was more appropriate in the rural regions. The implications of this split are manifold and contradictory. On the one hand, as novels like *No Longer at Ease*, *People of the City* and *Jagua Nana* show, the British encouraged an urbanising and 'civilising' aspiration through the variety of value markers it placed on financial accumulation, disposable commodities, cosmopolitanism and European cultural practices. On the other hand, the imposition of a fantasised version of pre-colonial legal structures sought, at best, to recognise the value of non-British cultural practice and, at worst, to establish an interim state through which, it was argued, the natives would eventually pass on their interminable journey towards the civilisation of their colonisers. Indeed, these arguments were often made in tandem and they changed very little throughout the period of twentieth-century colonisation in Nigeria. Thus, just as Wallace and others might express horror at the 'trousered ape' at the start of the century, Margery Perham, in 1941, claimed that African colonies 'must have foreign rulers, and for a long time to come', on the basis that 'the difficult yet exciting task of bringing Africa into the main movement of history and of training Africans to be full citizens of the civilized world' remained to be completed.[10] Nonetheless, Perham emphatically saw economic transformation through

---

[8] Achebe, *A Man of the People*, p. 98.
[9] See Mamdani, *Citizen and Subject*.
[10] Perham, *Africans and British Rule*, pp. 92, 93.

trade with Western Europe as key to the attainment of that civilisation, thus justifying the accompaniment of the colonial administration with (British-regulated) international trade.[11]

As a consequence of the paradoxes of the colonial administration, the problem of how power and law might be distributed and managed was not immediately resolvable following decolonisation. In *A Man of the People* we see the localised effects of this inheritance played out in the election contest for Anata, Odili's hometown. About halfway through the novel Achebe inserts one of the narrative's many scenes noted above in which events stand in for, but are not, a legal trial. Josiah the shopkeeper is accused of inviting a blind beggar into his shop, serving him food and wine, only to steal his stick. The villagers besiege Josiah's shop, hurling curses at him and retelling the story of his crime to all who come near. 'Within a week', Odili tells us, 'Josiah was ruined; no man, woman or child went near his shop ... Before the month was out the shop-and-bar closed for good and Josiah disappeared – for a while.'[12] The crowd are roused by a compelling story and act instead of the law to provide something that is not justice, but is made into its equivalent. Tellingly, Achebe has one of the villagers observe to Odili, in his explanation of the commotion, 'I have said that what the white man's money will bring about has not shown itself yet.'[13] This observation, we realise retrospectively, is all too true with regard to the politicking that follows.

One immediate sign of the continuing influence of 'the white man's money' is the social change that occurs in Anata over Christmas. The town's 'sons and daughters', we are told, 'who have gone out to work or trade in the cities usually return home with lots of money to spend'.[14] Their number is increased by holidaying students, whose presence, for Odili, had 'a way of immediately raising the general tone of the village, giving it an air of well-dressed sophistication'.[15] Here, Odili voices a 'progressive' postcolonial attitude that echoes directly the colonial ideal of civilised Western culture spreading from the cities to the rural communities through trade and education. Odili's focus on the luxury

---

[11] Even after independence Perham continued to express doubts about the validity of African nationalism on the grounds that independence had come too fast to West African nations. See Perham's 'The Psychology of African Nationalism' in *Colonial Sequence, 1949–1969* (first published in *Optima* in 1960), pp. 182–98.
[12] Achebe, *A Man of the People*, p. 86.
[13] Ibid. p. 86.
[14] Ibid. p. 96.
[15] Ibid.

commodities paraded by these returning students ('Italian-type shoes', 'lipstick', 'tight trousers', 'hair stretched with hot iron') reminds us of the commercialisation of 'civilisation' that accelerated in the post-war decades of colonialism and the first years of independence. As the *Unilever House Magazine* boasted in 1951, the United Africa Company 'now sells to the African everything from pins and padlocks to salt and sandals, biscuits and bulldozers'.[16]

Whilst colonisation of Nigeria, and West Africa more broadly, is frequently thought of in terms of the production and extraction of commodities for export to European markets, it is important to remember that the civilising mission of colonialism was also deployed in a calculated way to create new markets to which companies such as the UAC could sell. As the feature in the *Unilever House Magazine* makes clear, in the final decades of colonialism, when independence was increasingly on the cards, Britain fortified its commercial interests in West Africa through careful observation and cultivation of local appetites for imported commodities: 'attention to local variations in taste is most important,' the *Unilever House Magazine* explains to its employee-readers; '[f]or example, the Nigerian who works in an office likes to wear a felt hat, but it must have a particular type of stitching across both crown and brim.'[17] Moreover, as much as companies like the UAC used colonialism to develop new markets in disposable goods amongst individual consumers, colonial and neo-colonial nations were also quick to cash in on the larger markets in infrastructural development represented by newly independent governments. This was the case for both Eastern and Western bloc countries, as is made apparent in the advertisements carried in Nigerian newspapers, where Polish companies like Polservice advertised their capacity to contribute to building development alongside similar appeals from British firms. In an advertisement in the Nigerian *Daily Express*, for example, the construction company Taylor Woodrow included a miniature feature about 'Nigeria's Biggest Textile Mill': 'Taylor Woodrow are proud to have been associated with this important contribution to Nigeria's economic progress ... This fine Mill is one more example of the Taylor Woodrow policy of close co-operation with clients and consultants.'[18] In the rapidly expanding post-

---

[16] 'Biscuits and Bulldozers', p. 3.

[17] Ibid. p. 7. As the extensive advertisement sections in pamphlets such as the *Nigeria Handbook 1922–23* make clear, Nigeria had in fact long been seen as a rich market for European manufactured goods.

[18] *Daily Express*, 14 December 1962, p. 2. A month or so earlier Polservice offered their services in an advertisement 'to investors at all stages of building – from projects to realization',

war context of multinationals like Unilever, the companies that stood to gain from these various markets were frequently one and the same, as the title given to the *Unilever House Magazine* feature, 'Biscuits and Bulldozers', reminds us.[19]

We have seen already the significance of this colonial development on the individual consumer market in the metropolitan fiction of Ekwensi and Achebe, and in market literature more broadly. What differentiates its presentation here in *A Man of the People* is its continuation and expansion in the postcolonial state. Odili unquestioningly endorses the metropolitan embrace of Western goods and sees their influx during the festive season as a civilising influence on the village. As always, however, in the tight construction of this novel, Achebe doesn't allow this influence to go unchallenged for long. Whilst the 'Italian-style shoes' worn by the young hip students (and supplied by outlets such as the UAC's famous Kingsway stores) might seem innocuous enough, we are almost immediately introduced to Nanga's new four-storey house, which is a 'dash' from 'Antonio and Sons whom Nanga had recently given the half-million-pound contract to build the National Academy of Arts and Sciences'.[20] This is a rather different example of 'the white man's money', which gives an especially ironic lie to Nanga's early declared nativism in parliament.[21] The irony here is not only that Nanga awards the contract to a foreign rather than a local firm; it is also tangible in his involvement in establishing an institution like the 'National Academy of Arts and Sciences' that represents the very Western-orientated intellectual pretensions he has previously decried as evidence of anti-nationalist sentiment.

If Josiah's crime of tricking a blind man prefigures Nanga's kickback, to which the community turns a blind eye, Nanga's four-storey house in turn prefigures the ensuing exposure of similar graft between

---

indicating that they 'represent Polish Scientific – Technical institutes and planning offices' and could 'supervise the supplies of investment goods' such as factories and technical infrastructure (*Daily Times*, 15 November 1962, p. 2). Eastern bloc multinationals also regularly advertised commodity exports and imports, e.g. the Bulgarian firm Industrialimport, which traded in textiles, and the Polish firms Rolimpex, which traded in foodstuffs, and Ciech, which traded in pharmaceuticals.

[19] Unilever was, of course, intrinsically involved in the colonial-market nexus of Nigeria, since the UAC's predecessor had been the Royal Niger Company, whose non-commercial interests and activities were assumed by the British government when (to protect British commercial interests) it established its protectorates in Nigeria.
[20] Achebe, *A Man of the People*, p. 97.
[21] Ibid. p. 6.

the Foreign Trade department and 'British Amalgamated'.[22] Moreover, details in the press reveal that while head of the Foreign Trade department Nanga likewise had gained 'three blocks of seven-story luxury flats at three hundred thousand pounds each in the name of his wife and that these flats were immediately leased by British Amalgamated at fourteen hundred a month'.[23] Achebe's particular choice of property to illustrate political and economic corruption here recalls, of course, the very recent Coker Inquiry, which had occurred in the immediate wake of the Western Emergency in Nigeria. As we saw in the previous chapter, the inquiry was set up to investigate the large-scale siphoning of public funds by leading politicians in the Action Group through various businesses, primarily the Nigerian Investment and Property Company.[24]

But as well as alluding to recent political scandals, Achebe's focus on property reflects larger issues that were inherited from colonial rule. As Mamdani and Sara Berry have demonstrated, property was a fraught issue for the colonial administration. The negotiable and variable terms of access that characterised land rights and relationships in Nigeria were more or less intentionally misinterpreted over the years by the colonial government in various ways and with varying consequences. In the absence of recognised or consistent customs of individual property rights, the administration tended to treat native lands as communal and tribal. Having defined these lands as such, they sought to ascribe control over them to the often newly instated tribal leaders. Having thus identified a single figure responsible for 'tribal' lands, the administration sought to protect and regulate the land rights of the specified tribal community and its leader to the exclusion of all other claims or uses. Not only did this have the effect of essentially deterritorialising 'strangers', that is to say migrants from outside a particular community, in 'grounding the powers of the chiefs in the right to allocate customary land for use, customary law tended to fortify the position of Native

---

[22] Ibid. p. 100.
[23] Ibid. p. 101.
[24] Controversially, the inquiry concluded 'without doubt that Chief Awolowo has failed to adhere to the standards of conduct which are required for persons holding such a post. We take the view that there is no evidence sufficient, in our view, to say the same of Chief Akintola, and we absolve him on all grounds.' The absolution of Akintola and condemnation of Awolowo inevitably appeared politically motivated given the rivalry between them, and thus whilst it may have resolved one controversy, it perpetuated others in a manner recalled in *A Man of the People*.

Authorities'.²⁵ The relationship to the Native Authority that this management of land rights encouraged thus distorted and entrenched the local and familial dependencies and feuds that Achebe fictionalises in his early colonial fiction, such as *Arrow of God*, and that Orizu catalogues in *To Rule Is a Trouble*.

Following independence, tensions were inevitable between the Western model of individual property rights, already well established in the urban centres, and residual and/or ideological commitment to a communal understanding of land rights that had nonetheless been distorted by colonial regulation. Nanga's four-storey house crystallises these tensions in what appears a throwaway scene midway through the novel. On Christmas morning Odili finds Mrs Nanga besieged at home by a drunken relative of the chief. 'Look at the new house he is building,' the relative demands. 'Do I ask to share it with him when it is finished? No. I only ask for a common beer, common five shilling beer.'²⁶ When Mrs Nanga, humorously challenging him, asks if he shouldn't share the house with his kinsmen ('Does a man exclude his brother from his house?') he concludes, 'No, that is not done … It is my house; you have spoken the truth.'²⁷ The relative initially offers to substitute his kinship rights for the disposable commodity of a beer. On second thoughts, however, he reasserts his kinship rights through an invocation of the customary – what is 'done' or 'not done' – only to express those rights in singular terms: 'It is *my* house.' However, whilst dependency claims might traditionally be honoured when understood to be made earnestly and honestly, whether the need for a beer or a home, in this case neither beer nor home appears to be lacking for this relative, since he is already drunk and only claims his right to the house on the grounds of what is 'done' customarily. His demands abuse the customs of kinship dependency by repurposing them for his individual benefit. Light-hearted as this scene is, it nonetheless reflects once more Nanga's own corruption in repurposing international financial investment aimed at benefiting the nation towards his own individual aggrandisement. On an allegorical level, the conjunction of the relative and the house provides a metonymy for the ways in which both English and customary laws and practice have broken down under the

---

²⁵ Mamdani, *Citizen and Subject*, p. 140. See also Berry, 'Hegemony on a Shoestring', p. 336.
²⁶ Achebe, *A Man of the People*, p. 97.
²⁷ Ibid.

force of a self-interest that turns communities, both rural and urban, into individuals.

This sense of the abandonment of legal process, and the fracturing of communitarian culture, is likewise caught in another otherwise incidental Christmas scene in which a troupe of young boys appear at the doorstep to perform for money, with a dancing mask who brandishes an 'outsize matchet'.[28] This was a common enough occurrence in communities where young boys were encouraged to play at masquerade rituals using toys prior to their initiation into mask societies later in puberty. The attendant boys in this Christmas troupe tug at the mask's restraining ropes 'as adult attendants do to a real, dangerous Mask'; but when these come undone, rather than going on 'a wild rampage' with 'loss of life and property', as would be expected in such a situation in an adult masquerade, the 'Mask tamely put his matchet down, helped his disciples retie the rope, picked up his weapon again and resumed his dance'.[29] This vignette is comically charming but it allegorises the novel's larger dramatisation of the hollowing-out of traditional modes of social coercion and cohesion. The young mask's machete is a mere prop rather than a tool of his spiritual power. Moreover, the performance becomes a purely commercial affair with financial reward trumping wild abandon. This scene finds its inverse in the mob violence at the end of the novel, where the rampages of area boys cause exactly 'loss of life and property'. In both instances, the children's dance and the area boys' 'reign of terror', what is missing is the social regulation embodied in the traditional mask's threat of unrestrained violence. Emmanuel Chidi Onwuzolum argues that masking was commonly used to police villagers' activities and social conduct to the extent that the mask could even act as the 'executive arm of the *Oha* (Igbo legislative assembly)'.[30] Importantly, 'it was the spirits and ancestors that performed the police function through the mask.'[31] The disruptive rampage of the traditional masquerade is thus distinguished from that of the area boys by the ritual and social role it was understood to enact. Achebe characterises the mob violence of the area boys in direct contrast: 'What happened was simply that unruly mobs and private armies having tasted blood and power during the election had got out of hand and ruined their masters and employers. And

---

[28] Ibid. p. 98.
[29] Ibid.
[30] Onwuzolum, 'The Ritual-Theatricality of Igbo Masks and Masking', p. 91.
[31] Ibid.

they had no *public reason* whatever for doing it. Let's make no mistake about that.'[32] Public reason, by contrast, is exactly the rationale for masquerade violence, where justice is bacchanalian but restricted to the initiated and socially sanctioned. The absence from the novel of masquerade in its fully initiated adult form, like the absence of any legal trial, thus becomes another signifier of the deregulation and dissolution of the law, whether customary or (post)colonial.

Mob Violence

Book-ending the novel are two episodes that depict the political deployment of the riot and the mob as proxies for legal procedure. The premise for the first of these is the sacking of the finance minister, Dr Makinde, and others in the cabinet who support him. At issue is how the government is to respond to 'a slump in the international coffee market'.[33] Makinde has made a sound proposal (to drop coffee workers' wages and thereby the price of coffee on the international market) but it is likely to be unpopular in the lead-up to a general election. The Prime Minister proposes minting more money instead, a highly risky move that, while resolving the immediate cash flow problem, is likely to lead to hyperinflation and market volatility. Since Makinde cannot supply a plan that will both work and win the election, he and his supporters are dismissed as 'conspirators and traitors who had teamed up with foreign saboteurs to destroy the new nation'.[34] What follows is a persuasive media campaign that presents the Prime Minister's version of events and drowns out any voice of dissent. Amongst the ensuing protests and demonstrations against Makinde, Odili's Student Union 'met in emergency session … and called for a detention law to deal with the miscreants'.[35] Like Obi's suggestion of a benign dictator to resolve the problem of corruption in *No Longer at Ease*, the students' proposed detention law here reinstates the same colonial reliance on the states of emergency and exception to justify 'special laws' that independence was supposed to remove.[36]

---

[32] Achebe, *A Man of the People*, p. 145; emphasis added.
[33] Ibid. p. 3.
[34] Ibid. p. 4.
[35] Ibid. This call echoes the proposals for new preventative detention laws in the wake of the arrests of Awolowo and his colleagues. By contrast, however, the Nigerian Youth Congress opposed the proposal. See 'NYC predicts Detention Act', *Sunday Express*, 23 September 1962, p. 2.
[36] Hazzledine, *The White Man in Nigeria*, p. 94.

The outcry, however, becomes more capacious in its critique when the governing party's newspaper, the *Daily Chronicle*, carries an editorial calling for a purging of the been-tos and university-educated political class: 'Away with the damnable and expensive university education which only alienates an African from his rich and ancient culture and puts him above his people.'[37] It is no coincidence that it is only now that Odili notices 'a new, dangerous and sinister note in the universal outcry', since it is one that threatens him personally.[38] As a university student with ambitions that will soon take him into politics, he and his fellow Student Unionists fall under the definition the *Chronicle* provides of 'decadent stooges versed in text-book economics and aping the white man's mannerisms and way of speaking'.[39] Achebe here echoes very precisely the politically motivated anti-intellectualist rhetoric that rang through various factions of press and politics alike in the 1960s. In 1963, for example, the Western Regional Premier, Chief Samuel Ladoke Akintola, was reported to have 'criticised professors and lecturers in Nigeria's Universities for condemning politicians', commenting that '"These people go on annual globe-trotting in the name of glorified intellectualism. And some time [sic] they write glorified nonsense in classical-phraseology."'[40] Akintola's 'classical phraseology' is nothing but the 'white man's mannerisms' that Achebe's Prime Minister mocks. We can detect in both Akintola and the Prime Minister's rhetoric a desire to differentiate themselves from the coercion to 'civilisation', which earlier colonialism had imposed, as a way of appealing to voters.

Nonetheless, Odili is not excused from Achebe's satire. He is happy to share in the national indignation against Makinde right up to the point that he himself becomes suspect. Only when anti-intellectualism enters the discourse, indicting lecturers and by implication students, does he begin to question the Prime Minister's account. We may not notice at first reading, but this instance of Odili's flip-flopping suggests early on that even *his* political acumen is shaped, at least in part, by self-interest.

Odili sits in the public gallery at parliament on the day when the Prime Minister receives a vote of confidence and Makinde is booed out of the House. During the leader's three-hour diatribe against the minister, Odili observes, fascinated, both Makinde's 'grief-stricken figure' and the rabble-rousing Chief Nanga 'who, seeing the empty ministerial seats …

---

[37] Achebe, *A Man of the People*, p. 4.
[38] Ibid.
[39] Ibid.
[40] 'University Lecturers Attacked', *Daily Express*, 21 February 1963, p. 2.

yapped and snarled … shamelessly for the meaty prize'.[41] Makinde, 'tall, calm, sorrowful and superior', presents an early, idealised model to Odili of righteous intellectual suffering in the face of a baying political mob, embodied in Chief Nanga.

In many ways this is a trial scene: the charges are presented to cheers by the Prime Minister, Makinde's own statement of defence is drowned out by abuse, the Speaker is caught up in the fervour of the scene whilst 'ostensibly trying to maintain order', and the press (and 'the Hansard boys') inevitably misreport the evidence of the speeches the following day.[42] But, of course, taking place as it does in parliament, this is not in fact a trial scene. At the same time, however, the scene is *not* a parliamentary debate. If the law court is where the law is enacted, and parliament is where the law is originated, what we have here is a confused displacement of the law so that something that is like, but is not, the law is brought to bear as if it were, but is not, in a court. Legally, the charges against Makinde are the same as those brought against Awolowo, but with the key difference that the charges are not made in a legal setting. The Prime Minister claims that Makinde and his associates have been caught '"red-handed in their nefarious plot to overthrow the Government of the people … with the help of enemies abroad"'.[43] Instead of a year-long trial, however, Makinde is subjected to a ritual of humiliation before his peers, the public and the press. Legal process is replaced by the dispersal of judgement amongst the crowd. Even the Speaker breaks his mallet as he enthusiastically joins in the ruckus, while pretending to call the House to order. He becomes like the others, one of the crowd. And the press record their own hurled insults in the following day's report as if, caught up in the moment, they had ceased to be reporters and had become their own subjects.[44]

This scene finds a kind of repetition in Odili's own impromptu trial at the hands of Nanga and his area boys at the end of the novel. There, too, the regular machinations of the law, in this later instance represented by the police, are displaced by a violent force that is dispersed across the crowd. The final chapter encompasses Odili's fateful attendance at Nanga's rally, his recovery in hospital, and the political turmoil that follows the election leading to the declaration of a state of emergency.

---

[41] Achebe, *A Man of the People*, pp. 6, 7.
[42] Ibid. p. 6.
[43] Ibid. p. 5.
[44] Ibid. p. 6.

Interwoven with these events is the resolution of the novel's romantic plotline, which has seen Odili rival Nanga for the hand in marriage of an innocent young schoolgirl, Edna.

In essence the chapter illustrates three forms of political and state violence. The first of these is the violence that accompanies the political hustings and that is primarily meted out by the politicians' area boys. We meet Nanga's lead area boy, Dogo, at the start of the novel when Nanga visits the school at which Odili teaches. He is presented peripherally but his actions are significant. Firstly, he draws attention to Nanga's modesty in addressing the older but inferior schoolmaster as 'sir'; later he points out Nanga's generosity to the dancers who perform at the reception, explaining that although politicians are paid well by the government, the money is not for them but for the people. This scene of patronage, and the interpretation that Dogo provides for and requires of the onlookers, prefigures Nanga's later bribery of the same communities, accompanied and underwritten by the threat of violence from his area boys. That threat of violence, like Dogo's commentary at the school visit, forcefully directs the locals' interpretation of and response to Nanga's actions, requiring admiration and acquiescence.

When Odili joins Nanga's household in the city, Dogo and his fellow area boys act as guards to Nanga's property. Later they travel with Nanga as he lays the groundwork for his election campaign. By this time Odili has his own gang, which provides muscle to his campaign. The role of these area boys is obvious and yet remains officially undefined. Like the 'gifts' that Nanga bestows upon the village dancers at the start of the novel, their salaries come out of the politicians' pockets as an expense that might well be provided for in the generosity of the politicians' salary but which is not paid for directly by the political party.[45]

By the time we reach Nanga's rally the use of violent threat as a vehicle for policing political opinion is both ubiquitous and unregulated. When Odili is dragged from the crowd and up on to the stage, Nanga is the first to land a physical blow on Odili, but the violence rapidly escalates and in the process becomes depersonalised. 'Hands' hold Odili back for Nanga to strike him and soon the whole crowd at the rally 'roar … like a thick

---

[45] Such a situation was a familiar one in Nigeria at the time, with newspapers reporting accusations of the diversion of party funds to pay for violent disruption of political events, not least in the Western Region. Diversion of party funds was an explicit area of investigation in the Coker Inquiry too.

forest' and disembodied 'blows' fall 'fast as rain' on his head 'until *something* heavier than the rest seems to split [his] skull'.[46]

This brief scene illustrates the way in which the crowd, as a social form, is drawn into and thereby normalises the violence of political coercion that the area boys embody individually. Rather than a mode of opposition or protest, the riot here becomes an expression of political conformity. This is made possible by the gradual normalisation of violence in the social activity of politics where the presence of area boys presumes defence from and/or deployment of physical aggression. This normalisation of violence is in turn made possible by the very lack of regulation that attaches to it. Moreover, this lack of regulation is characterised not, or not only, by subversion or stealth, but is permitted by the 'cynicism' and 'apathy' of the populace.[47] Achebe provides a powerful metonymy for this state of affairs in Odili's final recollection of his assault at the rally: 'The last thing I remembered was seeing all the policemen turn round and walk away quietly.'[48] This image literalises the abandonment of the law, not as the abandonment of the law by the people, by which the scene of riot is usually read, but the abandonment of the law by the law, whereby the riot embodies the substitution of law with violent political conformity. The abandonment of the law in the riot scene is thus not so much a withdrawing of the law but a dispersal of the law into the crowd in the act of rioting.

When Odili comes round in hospital he notices that his room is constantly guarded by a pair of policemen. He assumes they are there to protect him from further attack, going so far as to wonder if 'it was their way of making amends for their desertion of me [at the riot] when I needed them'.[49] Later they disappear and he learns that, far from benevolent protection, the police were guarding him while he was under arrest, 'ostensibly for having weapons in my car but really to prevent me from signing my nomination paper'.[50] When, on the eve of the election, the charges are dropped, the policemen vanish. No rationale is given for withdrawing the case, emphasising the arbitrariness of both its construction and its withdrawal in the service of political ends. The police are thus characterised throughout as in hock to a political conformity that is embodied by the riot and by their self-recusal as regular legal actors in the scene of riot-

---

[46] Achebe, *A Man of the People*, p. 141; emphasis added.
[47] Ibid. p. 145.
[48] Ibid. p. 141.
[49] Ibid. p. 142.
[50] Ibid. p. 143.

ing. In such a context the declaration of a state of emergency that comes towards the end of the novel is pre-empted by the recusal of the rule of law itself from standing outside the riot.

Martial Law

Following the election, Nanga and his fellow politicians fail in their attempts to disband their 'private army' of area boys. The thugs instead run amok, 'sacking one market after another', inspiring other groups to follow suit until 'a minor reign of terror began'.[51] This second form of political violence is detached from political ambition, and the ensuing rampage makes visible the arbitrariness of the violence to which Nanga and his party had attempted to harness the crowd. In such conditions, the Prime Minister's claim 'that he intended to govern and stamp out subversion and thuggery without quarter or mercy' can only be heard as a restatement of the present violence. Thus, although the government attempts to reassure citizens and foreign investors of its commitment to the rule of law, the riots open up a space for an alternative legal mode: martial law – the very law that Awolowo's father had decried under colonial rule.

Martial law is the third form of political and state violence that the chapter depicts, following the political riot and the anarchic mob, and arises naturally from the prior two. As Odili explains, in the 'unrest and dislocation' caused by the thugs' rampage 'our young Army officers seized the opportunity to take over'.[52] These young officers embody an efficiency missing in the actions of the politicians and the area boys. They lock up 'every member of the Government' and move swiftly to put on trial 'all public servants who had enriched themselves by defrauding the state'.[53] Significantly, whereas Dogo points out the innumerability of money for Nanga, when he is handing out gifts to the dancers at the start of the novel ('You see how e de do as if to say money be san-san'[54]), the new regime is quick to calculate a specific total to be recuperated ('The figure involved was said to be in the order of fifteen million pounds'[55]). Moreover, this efficiency extends beyond the organs of government to curtail the democratic structure of the state itself, in the abolition of all political parties indefinitely.[56] The indefinite abolition is qualified, 'until

---

[51] Ibid. p. 144.
[52] Ibid. p. 148.
[53] Ibid.
[54] Ibid. p. 14. 'San-san' means 'sand' in Nigerian Pidgin English.
[55] Ibid. p. 148.
[56] Ibid.

the situation became stabilized once again', yet the conditions of the cessation of the ban are no longer determinable in the totalising environment of martial law.

In *The Jurisprudence of Emergency* Hussain unpacks the contradictory nature of martial law's version of the state of emergency. He draws our attention to how, in 'the legal maxim *Salus populi, suprema est lex* (safety of the people is the supreme law) ... martial law is the manifestation of both the highest law and of no law at all'.[57] Hussain demonstrates that much legal debate has therefore focused not on what constitutes the limits of martial law but on what constitutes an adequate necessity for which martial law can be justified. Those debates, as Hussain makes evident, are complicated in the colonial setting on the one hand by a desire to cultivate the supposed civilising influence of English law, and on the other by a persistent sense that the colonies require special treatment.[58] In the case of martial law this special treatment reflects a racial anxiety that justifies martial law as a preventative rather than simply a restorative mode of rule. Thus both Governor Eyre in Jamaica and General Dyer in Amritsar, for example, justified the violent extent of their imposition of martial law as necessary to prevent future social disorder.[59] In General Dyer's words, his use of violence was not 'a question of merely dispersing the crowd, but one of producing a sufficient moral effect ... not only on those present, but more especially throughout the Punjab'.[60] The colonial subject's propensity for disorder (the reasons for which are eternally sidestepped in such justifications because to examine them would be to admit the possibility that their cause was a justified objection to colonial occupation) requires that the extreme violence sanctioned under martial law be allowed to impose order, with the force of law that is not the law, where the usual constraints of civil law are no longer deemed effective. This imposition is both futuristic in its aim and declarative in its force. Order is what martial law makes it. As such, and as we have seen already, in the colonial setting the state of emergency is indefinite and enablingly indeterminate.

---

[57] Hussain, *The Jurisprudence of Emergency*, p. 102.
[58] We might think of Bulteel's 'special conditions' in Cary's *Mister Johnson* (p. 127).
[59] See Hussain, *The Jurisprudence of Emergency*, pp. 99–131.
[60] Report of General Dyer, 25 August 1919, to General Staff 16th Division. Reiterated in Great Britain, Parliament, *Army. Disturbances in the Punjab. Statement by Brig.-General R. E. H. Dyer, C.B.*, Cmd. 771 (1920), 10. Quoted in Hussain, *The Jurisprudence of Emergency*, p. 100.

At first sight the postcolonial martial law that is declared at the end of *A Man of the People* is distinct from its colonial predecessor. Within the world of the novel, the coup is presented rhetorically as a revolutionary act against the corruption of the previous government, rather than as a suspension of the law that permits the extra-legal enforcement of a self-defining order. Eunice is released from jail and Max is pronounced 'a Hero of the Revolution'.[61] In this regard both coup and martial law are declarative and manifestational: they create a new order that has the force of law and, in doing so, overturn the prior boundaries of the law by which crime and criminal are defined (Eunice is released, others are charged).[62] It might be tempting, then, to believe that the transformation that this instance of martial law embodies can extend to its own instantiation. Achebe is careful not to allow us to entertain this possibility for long.

Firstly, the indeterminacy of the party ban, which Achebe emphasises through Odili's use of quotation marks to mark off the phrasing from his own, recalls the preventative justification of colonial emergency violence. What, we might ask, constitutes a 'stability' that is adequate to the reintroduction of party politics following martial law? Who gets to decide on the adequacy of that stability? Secondly, the interweaving of Odili's romantic plotline into his account of the political revolutions subtly reiterates the scenario of apparently benevolent corruption with which the novel starts and, importantly, predicates this corruption on the very opportunities that arise from the political ban of martial law. For, having endeavoured to resist the temptation to embezzle the Soviet-sponsored party funds he has been provided with during his political campaign, Odili decides 'privately to borrow the money from C.P.C. funds' to pay the bride price for Edna on the basis that the ban on political parties means the funds 'were not likely to be needed soon'.[63] Thus the coup, even if unwittingly, creates space for the very corruption for personal gain and private satisfaction that rhetorically it claims to stamp out. The status of Odili's corruption here may be indeterminate insofar as the crime is hard to materialise if the victim (the political party) is itself rendered illegitimate by military rule; nonetheless, the irony is implicit in the parallels that Achebe draws between the financial wrangling of Odili and Nanga

---

[61] Achebe, *A Man of the People*, p. 148.
[62] I draw here on Walter Benjamin's 'Critique of Violence', in *Reflections: Essays, Aphorisms, Autobiographical Writings*, and on the discussion of Benjamin's essay in Hussain (*The Jurisprudence of Emergency*, pp. 122–4) and Agamben (*State of Exception*, p. 53ff).
[63] Achebe, *A Man of the People*, p. 148.

for Edna's hand, and in the repeated causal connections that he notes between Odili's success and the machinations of the coup. Edna's father is initially unwilling to accept him as a suitor, but 'the Army *obliged* [Odili and his family] by staging a coup' and Nanga is arrested.[64] Edna's father now sees him as 'a bird in hand' but Odili's family want to argue over the bride price. Tellingly, Odili comments, '[b]ut I was not interested in *legalistic-traditional arguments* just now, especially when they were calculated to delay things (a coup might be followed by a counter coup and then where would we be?)'.[65] Odili sees the coup as an opportunity for personal fulfilment that must be seized, even if doing so means breaking the legal tradition of local custom. In this Odili's embezzlement and disregard for (familial) law echo clearly the very corruption and hypocrisy he had despised in Nanga and that is quietly satirised in the scene in which Nanga's drunk relative demands a beer as a Christmas day 'dash'. Neither customary practice nor the rule of law is heeded.

Assassination

If the political riot, mob violence and martial law are shown to fail in their attempt to provide a cohesive justice through social coercion that might effectively replace the (pre)colonial operations of the mask, one last form of extra-legal violence remains open: assassination. Achebe explores this possibility with an ambiguous sympathy that is otherwise, and unsurprisingly, withheld from the political riot, mob violence and martial law. Nevertheless, like these earlier forms of violent substitution for the law, the act of assassination is subjected to an iterative narration which ironises its force. At the start of the novel, when Nanga visits the school at which Odili teaches, he offers to help Odili in attaining a scholarship for overseas postgraduate study. Odili takes up Nanga's offer to stay with him and to meet with Chief Koko, the Minister for Overseas Training. Odili and Nanga's visit, however, takes an unexpected turn when Koko believes his coffee has been poisoned by one of his servants, only to be reassured by his cook that it is simply a different brand of coffee. The whole episode is presented in highly comic, almost slapstick terms. Koko's bodyguard is dressed as a cowboy and Koko himself is wearing 'an enormous homeknitted red-and-yellow sweater'.[66] When he tastes the coffee he jumps as if bitten by a scorpion and immediately performs a dramatic death

[64] Ibid. p. 147; emphasis added.
[65] Ibid. p. 148; emphasis added.
[66] Ibid. pp. 34, 33.

scene: wailing, 'wringing his hands, breathing hard and loud and rolling his eyes'.[67] His use of the past tense to describe this apparent assassination ('they have killed me') and his rhetorical questions ('what have I done?') add to the paranoia and hyperbole of the scene.[68] Once the issue is resolved, this comedy passes from the reader (and the recollection of Odili, our narrator) to Koko and Nanga, who banter between themselves with chauvinistic bravura about the incident.

As Odili points out, the joke, which neither Koko nor Nanga reflects on, is that the questionable coffee is one of the many locally produced brands that the government has been promoting in competition with the products of multinationals, like Koko's preferred Nescafé. Koko's preference for a European brand of coffee is further ironised by the fact that the influence of multinationals like Nestlé on the global coffee market is what precipitates the political crisis of the collapsed coffee market on which the whole narrative rests. More broadly, Koko's preference, like his bodyguard's cowboy outfit, gestures to the imbrication of Western consumer commodities in the pursuit of local prestige and affluence. Nonetheless, this imbrication signifies in different directions at once. Koko's Nescafé is used explicitly to ironise the hypocrisy of the politicians who indulge in multinational imports while exhorting the populace to buy local products, as the 'key to economic emancipation without which our hard-won political freedom was a mirage'.[69] The bodyguard's garb is a little more abstruse, referencing a particular kind of gang-culture that originally emerged in Nigeria (and elsewhere in West Africa) in the 1930s, in which groups of young men adopted uniforms inspired by Western films, and organised themselves for musical performance, military training and occasional gang fights.[70]

Koko and his cowboy bodyguard present a comic but telling representation of the extra-legal operations of justice that ensue in the novel. Whether as sheriff or outlaw, the cowboy mirrors the creative approach to justice fantasised by Wallace in the Sanders series. Meanwhile, Koko's paranoia suggests he already believes that any enemies he might have will seek retribution by foul play rather than justice through the courts. In

---

[67] Ibid. p. 33.
[68] Ibid. p. 34.
[69] Ibid. p. 35. While coffee production was at an all-time high in Nigeria in the 1960s, Nestlé appear not to have bought from Nigerian producers in this period. The International Coffee Agreement of 1963 did little to shore up Nigerian coffee production and it dwindled from the 1970s onwards.
[70] See Hair, 'The Cowboys'.

this, of course, he is not wrong. When Max goes to investigate ballot fraud in the elections, one of Koko's jeeps runs him down, missing Eunice by inches. When Koko comes forward to 'handle the matter', Eunice shoots him twice with a pistol kept in her handbag. Her retribution is swift, complete and beyond the law.

As I indicated at the start of this chapter, Koko's assassination was not exactly an imaginative liberty: the assassinations of Lumumba and Olympio, not to mention John F. Kennedy, were matters of regular discussion in the Nigerian media when they occurred a few years prior to the publication of *A Man of the People*. Moreover, as we have noted, the assassinations of the Sardauna, Alhaji Sir Ahmadu Bello, and Chief Samuel Ladoke Akintola, Premiers of the Nigerian Northern and Western Regions respectively, occurred just as the novel was going to print. Where Achebe is more inventive is in the fact that Koko's assassination is carried out by a lone civilian woman rather than a group of military men. This gives the scene a particular charge and encourages us to consider the assassination as not simply another instance of political realism but significant of something more.

Eunice is not like other women in the novel and is presented as exceptional from the start. We encounter her first as 'a very beautiful lawyer', the only woman amongst the group of young men who meet with Max to found the new party. Later Odili observes her 'forming the same words that [Max] was uttering' as her fiancé makes a political speech.[71] Odili is drawn to her beauty but alarmed by her intelligence and his reactions to her barely sublimate his gendered prejudices. In this scene he reduces her in his narrative to 'a nervous schoolgirl' and a 'delicious picture of feminine loyalty'.[72] Nonetheless, as Osinubi suggests, Eunice is clearly the moving force behind Max's political ambition, and despite the fact that Koko's assassination can be read as a crime of passion it is also unmistakably political.[73] Indeed, whilst politics is a frequent pander to Odili's love life (the scene in which Eunice quietly speaks Max's speech with him, quoted above, inspires Odili the next day to 'abandon [his] carefully worked out strategy and go in search of Edna'[74]), for Eunice love instigates political action. Her response to Max's murder is swiftly calculated to create the kind of political short-circuiting of the election that her assassination creates in the processes of legal justice. Eunice's murder of Koko represents yet another kind of political violence,

---

[71] Achebe, *A Man of the People*, p. 128.
[72] Ibid.
[73] Osinubi, 'Cold War Sponsorships', pp. 415–16.
[74] Achebe, *A Man of the People*, p. 128.

one that mimics yet disrupts both the politically coercive violence of the novel's scenes of electioneering and the socially coercive violence of the mask. The singularity of her act, however, sets it apart from these other communal modes of extra- or para-legal regulation. An end in itself as a non-legal form of retributive justice for Max's murder, it is also the catalyst for the ensuing social disorder that results in the state of emergency.

Eunice's role in the novel is emphasised by her name, which is derived from the Greek Εὐνίκη, meaning good or happy victory. Without alluding to the Greek overtly, Odili attributes just such a victory to her actions in the final sentence of the novel, in which he reflects, 'in such a regime, I say, you died a good death if your life had inspired someone to come forward and shoot your murderer in the chest – without asking to be paid.'[75] Odili, and to a large extent Achebe, raises Eunice's action to a level of purity, but this also keeps it in a state of impossibility. This is a different kind of exceptional state to those we have encountered before, since her actions cannot be translated, or extrapolated from, as a model for political or social reform. Of all the political actors in the novel Eunice is the most free, in her willingness to substitute pure violence for justice. Nevertheless, the absoluteness of her freedom places it beyond the reach of our protagonist, who remains to the end mired in the all-too-human realities of personal cupidity and self-preservation. Achebe thus posits the assassination as a fourth form of political violence. Even more efficient than the martial law of the 'young army officers', assassination contains within it the most lethal and concentrated form of exceptionalism of all those explored in the novel's final chapter. Achebe's choice of a lone female as the emblem of political assassination, rather than the more realistic, and far more common, gang of (military) men, is thus, like her name, used to emphasise her particular form of exceptionalism.

The ending of the novel fails to provide a resolution to the political disarray that Achebe diagnoses in newly independent West Africa. While Odili's own romantic plot is brought to a satisfactory conclusion, the state remains under the indefinite imposition of martial law, with no indication that corruption will be stamped out. Odili's embezzlement of party funds demonstrates how martial law has already provided opportunity for new instances of corruption. Moreover, the decision of the new military power to pardon Eunice and to celebrate Max as a martyr neutralises the revolutionary potential of Koko's assassination and reincorporates its singular expression of freedom into the structures of political conformity.

---

[75] Ibid. p. 150.

'In the Affairs of the Nation There Was No Owner'[76]

In the scene of Josiah's non-trial by the villagers of Anata, one observes to Odili: 'Josiah has taken away enough for the owner to notice.'[77] At the end of the novel Odili's father applies the same phrase to Chief Koko. The implication in each case is that helping oneself a little to the goods on offer (in whatever context) is only to be expected; what matters is doing so with enough respect and moderation not to get caught nor to offend. Comparing these two instances, Odili reflects that for Josiah '[t]he owner was the village, and the village had a mind; it could say no to sacrilege. But in the affairs of the nation there was no owner, the laws of the village became powerless.'[78]

This comparison gets to the heart of the problems to which the varieties of political violence we have scrutinised are the chaotic response. The structures of the nation state that countries like Nigeria inherited from the endless reorganisations of colonial rule could not translate, or extrapolate from, the local practices enshrined by indirect rule, and which those very structures sought to protect. Although, as Achebe repeatedly shows in the novel, Anata is less coherent than Odili credits it here, its capacity for coherent action can be mobilised towards the preservation of social unity. This is what distinguishes, for Odili, the village mob from the political mob: the former punishes actions that harm the sanctity of communal good faith; the latter simply punishes the opposing voice. Of course, Nanga and others borrow the language of community to incite the mob, but this language becomes merely rhetorical, a way of communicating in customary terms the needs of a political conformity.

Odili's distinction is neat but it gestures to the far messier tangle of power and administration that evolved through the period of transition to independence for Nigeria as for other postcolonial nations. This included the elementary incoherence of indirect rule, which imposed and repeatedly reformulated particular forms of the customary that created or exacerbated divisions of ethnicity, geography, metropolitanism and education. The immediate consequences were a polarisation of nativism and intellectualism, the deracination of minority groups, urban-rural tensions, and bloody intra- and inter-regional rivalries. Added to this was the transformation of the state into an international marketplace, for which the retreating colonial powers acted as eager midwives. Although the

---

[76] Ibid. p. 149.
[77] Ibid. p. 87.
[78] Ibid. p. 149.

commodification of civilisation through European-sold goods was countered by ardent nativist marketing (represented in *A Man of the People* by the OHMS coffee that Koko presumes is poisoned), the colonial rhetoric of Westernisation remained powerful and was underpinned by the financial advantage that international firms could leverage in their advertising campaigns. At the same time West African countries were increasingly exposed to the volatility of the international market for their export products like coffee and cocoa, a fact further complicated by the expansion of multinational companies, many of which, like Unilever, already had a colonial presence in the region. These two factors – the colonial fantasy of customary law and the marketisation of decolonisation – inevitably intertwined, leading to corruption scandals such as those investigated by the Coker Inquiry and fictionalised in Nanga's dash from Antonio and Sons.

John Pepper Clark-Bekederemo was right when he said that everything that Achebe had written had already happened – even the coup, as they were soon to discover. And to that extent the novel might be thought of as purely realist. It is certainly possible to go through the novel and point to equivalent historical events and sources, as much using the novel as a guide to historical events as those historical events might be used as a guide to the novel. But as my allusions to historical context make clear, the novel is not simply such a realist account. Instead, Achebe distils from the political turmoil of mid-1960s West Africa particular concerns, notably corruption, political violence, and the nation state's new relationships with international economies and powers. In doing so, he dramatises new forms of extra-legal performance, states of exception, and abandonments of the law as problems arising from these particular concerns. These problems are structured through ironising iterative narration, such as the parallels used to highlight the arbitrariness of the distinction between Odili's success in repurposing party finances secretly, and the public exposure of Nanga's earlier siphoning of funds. Moreover, the law provides the grounds for reflecting the contradictions of statehood inherited at independence and the dissolution of social coherence under the pressures of political conformity. The law therefore becomes the site for engaging *fictively* with the realities of the moment, crystallising for Achebe and for his readers the implications of those realities.

Conclusion: Imagined States

In 2000 Ambreena Manji observed that 'whilst the study of law and literature is now well established in the western academy, little attention has been paid to portrayals of law in African literature ... [and] studies of the state by lawyers, political scientists, and historians have neglected African fiction's long engagement in this area'.[1] In the two decades since Manji made this observation scholarly engagement in West African law and literature has remained incremental. As the preceding chapters have shown, however, attending to the narrative threads of law and the imagination provides significant new insights into the operations of both the law and fiction in colonial and postcolonial Nigeria. In particular, such attention helps us to recognise the *a priori* of the state of exception for indirect rule and the power of fiction to reveal that *a priori* through its mirroring of law's imaginative processes. It also helps us to recognise how law and literature became crucial sites for thinking through the challenges of nationhood and the limits of statehood in the years immediately prior to and following independence. More broadly, tracing the place of law through a range of high- and lowbrow publications from Britain and Nigeria, as I have done here, makes visible the intricate relationships and fraught inheritances between colonial and postcolonial legal practice and literary imagination.

The period covered by these previous chapters is precisely and legally demarcated by the British government's revocation of the Royal Niger Company's charter in 1900 and the collapse of the first Republic at the start of 1966. In drawing my discussion to a close, however, I want to consider in a little more detail the impact of the events of 1966 and the fiction that emerged in the ensuing years, before returning to a fuller reflection on the significance of the law for Nigerian fiction.

---

[1] Manji, "'Like a Mask Dancing'", p. 626.

'Annoyingly Predictable' Plots [2]

In 1966 the South African author Lewis Nkosi wrote an intentionally provocative review of recent African anglophone fiction for the *Africa Report*. The review opens:

> In African literature, as in African politics, the excitement that marked the beginning of the decade is wearing off. The novels continue to flow from the presses, of course, but their plots are annoyingly predictable …
>
> … the endless parade of heroes caught between the old order and the new, of young lovers divided by tribal barriers which they are unable to breach however large their nobility and fierce their passion … the Utopian novels of the independence struggle, and the equally simplistic tales of a post-independence world gone sour. One longs not so much for new themes as for fresh treatment.[3]

Nkosi's summary demonstrates how familiar, even over-familiar, the plots of Ekwensi, Achebe and their market literature peers had become by the mid-1960s, not only for Nigerians but also for international audiences.

Nkosi's criticism implies that the problem for African literature was hackneyed treatment of over-familiar themes. Of course, to some extent such a predicament was inevitable. International publishers and series such as the Heinemann African Writers series bestowed visible success on those authors they produced. These series were shaped by international tastes and interests – not least a curiosity about African life told from African perspectives, a view that had been obscured and ignored during earlier colonial rule. The success of literature working in this mode encouraged imitation and fed what Nkosi rather exaggeratedly characterises as a glut in the market. This glut, however, was only half the story.

Surprisingly, Nkosi avoids almost all reference to the coups in Nigeria that had taken place over the twelve months prior to his review. There is a faint allusion to the political turmoil in his discussion of *A Man of the People* but otherwise it remains invisible. There are, I think, several reasons for this omission. Firstly, Nkosi's own politics had led to his exile from South Africa, where he had been blacklisted as a communist. Nonetheless, he was writing in the *Africa Report*, a journal produced by

---

[2] Nkosi, 'Where Does African Literature Go from Here?', p. 7.
[3] Ibid.

the Africa America Institute, founded with support from the CIA, and Nkosi himself had previously held a Nieman fellowship in the United States when he first left South Africa, which was also funded through CIA conduits. These politics, and the potentially compromised position they placed him in, may have encouraged him to sidestep the political crisis in Nigeria, fomented as it was in part by disagreement about Eastern/Western bloc alignment. Less speculatively, we should remember that Nigeria's political crisis would have been very familiar to Nkosi's immediate audience. Indeed, Nkosi's one glancing reference to it is to complain that it has become *the* focal point for readings of *A Man of the People* at the expense of appreciating its wider satirical scope. As an African news item the coups in Nigeria were themselves in this period an over-familiar narrative, coming as they did only a few years after the assassinations of Lumumba and Olympio. Nkosi's silence reflects a desire to avoid reinforcing what was already becoming a stereotype of African postcolonial politics. As his review makes evident, Nkosi wanted those stereotypes to be challenged rather than repeated and we can read this omission as a refusal to engage with them in his own discussion of African fiction.

Nonetheless, in ignoring the coups Nkosi misses out a key reason why the themes of African fiction at this time, and of Nigerian fiction in particular, felt hackneyed: the coups literalised the themes of tribalism, the tensions of modernity and the traps of utopian and dystopian politics, which he complains have been dulled by familiarity. These ideas were no longer implicit in the dysfunction of colonial inheritance but had become absolutely explicit in the rhetoric and actions of those struggling to gain and maintain sovereign power. Reality had caught up with fiction. Fiction, therefore, no longer had recourse to pointing up these implicit themes in current affairs. To write of them in 1966 was to record the obvious rather than to reveal an unspoken yet deeply felt experience. In 1966 this discourse was no longer the prerogative of the author; instead it was taken up by the press and the politicians, who spoke of almost nothing else. This is not to suggest that the themes that Nkosi enumerates had not been expressed before by press and politicians; the discussions of the previous chapters illustrate their presence from early on in the development of the Nigerian political parties and press. Rather, what happened in 1966 made these issues the structuring principles *par excellence* of public debate, with increasingly devastating effects.

'Nigeria Is Not a Nation'[4]

When Major Chukwuma Kaduna Nzeogwu attempted the first coup on 15 January, in which the Prime Minister, Alhaji Sir Abubakar Tafawa Balewa, the Northern Premier, Alhaji Sir Ahmadu Bello, and the Western Premier, Samuel Ladoke Akintola, were murdered, he declared that the goal of the coup was unification and to counteract the deleterious influence of the North, which had in Nzeogwu's words 'put the Nigerian calendar back by their words and deeds'.[5] In the wake of the assassinations, executive power was handed to Major General Aguiyi-Ironsi, Nigeria's first Nigerian head of the military.[6] Aguiyi-Ironsi swiftly detained Nzeogwu and his conspirators; nevertheless, on taking power his rhetoric echoed Nzeogwu's. Aguiyi-Ironsi, like Nzeogwu, sought to dismantle the federal structure of the Republic in favour of a unified nationalist government. His argument for doing so was that the regionalism of the federation had entrenched tribal differences that in turn had led to simmering resentments and local discord. By doing away with regional assemblies, unification would create a sense of national coherence through shared governance, law and infrastructure. This aim was radical, challenging Northern politics particularly, but also the federalism that Awolowo had promoted twenty years earlier in *Path to Nigerian Freedom*. Here Awolowo argues: 'If rapid political progress is to be made in Nigeria it is high time we were realistic in tackling its constitutional problems. Nigeria is not a nation. It is a mere geographical expression. There are no "Nigerians".'[7] Nzeogwu and Aguiyi-Ironsi were thus asking the Republic's subjects to do nothing less than reimagine the very structure of the nation state in a completely new way. Importantly, this invitation, or rather this command, to reconceive what 'Nigeria' meant was wholly ideological. This was not a response to changed geographical boundaries or the integration of new migrant populations; it was about how Nigerians imagined the nature of sovereign power. Thus we see in action the very utopianism that Nkosi critiques in African fiction.

Unification was enforced in several ways. Firstly, the declaration of military rule under Aguiyi-Ironsi was followed by the Suppression of

---

[4] Awolowo, *Path to Nigerian Freedom*, p. 47.
[5] Quoted in Adebanwi, *Nation as Grand Narrative*, p. 111.
[6] Following independence and the declaration of the Republic, Nigeria's military had continued to be led by a British-born soldier, Major General C. E. Welby-Everard, until 1965 when he was replaced by Aguiyi-Ironsi.
[7] Awolowo, *Path to Nigerian Freedom*, p. 47.

Disorder decree in February, which provided for the enforcement of what amounted to martial law at the discretion of the head of state.[8] Military rule also effectively abolished the party system, replacing government by elected representatives with appointments made from the military and the civil service. Decree No. 1 of 1966 suspended the legislative assemblies and assigned plenary legislative power to the Federal Military Government. The decree also provided for all future legislation to be issued by decree and edict. These rendered all other legislation *pro tanto* void where it was inconsistent with any given decree or edict. Moreover, as E. A. Keay explained at the time, 'since no court can entertain any questions as to the validity of either a Decree or an Edict no remedy on the ground of invalidity is available by judicial process.'[9] Practically speaking, as Keay notes, 'the main direction of effort [was] not to abolish institutions but to replace membership of them wherever the politics of the past [had] played a part whether legitimate or illegitimate in the selection of personnel, or wherever corruption and inefficiency [had] become evident.'[10]

Significantly, politics and politicians were held responsible for the regional and tribal strife, which the military government now claimed to eradicate. The government-sponsored *Morning Post*, changing its stripes to fit the rhetoric of its new paymaster, declared that 'the trouble with this country has been the over-present surfeit of politics'.[11] Unification, then, was to be achieved by making all alike subject to the force of a singular military rule. The state of exception that the military government established for itself through Decree No. 1 was to be the form by which unification could finally be achieved following the failure of the party system to synthesise regional and tribal differences. On 24 May 1966 this argument was translated into law through Decrees 33 and 34. Decree 33 dissolved eighty-one political associations and twenty-six tribal and cultural associations. Decree 34 abolished the federal regions and established in their place thirty-five provinces under a unified civil service. As Adebanwi reminds us, 'unification, in itself, is a narrative'.[12] The unification decree made explicit a new narrative for Nigeria, one in which the

---

[8] See Nwabueze, *A Constitutional History of Nigeria*, p. 216. As Nwabueze notes, the powers of this decree were never in fact invoked by Aguiyi-Ironsi.
[9] Keay, 'Legal and Constitutional Changes in Nigeria under the Military Government', p. 104.
[10] Ibid. p. 97.
[11] 'Best Hope for Democracy', *Morning Post*, 20 January 1966, p. 1; quoted in Adebanwi, *Nation as Grand Narrative*, p. 114.
[12] Adebanwi, *Nation as Grand Narrative*, p. 116.

values enshrined by indirect rule were overturned in favour of an ideology of nationalism and modernity.

Unity was valorised in the Southern and governmental press, whilst those in the North who argued for federalism were labelled 'Pakistanists', alluding to the violence of partition in British India in 1947 (and reminding us of another trope noted by Nkosi). Nonetheless, criticism of unification persisted in the North, frequently expressed in the press as an anxiety about Southern 'colonisation' of the North.[13] This anxiety stemmed from a sense in both the North and the South that the North was educationally and developmentally inferior to the Southern regions. We see here the far-reaching consequences of the policy of indirect rule, which had supported a varied approach to the provision of education in the regions on the basis of what was customarily appropriate. The effects of the limited development of educational provision in the North, which we noted in Chapter 3, were thus felt as a problematic deficit in the postcolonial era (see again Nkosi's critique). Those in the North, which had in effect led the Republic's government under the Prime Minister, Balewa, feared that their voice would be sidelined by the new Igbo-led military regime. In particular, the unification of the civil service under Decree 34 was seen as paving the way for the deployment of Southern civil servants in the North on the basis of their more advanced training. Read in this light, the accusation of 'colonisation' pinpoints the crux of the North's anxiety. The idealised principle of 'talent' becomes a postcolonial revision of the old model of 'civilisation' that had been used in the previous decades by the colonial regime to exclude Nigerians from power. Northerners were always going to be catching up with their more 'civilised' and 'talented' compatriots in the South, endlessly deferring their claim to power as they sought and failed to embody the right kind of educated culture valorised in the metropolitan centres of the South. Placed in this position, the North understandably favoured the federal system that had provided for independent regional development, as it had been enshrined in indirect rule.

The failure of the Aguiyi-Ironsi regime to reassure those in the North of the benefits of unification was the fundamental cause of the counter-coup in July 1966. Aguiyi-Ironsi was killed in Ibadan, but before his fate was made public Lieutenant Colonel Yakubu Gowon took control as

---

[13] See ibid. p. 117.

head of state and in his first public broadcast overturned Aguiyi-Ironsi's decree of unification. Yet the counter-coup did little to defuse the increasingly violent tensions between North and South, particularly between the Northern and Eastern Regions. Greeted with relief and celebration in the North, Gowon's new military regime was rebuffed by Lieutenant Colonel Odumegwu Ojukwu, leader of the military in the East, who refused to acknowledge Gowon as the national leader. Moreover, in the months following the counter-coup deadly violence against Igbo in the North gathered pace, leading to mass migrations of Igbo from across the country back to the Eastern Region to escape the Northern massacres. Thus the violence of tribalism that both Gowon and Aguiyi-Ironsi aimed to eradicate through their divergent policies of federalism and unification was in fact exacerbated by their actions (enacting Nkosi's final trope of 'a post-independence world gone sour'). The press, like the politicians, repeated a desire for good sense to prevail and for time to heal the 'bitterness' felt on all sides; nonetheless, such calls became increasingly hard to sustain. The *West African Pilot*, for example, wrote in September:

> The facts as they are today, are that Nigerians are haunted by fear of domination of one section by another, by fear of insecurity of life and property, by fear of molestation. These are basic human freedoms which, lacking in a country makes a nonsense of united nationhood.[14]

As this account makes clear, the 'themes' that had become so familiar as to feel trite to Nkosi in December of 1966 were at the heart of the Nigerian crisis of the same year. The violence and disruption of tribal difference was the motivating force behind both federalism and unification. Moreover, the discord between traditional and modern forms of sociability and education shaped the character of North-South rivalries and distrust. These translated into the utopian and dystopian rhetoric of both politicians and the press, in their daily attempts to provide an organising narrative that might make sense of the chaos unfolding. Nowhere is this clearer than in the endless ideological recalibrations of the *Morning Post*, whose financial ties to the government's administration meant it was obliged, by and large, to support whichever policy was promulgated by the head of state. Thus following the announcement of Aguiyi-Ironsi's leadership, the *Post*, which had previously sung the praises of Balewa's federal government, proclaimed that it joined 'all lovers of peace in this country in welcoming the Military Government' and, in an article

---

[14] 'When our £-o-v-e is tied to the Pound', *West African Pilot*, 19 September 1966; quoted in Adebanwi, *Nation as Grand Narrative*, p. 131.

entitled 'Civis Nigerianus Sum', went so far as to greet unification under Decree 34 as 'a thing that all true patriots of this country have eagerly looked forward to'.[15] Only three months later, however, it stridently declared: 'WE ARE CONVINCED THAT FEDERALISM WOULD SUIT A SOCIETY SUCH AS OURS BETTER THAN A UNITARY GOVERNMENT.'[16]

Adebanwi characterises the press reports at this time as speaking for and affirming 'different kinds of collective identity – national, regional, or ethnic – while simultaneously emphasizing the differences and divisions among the national, regional, or ethnic collective and the imagined other(s)'.[17] This became even more complicated when newspapers tried to appeal to multiple collective identities, whether for profit or for expediency, as was the case for the *Morning Post*, for example.[18] These expressions of division gave rise to narratives in the media that echoed the very concerns that had already been dramatised in much Nigerian and colonial fiction over the previous decades. As early as Wallace's Sanders series we meet the problems of imposed leadership in the figure of Bosambo, the Monrovian krooboy, conflicts arising from unequal education, and concerns for the 'traditions' that indirect rule was supposed to preserve. In *Mister Johnson* the perennial anxiety about Southern civil servants in the North is the underpinning premise of the whole novel. Ekwensi and Achebe's urban fiction expands upon these issues, exposing the incongruent loyalties to national, regional and ethnic collective identities required of young people trying to negotiate a new metropolitan life for themselves. Occasionally we even find alternative collective identities imagined, such as the gynocentric civility that Jagua creates for herself with her mother and Rosa at the end of *Jagua Nana*. These challenges of identity and difference, and their mediation through the legal structures and inheritance of colonialism, had informed fiction from and about Nigeria for several generations before the crisis of 1966.

---

[15] 'Road to Survival', *Morning Post*, 19 January 1966, p. 1; 'Civis Nigerianus Sum', *Morning Post*, 26 May 1966, p. 1; both quoted in Adebanwi, *Nation as Grand Narrative*, pp. 114, 119.

[16] 'This is No Time to Kid', *Morning Post*, 6 August 1966, p. 5; quoted in Adebanwi, *Nation as Grand Narrative*, p. 126.

[17] Adebanwi, *Nation as Grand Narrative*, p. 116.

[18] As we saw in Chapter 6, the ties between politics and the press here offer a useful complication to Anderson's account of the role of the press in nation formation in *Imagined Communities*. When even 'official nationalism' is in a state of flux, the press's capacity to invoke community can be compromised.

Biafra and After in Nigerian Fiction

Nkosi was, of course, expressing his desire for new approaches to the over-familiar themes that he delineates on a continental basis. In Nigeria, however, the civil war that broke out at the start of 1967, barely a month after Nkosi's review, gradually prompted not simply new approaches but new themes too. Civil war novels and memoirs began to appear in the 1970s, and the events of the war have continued to inspire several generations of writers from Elechi Amadi's *Sunset in Biafra* (1973) to Chimamanda Ngozi Adichie's *Half of a Yellow Sun* (2006). The war was not the only prompt to new fiction, however. In his review, Nkosi gives short shrift to Flora Nwapa's first novel, *Efuru*, which had appeared in 1966:

> Nigeria's Flora Nwapa attracted a certain amount of attention [in 1966], but this was mostly because she was Nigeria's first woman novelist. To the debt she owes Chinua Achebe, she had added nothing but tedium and a few more details about the social relations in an Ibo community … *Efuru* is a competent and straightforward, but excessively dull, narrative about the marital troubles of an Ibo woman.[19]

Promoted by Achebe, Nwapa's novel certainly ploughs the furrow of revealing Nigerian life to European readers that characterised much of the Heinemann African Writers series. Nkosi's dismissal of Nwapa, however, fails to recognise the significance of Nwapa's focus on women's lives in Nigeria, and the signal she gave as a woman writer in Nigeria of a change in the literary landscape. Nwapa went on to clear a path to international recognition and publication for a number of other female authors in the following years, not only as a role model for younger writers but also practically through her two publishing ventures, Tana Press and Flora Nwapa Books. Close behind in Nwapa's footsteps came Buchi Emecheta, for example, whose *The Bride Price* (1976) and *The Joys of Motherhood* (1979) led the way in feminist fiction from and about Nigeria.[20]

Following the end of the civil war a number of new writers emerged in the North, many under the aegis of the Gaskiya Corporation. Originally an experimental colonial project, which brought Hausa and British administrators together to publish Hausa language books and the first Hausa newspaper, *Gaskiya Ta Fi Kwabo*, Gaskiya continued to promote Hausa writing through competitions and its press following independence (later

---

[19] Nkosi, 'Where Does African Literature Go from Here?', p. 8.
[20] Emecheta wrote her first novels in the UK rather than in Nigeria.

as the Northern Nigerian Publishing Company).²¹ Sulaiman Ibrahim Katsina and Hafsatu Abdulwahid, for example, found their first success with Gaskiya in 1979, the same year that Labo Yari published *Climate of Corruption*, often hailed as the first Hausa novel in English. *Climate of Corruption* depicts the familiar satirical scene of young professionals negotiating the challenge of urban living from a new Hausa perspective. At the same time, while Onitsha's market waned following the civil war, the market for popular literature blossomed in the North. Here the familiar theme of love re-emerges in soyayya novels, which negotiate many of the same challenges with which Onitsha market literature had engaged in the 1950s and 1960s.

One author on whom Nkosi alights as an example of the change necessary to style if not to theme in the African novel is Chukwuemeka Ike. Ike's *Toads for Supper* (1965) drew on his own experience at the University of Nigeria, Nsukka, to satirise contemporary culture, in a manner that echoes Achebe's *No Longer at Ease*. The corruption of university life was a topic to which Ike returned several times over the ensuing years, notably in *Expo '77* (1980). Ike and Yari, in particular, demonstrate how the law remained a key narrative trope for Nigerian writers in the decades following the civil war. This was in part a result of the ways in which the various military regimes of the 1970s and onwards focalised the significance of the law through their suspension of it in declarations of emergency and martial law. It was also a response to the persistence of corruption as a structuring function of the state during these years. More broadly, we can also see the continued presence of the law in Nigerian fiction as a reflection of the repeated shifts in imagining what 'Nigeria' was with each reconfiguration of Nigerian sovereignty.

'Imagining Justice'²²

While scholarship in law and literature has tended to neglect Nigeria, the history of how the law has been presented in literature from and about Nigeria is important. The law has been a crucial site for Nigerian and British writers throughout the decades of late colonialism and early independence, and continues to be so for Nigerian writers today such as Adichie and Helon Habila. This is because, as Mamdani and others have shown, indirect rule created an extraordinary complex of legal structures

---

[21] For an account of the origins of the Gaskiya Corporation, see Furniss, 'On Engendering Liberal Values'.

[22] Berman, *Modernist Commitments*, p. 6.

whose framework shapes the operations of the law in Nigeria to this day. As we noted in Chapter 1, indirect rule resulted in multiple legal systems (customary, Islamic, English) and in doing so also reconfigured and multiplied the administrators of those legal systems. Moreover, an extensive process of mediating between these different systems was also necessary in order to ensure that colonial rule was not undermined. But these systems were a fiction; they obscured the reality of the essential state of exception that colonial rule maintained through the exempting rhetoric of civilisation. The rhetoric of civilisation bestowed sovereign power on the 'civilised' so that any act became as if it were law even as it passed the bounds of law. Thus indirect rule constructed, and repeatedly restructured through endless inquiries and commissions, baroque edifices of the law that became the legal inheritance of colonial rule at independence.

What the preceding chapters have shown is how novels and press narratives were crucial sites for thinking through the edifices of the law during colonial rule and after. This is because fiction operates like the law in that it is an imaginative response to the world. Although one of the fictions of the law is its lack of creativity, the law is nothing if not imaginative. The law imagines transgression and makes it visible, for example through the body of the treasonable felon; the law imagines the boundary of its own extent and describes that boundary through the construction of the nation state; and, as Hussain argues, the law imagines its own failure in its provision for the state of exception.[23] Likewise, fiction's fictionality has the power to make visible the suspension of the law – the state of exception as the *real* behind the prosthesis of the legal state. What I hope to have demonstrated here is how fiction returns again and again, whether sincerely or satirically, to this scene in which the law absents itself, as we saw not only in Odili's abandonment by the police but also in Rudbeck's extra-legal killing of Mr Johnson. In British colonial fiction this is the fantasy of the benevolent force of civilisation; in Nigerian fiction the violence of the law's suspension is more frequently exposed and critiqued.

Fiction is thus an essential locus for an investigation of the law in colonial and postcolonial Nigeria because it repeatedly makes visible the particular fictions of the law itself. That this matters is clear from the place that literature occupied in the machinations of colonial rule and in the response of governments to writers in both the colonial and the

---

[23] Hussain, *The Jurisprudence of Emergency*, p. 9.

postcolonial period. Most obviously, the history of writers courting the law or persecuted by the state stretches from the early trials of Azikiwe in Sierra Leone, which Stephanie Newell records in *The Power to Name*, through the suspicion that fell upon Achebe following the publication of *A Man of the People*, to the imprisonment of Wole Soyinka in 1967 and the execution of Ken Saro-Wiwa in 1995.[24] Beside these instances, and more like them, however, novels themselves gestured to and depicted the close relationship between law and literature that characterised Nigeria in the period between 1900 and 1966. As I noted in Chapter 2, it is telling that Margery Perham's first attempt to justify the benevolent civilising influence of colonialism was through fiction. Her missionary zeal for indirect rule continued up to Nigerian independence and is evident even in her foreword to Awolowo's *Path to Nigerian Freedom*, in which she takes issue with Awolowo's measured but forceful calls for independence in 1947. Her novel, *Major Dane's Garden*, allowed Perham to hypothesise the triumph of the ideals of indirect rule and thereby to present its justification in a seductive form. As Jessica Berman observes, 'in narrative we put ethics into play and begin to imagine justice, acting to generate and respond to the social relationships and obligations that shape the future of our common world.'[25] Berman is imagining a different sort of justice here, one that challenges rather than endorses colonialism, but her account is striking for the way it also captures the aims of Perham in her novel. For Perham, 'imagining justice' means imagining the colonial state of exception as *the* vehicle for the civilisation that will 'shape the future of our common world'. Perham, in turn, inherits this romance of justice from the St Crispin's Day inflections of memoirs by those like Hazzledine and Flora Shaw who valorised the early years under Lugard's governorship.

Elsewhere, more subtly, we see how fiction is imbricated in the operations of the law through the significance that the reading matter of administrators is made to carry in novels such as *No Longer at Ease*, *The Heart of the Matter*, *Mister Johnson* and *Arrow of God*. Edgar Wallace's fiction, for example, is repeatedly mentioned as the preferred reading of young administrators, men whose imagination was vivid enough to romanticise their own activities but not critical enough to recognise their own

---

[24] General Sani Abacha's government was responsible for the military trial and execution of Saro-Wiwa as well as the death sentence passed against Soyinka *in absentia* on the charge of treason.
[25] Berman, *Modernist Commitments*, p. 6.

CONCLUSION

self-deception in doing so. These intertextual references alert us to the mutual seduction between the law and fiction to which these novels allude (and that *Major Dane's Garden* enacts on a grand scale). They encourage us to recognise the problematic limits to the imagination of these young administrators, effectively inviting us to imagine for ourselves an alternative world in which such administrators were not seduced by the romance of exceptionalism and imagined justice on other grounds. Berman invokes Paul Ricoeur's characterisation of imagination as a state of 'as if' (*comme si*), where in Berman's words 'new possible worlds make ethical and political claims upon our understanding of this one'.[26] The challenge can be more complicated than this, though, as Berman acknowledges. Where fiction presents the artifice of 'real' life – the reality, for example, of the state of exception – the ethical and political claims upon our understanding are to imagine a more just alternative than the novel provides. Thus, in the arresting officer in *No Longer at Ease*, who addresses Obi like 'a District Officer ... reading the Riot Act', we might read an alternative to Ricoeur's 'as if'. *What* if, Achebe challenges us, the colonial administration did not read itself in terms of *Sanders of the River*?

In May 1967, a year after the publication of *A Man of the People*, the people of the Eastern Region of Nigeria imagined a 'new possible world' for themselves and declared the Republic of Biafra. This literal state of 'as if' held out against the Nigerian military until January 1970. This period of nominal independence was in Nigerian terms nothing other than civil war. For those in the Eastern Region Biafra was now their nation state; for the rest of the geographical territory of Nigeria this was a state of rebellion. Competing narratives brought into being competing states, competing ways to imagine the nation.

The failure of the 'as if' of Biafra was a failure first and foremost because the Nigerian Federal Military Government blockaded the state until famine forced the Biafran leadership to capitulate. The blockade was one of the most extreme examples of the state of exception in Nigeria in the twentieth century, symbolically and literally reducing the Biafran population to bare life: on the one hand Biafra represented a territory to be reintegrated within the state, and yet for this to happen it was excluded from the state, a body (conceptual and literal) that in Agambenian terms could be killed but not sacrificed. The famine was decried in the international press but Biafra remained unrecognised as a state by all but a handful of countries, reinforcing its status as bare life. Capitulation did

---

[26] Ibid. p. 7. See Ricoeur, *Time and Narrative*, vol. 1.

not, however, mean complete reintegration. The 'as if' of Biafra continued, and continues, to signify differently under the ensuing regimes. Moreover, the anxiety to secure the limit of the state, whether through the identification of the treasonable act or through the delineation of borders, likewise continues to this day.

Biafra, and the larger history of colonialism and its inheritance in Nigeria, reminds us that how we imagine the law and the state matters. Equally, how the law imagines the state, and how the state imagines the law, are foundational to justice. The relationships of law and state, and our relationships to them, are not a given. They take on conflicting and contradictory forms, and mobilise complex rhetorics that obscure the realities of their (dys)function. Fiction, with its premise of 'as if', creates the space to dramatise these relationships, enabling us to recognise their implications and to entertain alternatives. This dramatisation is writ large in a novel like *A Man of the People*, but it is as much at the heart of the fictional letters of Beatrice and Gabriel in Okonkwo's market publication *Never Trust All that Love You*. In this correspondence the legal discourse, the accusations of forgery and the expressions of mistrust call into question the relationship not only of Beatrice and Gabriel but also of Okonkwo and his audience, of the reader and the text, of love and the law. Likewise, the 'as if' of Jagua's new community at the end of *Jagua Nana* imagines, however briefly, an alternative to the failure of the law in the novel's prior action. Such narratives reorient our thinking about the law by making visible its fictions and its limits. They remind us of the foundational 'as if' on which the edifices of the law are premised.

Bibliography

Achebe, Chinua, *Arrow of God* (New York: Anchor Books, 1974).
—— *A Man of the People* (Garden City: Anchor Books, 1989).
—— *No Longer at Ease* (New York: Anchor Books, 1994).
—— 'The Novelist as Teacher', *New Statesman*, 29 January 1965, pp. 161–2.
—— *There Was a Country: A Personal History of Biafra* (London: Allen Lane, 2012).
—— *Things Fall Apart* (London: Penguin, 2001).
Adebanwi, Wale, *Nation as Grand Narrative: The Nigerian Press and the Politics of Meaning* (Rochester: University of Rochester Press, 2016).
Aderinto, Saheed, 'Modernizing Love: Romantic Passion and Youth Literary Culture in colonial Nigeria', *Africa: The Journal of the International African Institute* 85:3 (2015), pp. 478–500. DOI: 10.1017/S0001972015000236.
Agamben, Giorgio, *Homo Sacer: Sovereign Power and Bare Life*, trans. Daniel Heller-Roazen (Stanford: Stanford University Press, 1998).
—— *State of Exception*, trans. Kevin Attell (Chicago: University of Chicago Press, 2005).
Agbaje, Adigun, *The Nigerian Press, Hegemony, and the Social Construction of Legitimacy* (Lewiston: Edwin Mellen Press, 1992).
Allott, A. N., 'The Common Law of Nigeria', *International and Comparative Law Quarterly* Supplement Publication 31 (1965), pp. 31–49.
Anderson, Benedict, *Imagined Communities: Reflections on the Origin and Spread of Nationalism*, rev. edn (London: Verso, 2006).
Awolowo, Obafemi, *Awo: The Autobiography of Chief Obafemi Awolowo* (Cambridge: Cambridge University Press, 1960).
—— *Path to Nigerian Freedom* (London: Faber & Faber, 1947).
Babalola, C. A., 'A Reconsideration of Achebe's *No Longer at Ease*', *Phylon* 47:2 (1986), pp. 139–47. DOI: 10.2307/274540.
Ballentyne, R. M., *The Gorilla Hunters* (London: T. Nelson & Sons, 1861).
Barber, Karin (ed. and trans.), *Print Culture and the First Yoruba Novel: I. B. Thomas's 'Life Story of Me, Sẹgilọla' and Other Texts* (Leiden: Brill, 2012).
Becke, Louis, *By Reef and Palm* (London: Fisher Unwin, 1894).
Benjamin, Walter, *Reflections: Essays, Aphorisms, Autobiographical Writings*, ed. Peter Demetz, trans. Edmund Jephcott (New York: Schocken Books, 1986).
Bennion, F. A. R., *The Constitutional Law of Ghana*, African Law Series (London: Butterworths, 1962).

Berman, Jessica, *Modernist Commitments: Ethics, Politics and Transnational Modernism* (New York: Columbia University Press, 2011).

Berry, Sara, 'Hegemony on a Shoestring: Indirect Rule and Access to Agricultural Land', *Africa: Journal of the African Institute* 62:3, Rights over Land: Categories and Controversies (1992), pp. 327–55. DOI: 10.2307/1159747.

'Biscuits and Bulldozers', *The Unilever House Magazine* 4:3 (March 1951), pp. 3–8.

Bourgault, Louise, *Mass Media in Sub-Saharan Africa* (Bloomington: Indiana University Press, 1995).

Brown, Bernard, 'The "Ordinary Man" in Provocation: Anglo-Saxon Attitudes and "Unreasonable Non-Englishmen"', *International and Comparative Law Quarterly* 13 (January 1964), pp. 203–35. DOI: 10.1093/iclqaj/13.1.203.

Cary, Joyce, *Mister Johnson* (Harmondsworth: Penguin, 1970).

Chamberlain, M. E., *The Scramble for Africa* (Harlow: Longman, 1984).

Christelow, Allan, 'Islamic Law and Judicial Practice in Nigeria: An Historical Perspective', *Journal of Muslim Minority Affairs* 22:1 (2002), pp. 185–204. DOI: 10.1080/13602000220124908.

Coleridge, Samuel Taylor, *Biographia Literaria* (New York: Leavitt, Lord & Co., 1834).

Conrad, Joseph, *Youth and Two Other Stories* (Garden City: Doubleday, Page & Co., 1920).

Crocker, W. R., *Nigeria: A Critique of British Colonial Administration* (London: George Allen & Unwin, 1936).

Cunninghame Graham, R. B., 'Introduction', in A. C. G. Hastings, *Nigerian Days* (London: John Lane, The Bodley Head, 1925).

Dodson, Don, 'The Role of the Publisher in Onitsha Market Literature', *Research in African Literatures* 4:2 (1973), pp. 172–88.

Dwyer, Philip and Amanda Nettelbeck (eds), *Violence, Colonialism and Empire in the Modern World* (London: Palgrave Macmillan, 2018).

Eaglestone, Robert, 'On Giorgio Agamben's Holocaust', *Paragraph: Journal of Modern Critical Theory* 25:2 (2002), pp. 52–67. DOI: 10.3366/jsp.2002.25.2.52.

Ekwensi, Cyprian, *Jagua Nana* (Oxford: Heinemann, 1987).

—— *People of the City* (Toronto: African World Press, 2004).

Foster, Malcolm, *Joyce Cary: A Biography* (London: Michael Joseph, 1969).

[Freeman, Thomas Birch,] *Missionary Enterprise No Fiction: A Tale Founded on Facts* (London: Elliott Stock, 1871).

Furniss, Graham, 'On Engendering Liberal Values in the Nigerian Colonial State: The Idea behind the Gaskiya Corporation', *The Journal of Imperial and Commonwealth History* 39:1 (2011), pp. 95–119. DOI: 10.1080/03086534.2011.543796.

Gordon, Michelle, 'The Dynamics of British Colonial Violence', in Philip Dwyer and Amanda Nettelbeck (eds), *Violence, Colonialism and Empire in the Modern World* (London: Palgrave Macmillan, 2018), pp. 153–74.

Hair, P. E. H., 'The Cowboys: A Nigerian Acculturative Institution (Ca. 1950)', *History in Africa* 28 (2001), pp. 83–93. DOI: 10.2307/3172209.

Hastings, A. C. G., *Nigerian Days* (London: John Lane, The Bodley Head, 1925).

Hazzledine, George Douglas, *The White Man in Nigeria* (London: Edward Arnold, 1904).

Hodges, Hugh, 'Beasts and Abominations in *Things Fall Apart* and *Omenuko*', *ARIEL: A Review of International English Literature* 43:4 (2013), pp. 49–68.

Howarth, Patrick, *Play Up and Play the Game: The Heroes of Popular Fiction* (London: Eyre Methuen, 1973).

Hunter, William Wilson, *A Life of the Earl of Mayo, Fourth Viceroy of India*, 2 vols (London: Smith, Elder, 1875).

Hussain, Nasser, *The Jurisprudence of Emergency: Colonialism and the Rule of Law* (Ann Arbor: University of Michigan Press, 2003).

Jenkins, George D., Papers, Hoover Institution Archives, Stanford University, California.

Keay, E. A., 'Legal and Constitutional Changes in Nigeria under the Military Government', *Journal of African Law* 10:2 (Summer 1966), pp. 92–105. DOI: 10.1017/S0021855300004551.

Kerr, Douglas, *Conan Doyle: Writing, Profession, and Practice* (Oxford: Oxford University Press, 2013).

Korda, Zoltán (dir.), *Sanders of the River* (London Film Productions, 1935).

Kortenaar, Neil ten, 'The Rule, the Law, and the Rule of Law in Achebe's Novels of Colonization', *Cambridge Journal of Postcolonial Literary Inquiry* 2:1 (2015), pp. 33–51. DOI: 10.1017/pli.2014.23.

Lawrence, Benjamin N., Emily Lynn Osborn and Richard L. Robert (eds), *Intermediaries, Interpreters, and Clerks: African Employees in the Making of Colonial Africa* (Madison: University of Wisconsin, 2006).

Lefebvre, Alexandre, *The Image of Law: Deleuze, Bergson, Spinoza* (Stanford: Stanford University Press, 2008).

Mackintosh, John P., 'Politics in Nigeria: The Action Group Crisis of 1962', *Political Studies* 11:2 (1963), pp. 126–55. DOI: 10.1111/j.1467-9248.1963.tb01055.x.

Mamdani, Mahmood, *Citizen and Subject: Contemporary Africa and the Legacy of Late Colonialism* (Princeton: Princeton University Press, 1996).

—— *Define and Rule: Native as Political Identity* (Cambridge, MA: Harvard University Press, 2012).

Mangan, J. A., *The Games Ethic and Imperialism: Aspects of the Diffusion of an Ideal* (Harmondsworth: Viking, 1986).

Manji, Ambreena, '"Like a Mask Dancing": Law and Colonialism in Chinua Achebe's *Arrow of God*', *Journal of Law and Society* 27:4 (2000), pp. 626–42. DOI: 10.1111/1467-6478.00170.

Mason, Michael, 'The History of Mr Johnson: Progress and Protest in Northern Nigeria, 1900–1921', *Canadian Journal of African Studies/Revue canadienne des études africaines* 27:2 (1993), pp. 196–217.

Mbembe, Achille, 'Necropolitics', *Public Culture* 15:1 (2003), pp. 11–40. DOI: 10.1215/08992363-15-1-11.

Miller, Carroll, 'Colonial West African Fiction, 1823–1914: An Annotated Bibliography', *Research in African Literatures* 4:2 (1973), pp. 199–203.

Morton, Stephen, *States of Emergency: Colonialism, Literature and Law* (Liverpool: Liverpool University Press, 2013).

Motha, Stewart, 'Colonial Sovereignty, Forms of Life and Liminal Beings in South Africa', in Marcelo Svirsky and Simone Bignall (eds), *Agamben and Colonialism* (Edinburgh: Edinburgh University Press, 2012), pp. 128–51.

Newell, Stephanie, 'Dirty Whites: "Ruffian-Writing" in Colonial West Africa', *Research in African Literatures* 39:4 (2008), pp. 1–13. DOI: 10.2979/RAL.2008.39.4.1.

—— 'From the Brink of Oblivion: The Anxious Masculinism of Nigerian Market Literatures', *Research in African Literatures* 27:3 (1996), pp. 50–67.

—— 'Petrified Masculinities? Contemporary Nigerian Popular Literatures by Men', *Journal of Popular Culture* 30:4 (1997), pp. 161–82. DOI: 10.1111/j.0022-3840.1997.3004_161.x.

—— *The Power to Name: A History of Anonymity in Colonial West Africa* (Athens: Ohio University Press, 2013).

—— (ed.), *Readings in African Popular Fiction* (Oxford: James Currey, 2002).

Nkosi, Lewis, 'Where Does African Literature Go from Here?', *Africa Report* 11:9 (December 1966), pp. 7–11.

Nnadozie, J. O., *Beware of Harlots and Many Friends: The World Is Hard* (Fegge-Onitsha: J. O. Nnadozie, n.d.).

Nwabueze, Benjamin Obi, *A Constitutional History of Nigeria* (London: C. Hurst, 1982).

Nwoga, Donatus, 'Onitsha Market Literature', *Transition* 19 (1965), pp. 26–33. DOI: 10.2307/2934655.

Nwogugu, E. I., 'Abolition of customary Courts – A Nigerian Experiment', *Journal of African Law* 20:1 (1976), pp. 1–19. DOI: 10.1017/S0021855300006689.

Nwosu, Cletus Gibson, *Miss Cordelia in the Romance of Destiny* (Port Harcourt: Vincent Okeanu [1960]).

Obiechina, Emmanuel, 'Market Literature in Nigeria', *Kunapipi* 30:2 (2008), pp. 108–25.

Ocheje, Paul D., 'Law and Social Change: A Socio-Legal Analysis of Nigeria's Corrupt Practices and Other Related Offences Act, 2000', *Journal of African Law* 45:2 (2001), pp. 173–95. DOI: 10.1017/S0221855301001687.

Odim, Cheryl Johnson, and Nina Emma Mba, *For Women and the Nation: Funmilayo Ransome-Kuti of Nigeria* (Urbana: University of Illinois Press, 1997).

Okonkwo, R., *Never Trust All that Love You: The world is so corrupt, that it has became [sic] difficult to trust all people*, foreword by S. A. Egwuonwu (Fegge-Onitsha: [S. A. Egwuonwu] [1961]).

Onwuzolum, Emmanuel Chidi, 'The Ritual-Theatricality of Igbo Masks and Masking,' PhD thesis, University of British Columbia, 1977.

Orizu, Okwudili, *To Rule Is a Trouble* (Onitsha: Onwudiwe & Sons, [1960]).

Osinubi, Taiwo Adetunji, 'Abolition, Law, and the Osu Marriage Novel', *Cambridge Journal of Postcolonial Literary Inquiry* 2:1 (2015), pp. 53–71. DOI: 10.1017/pli.2014.24.

—— 'Cold War Sponsorships: Chinua Achebe and the Dialectics of Collaboration', *Journal of Postcolonial Writing* 50:4 (2014), pp. 410–22. DOI: 10.1080/17449855.2014.925695.

Patterson, Charles J., 'Anniversaries, Emergencies and Teething Troubles', Report to Richard Nolte, Institute of Current World Affairs, New York, 15 October 1962, <http://www.icwa.org/wp-content/uploads/2015/09/CJP-8.pdf> (last accessed 27 March 2019).

Perham, Margery, *Africans and British Rule* (London: Oxford University Press/ Humphrey Milford, 1941).

—— *Colonial Sequence 1949–1969: A Chronological Commentary upon British Colonial Policy in Africa* (London: Methuen, 1970).

—— *Major Dane's Garden* (London: Rex Collings, 1970).

Ricoeur, Paul, *Time and Narrative*, trans. Kathleen McLaughlin and David Pellauer, 3 vols (Chicago: University of Chicago Press, 1984).

Rowell, Charles H., 'An Interview with Chinua Achebe', *Callaloo* 13:1 (Winter 1990), pp. 86–101. DOI: 10.2307/2931612.

Ryan, Lyndall, 'Martial Law in the British Empire', in Philip Dwyer and Amanda Nettelbeck (eds), *Violence, Colonialism and Empire in the Modern World* (London: Palgrave Macmillan, 2018), pp. 93–109.

Schmitt, Carl, *Political Theology: Four Chapters on the Concept of Sovereignty* (1922), trans. George Schwab (Cambridge, MA: MIT Press, 1985).

Shaw, Flora Louise (Lugard), *A Tropical Dependency: An Outline of the Ancient History of the Western Soudan, with an Account of the Modern Settlement of Northern Nigeria* (London: James Nisbet & Co., 1905).

Shirley, Edward, *Up the Creeks: A Tale of Adventure in West Africa* (London: Thomas Nelson and Sons, 1900).

Sklar, Richard L., *Nigerian Political Parties: Power in an Emergent African Nation* (Princeton: Princeton University Press, 1963).

Southon, Arthur E., *The Laughing Ghosts* (London: Sheldon Press [1928]).

—— *The Taming of a King: A West African Story* (London: Cargate Press [1927]).

—— *A Yellow Napoleon* (London: Hodder & Stoughton, 1923).

Speed, Edwin Arney, *Richards's Table of Offences in their relation to the jurisdiction of district commissioners as commissioners of the supreme court of Southern Nigeria with notes on the criminal jurisdiction and procedure. Revised and Enlarged* (London: Steven and Sons, 1908).

Svirsky, Marcelo, and Simone Bignall (eds), *Agamben and Colonialism* (Edinburgh: Edinburgh University Press, 2012).

Taiwo, E. A., 'Repugnancy Clause and its Impact on Customary Law: Comparing the South African and Nigerian Positions – Some Lessons for Nigeria', *Journal for Juridical Science* 34:1 (2009), pp. 89–115.

Thomas, Martin, *Violence and Colonial Order: Police, Workers and Protest in the European Colonial Empires, 1918–1940* (Cambridge: Cambridge University Press, 2012).

Wallace, Edgar, *Bosambo of the River* (London: Ward, Lock & Co. [1956]).

—— *The People of the River* (London: Ward, Lock & Co. [1949]).
—— *Sanders of the River* (London: Ward, Lock & Co. [1952]).
Zachernuk, Philip S., 'Of Origins and Colonial Order: Southern Nigerian Historians and the 'Hamitic Hypothesis' c. 1870–1970', *The Journal of African History* 35:3 (1994), pp. 427–55. DOI: 10.1017/S0021853700026785.

Index

Abacha, Sani, 192n
Abdulwahid, Hafsatu, 190
Abinsi, 66
Achebe, Chinua, 102, 104–5, 129, 156,
    182, 188, 189
    Arrow of God, 18–19, 28n, 86, 88, 90,
        165, 192
    A Man of the People, 10–11, 25, 157–80,
        182, 183, 191, 193, 194
    No Longer at Ease, 9, 85–106, 108, 111,
        112, 119–20, 125, 127, 132, 160,
        167, 190, 192, 193
    Things Fall Apart, 14n, 86, 87, 88, 90,
        105
    There Was a County, 157
Action Group, 21, 130, 132–7, 140, 141,
    144, 146, 147n, 149–53, 156, 164
Adadipe, B. A., 141
Adegbenro, Dauda Soroye, 142
Adichie, Chimamanda Ngozi
    Half of a Yellow Sun, 189
Africa America Institute, 183
Africa Report, 182–3
African Messenger, 134
African Morning Post, 134
African Press, 134
Agamben, Giorgio, 2–3, 27
    Homo Sacer, 25n, 73, 76, 84n
    State of Exception, 2, 24–5, 26, 27, 40,
        46, 66, 85, 101, 174n
Agbaje, Adigun, 1
Agbani, 113
Aguiyi-Ironsi, Johnson, 184, 186–7
Akede Eko, 116
Akinsanya, Ayo, 150
Akintola, Samuel Ladoke, 135–6, 142, 156,
    164n, 168, 177, 184
alkalai, 4, 24
Allied Newspapers Limited, 134, 136

Amadi, Elechi
    Sunset in Biafra, 189
Amalgamated Press of Nigeria, 134, 136
Amritsar, 173
Anambra, 110
Anderson, Benedict, 1, 2, 106n, 108, 121,
    122, 131, 135n, 154n, 188n
Anglo-Aro War, 16–17
Apapa, 137, 138
Arabic, 23
Aro, 16–17
Awolowo, Obafemi, 7, 10, 21, 22n, 25,
    129, 130, 132, 133–6, 138–45, 147,
    148–9, 154, 155, 156, 164n, 167n,
    169, 172
    Awo, 7, 12–13, 20
    Pathway to Nigerian Freedom, 133–4,
        184, 192
Azare, 65, 66
Azikiwe, Nnamdi, 10, 20, 21, 132, 133,
    134, 136, 137, 145, 155, 156, 192

Babalola, Richard, 141
Balewa, Abubakar Tafawa, 132, 133, 136,
    137, 145, 155, 156, 184, 186, 187
Bello, Ahmadu, 21, 132, 137, 156, 177, 184
Benjamin, Walter, 25n, 129n, 174n
Benue River, 16
Berlin Conference, 16
Biafra, Republic of, 21, 157, 189, 193, 194
Bonny, 15
Borgu, 60–1
Boy Scouts, 92
Buchan, John, 30
Burkina Faso, 14

Cameroons, 14, 60, 100, 131
Cary, Joyce, 52, 55, 56, 59–61, 85, 86,
    91, 104

Mister Johnson, 8, 54–84, 86n, 100, 173n
Casement, Roger, 35
Ceulemans, Edward, 149, 150, 151
Christianity, 12, 14, 30, 47n, 48, 87, 92
CIA, 183
Clark-Bekederemo, John Pepper, 157, 180
Coker Commission *see* Coker Inquiry
Coker Inquiry, 136, 137, 139, 148, 164, 170n, 180
Commoners' People's Party, 159
Congo, 35, 37, 52, 158, 159
Congo Free State *see* Congo
Congo River, 35
Conrad, Joseph, 86
  'Heart of Darkness', 5n, 31, 72, 79
Convention People's Party (CPP), 141
Crocker, W. R., 58–9, 61, 65–6, 68
Cunninghame Graham, R. B., 33, 35, 36, 37n, 49, 51, 52

Daily Express, 94, 95, 134, 138, 141, 143, 144n, 146–8, 149–51, 152–3, 162, 168
Daily Service, 134
Daily Times, 139–40, 142, 143, 146, 162–3n
District Commissioners, 4, 7–9, 17, 18, 19, 24, 25, 26–53, 85, 104, 117
dogarai, 61, 67
Doyle, Arthur Conan, 30–1
Dyer, Reginald, 173

East India Company, 16
Eastern Assembly, 110, 133
Eastern Region, 21, 22, 23, 85, 110, 132, 134, 157, 187, 193; *see also* Biafra, Republic of
Ebido, Samuel Itse, 151–2
Edo Empire, 15
Egbe Omo Oduduwa, 132
Ekiti, 145
Ekwejunor-Etchie, Gabriel, 142, 143
Ekwensi, Cyprian, 9, 10, 25, 90, 106, 108, 118, 163, 182, 188
  Ikolo the Wrestler and Other Ibo Tales, 118
  Jagua Nana, 118–20, 122–5, 127–9, 132
  People of the City, 118–22, 123–5, 126–7, 129, 134n
  When Love Whispers, 118

Elizabeth II, Queen, 10, 155
Emecheta, Buchi
  The Bride Price, 189
  The Joys of Motherhood, 189
Enahoro, Anthony, 137, 138, 142–3, 144n, 146, 148, 154–5
Enugu, 134
Eric, Speedy
  Mabel the Sweet Honey That Poured Away, 107
Eyre, Governor Edward, 173

First World War, 52, 55, 57, 60, 65, 78
Flora Nwapa Books *see* Nwapa, Flora
Foot, Dingle, 142
France, 32, 38

Gaskiya Corporation, 189–90
Gaskiya Ta Fi Kwabo, 189
Germany, 38, 60
Ghana, 15, 23, 38, 47, 102, 118, 139, 140–2, 146, 151, 158–9
Ghory, R. A., 142
Gold Coast *see* Ghana
Goldie, George Taubman, 15–16, 33
Gowon, Yakubu, 186–7
Gratiaen, E. F. N., 142–4
Great Depression, 59, 65, 66
Greene, Graham, 91
  The Heart of the Matter, 88–90, 91n

Habila, Helon, 190
Haggard, Rider, 30, 31, 33, 55
Harding, A. J., 56, 58, 59
Hastings, A. C. G., 29, 34, 36, 37, 39, 40, 41–2, 43, 44, 48, 49, 52, 53, 60, 61
Hausa, 21, 36, 40, 41, 133, 189–90
  Hausa language, 23, 37n, 62, 74, 189
Hazzledine, George Douglas, 33, 39–40, 41, 53, 68, 98, 167, 192
Heinemann African Writers series, 182, 189
high life, 111, 118, 119, 124n
Howarth, Patrick, 29–30, 31, 32
Hughes, Thomas, 30
Hussain, Nasser, 3–4, 5n, 173, 174n, 191

Ibadan, 38, 91, 92, 134, 135, 186
Ibadan Association of Chartered Secretaries, 92

Ibo *see* Igbo
Igbo, 10, 14, 16–17, 21, 86, 89, 104, 133, 156, 157, 166, 186, 187
Igbo Women's War *see* Ògù Umùnwaàyi
Ijebu Remo, 12–13
Ike, Chukwuemeka
   Expo '77, 190
   Toads for Supper, 190
Ikoli, Ernest, 134
Ikoyi, 157
India, British, 186
indirect rule, 8, 12–13, 17–20, 21, 25, 31, 33, 42, 45, 52, 56–9, 63, 67–8, 71–2, 83, 105, 128, 155, 159, 160, 179, 181, 185, 186, 188, 190–1, 192
Institute of Current World Affairs, 136
Islam, 14, 92
   Islamic law, 4, 8, 14, 18, 22–3, 24, 43, 61, 191
Ithiala, 123
Iweala, Uzodinma, 103n

Jakande, Lateef Kayode, 148n
Jamaica, 173
Jenkins, George D., 91, 92, 131n

Kano, 65, 134
Katsina Ala, 66
Katsina, Sulaiman Ibrahim, 190
Kennedy, John F., 177
Kingsley, Charles, 30
Korda, Zoltán and Alexander
   Sanders of the River, 83, 90
Kuti, Fela, 103n
Kuti, Funmilayo Ransome, 128, 129, 159, 159n

Lagos, city of, 10, 20, 85, 87, 94, 95, 118, 119, 120, 121, 123, 129, 132, 135, 137, 138, 147n, 157, 160
Lagos Colony, 12, 15, 16, 34, 57, 77
Lagos Herald see *Akede Eko*
Lagos High Court, 137, 151
Lambo, Sigismund Olanrewaju, 154
Lefebvre, Alexandre, 24, 113
London, 20, 88, 92, 97, 120, 132, 142, 144n
Lowe, John, 144n
Lowe, Josephine, 144n
Lugard, Flora *see* Shaw, Flora

Lugard, Frederick, 16, 17–18, 21, 28, 33, 37, 63, 104, 192
Lumumba, Patrice, 158, 159, 177, 183
Lynn, John, 149, 150, 151, 152, 153

Maja, Oladipo, 141
Majekodunmi, Moses Adekoyejo, 135–6, 137
mallam, 61
Mamdani, Mahmood, 19, 44–5, 57–8, 63, 70n, 160, 164, 190
market literature, 9, 90, 102, 105, 106, 107–18, 119, 123, 124n, 125–7, 129, 163, 182, 190; *see also* popular fiction *and* soyoyya
market princess *see* market women
market women, 128, 129, 147n
martial law, 12, 13, 157, 158, 172–4, 175, 178, 185, 190
Mbembe, Achille, 3, 11, 12
Middle Belt Region, 132, 156
Monrovia, 45
Morel, E. D., 35
Morning Post, 134, 136, 137, 142, 143, 145, 146, 151, 152n, 153, 155–6, 185, 187–8

National Bank of Nigeria, 136
National Council of Nigeria, 131
National Council of Nigeria and the Cameroons (NCNC), 20, 21, 131–2, 133, 134, 135, 151, 156
New Statesman, 102
Niger River, 15, 16, 32, 35
Nigeria
   Federal House of Assembly of, 135
   Federal Military Government of, 185, 187, 193
   First Republic of, 10, 21, 130, 131, 139, 140, 142, 154, 155–6, 181, 184
Nigerian Economic Society, 92
Nigerian Investment and Properties Company, 136, 164
Nigerian Tribune, 134, 144, 145, 154
Nigerian Union of Students, 92, 131
Nigerian Women's Union, 128, 129
Nigerian Youth Congress, 138, 167n
Nigerian Youth Movement, 132, 134
Nkosi, Lewis, 182–3, 184, 186, 187, 189, 190

Nkrumah, Kwame, 141–2, 146, 159
Nnadozie, J. O.
  Beware of Harlots and Many Friends 109–10, 115–17, 119, 129
Northern Assembly, 133
Northern Elements Progressive Association, 132
Northern Nigerian Protectorate, 6, 8, 16, 17, 19, 39, 48, 57, 69
Northern Nigerian Publishing Company *see* Gaskiya Corporation
Northern People's Congress (NPC), 21, 132, 133, 151
Northern Region, 21, 110, 132, 156, 177, 186, 187
Northern Teachers' Association, 132
Nwapa, Flora, 189
  Efuru, 189
Nzeogwu, Chukwuma Kaduna, 157, 184

Oba, 7, 13, 14
Obalende, 150
Obi, Chike, 137, 152
Odesanya, Michael Adeyinka, 152
Odinani, 14
Ògù Umùnwaàyi, 128
Ohaegbula, Joseph, 152, 153
Ojukwu, Odumegwu, 187
Okonkwo, R.
  Never Trust All that Love You, 112, 113–15, 116, 117, 119, 126, 127, 194
Okotie-Eboh, Festus, 137
Olympio, Sylvanus, 141n, 142, 158, 159, 177, 183
Omisade, Michael, 148
Omo-Eboh, Modipe, 21
Onitsha, 14, 107, 108–9, 110, 118, 134, 190
Orizu, Okwudili
  To Rule Is a Trouble, 110–11, 122–3, 129, 158, 165
Osu, 88, 94, 104–5, 120
Oyo Empire, 15

palm oil, 15, 107
Patterson, Charles, 136–7, 138
People's Union, 131
Perham, Margery, 28, 76, 133, 160–1
  Major Dane's Garden, 28–9, 33–4, 50n, 52, 53, 56, 68n, 192

Polservice, 162
popular fiction, 5, 26, 60, 86, 94–5, 129, 190; *see also* market literature *and* soyoyya
Port Harcourt, 85, 134
Portugal, 32
Punjab, 173

Rewane, Alfred, 142, 143
Ribadu, Muhammadu, 137
Ricoeur, Paul, 193
Rohmer, Sax
  Fu Manchu series, 30, 31, 49n
Royal Niger Company, 6, 8, 16, 17, 33, 35, 38, 69, 163n, 181; *see also* United Africa Company

Saro-Wiwa, Ken, 192
Schmitt, Carl, 2, 3
Second World War, 20, 21, 107, 124n, 131, 132
Selassie, Haile, 55
Serakin Mata, 61
Shango, 14
Shaw, Flora, 33
  A Tropical Dependency, 33, 35, 37, 192
Sierra Leone, 15, 16, 32, 44n, 57–8, 90, 192
slave trade *see* slavery
slavery, 12, 15, 16, 17, 35, 36, 69, 104
Society of Nigerian Authors, 157
Sokoto Caliphate, 14, 17–18
Somaliland, British, 28, 52
South Africa, 5, 182–3
Southern Nigerian Protectorate, 6, 8, 16, 38, 57, 69
Southon, Arthur E., 9n, 29, 43, 52, 56, 60, 61, 64
  The Laughing Ghosts, 36, 41
  The Taming of a King, 32n, 34, 37
  A Yellow Napoleon, 50
Sowemimo, George Sodeinde, 138, 146, 154
soyayya, 190
Soyinka, Wole, 103n, 192
Speed, Edward Arney, 24, 38, 39, 41, 43, 61
Stanley, Henry Morton, 8, 35, 52
Stephen, James Fitzjames, 1, 4
Storey Report, 85
Sudan, 18n

Political Service, 48
Sule, Maitama, 137

Tabansi Press, 118
Tana Press *see* Nwapa, Flora
Tanganyika, 61
Taylor Woodrow, 162
Temple Bar, 39
Thomas, Isaac B.
  'Sẹgilọla of the Fascinating Eyes', 116
Thomas, Stella, 21
Thorne, Isabel, 35
Togo, 141, 142, 159
Tutuola, Amos
  Palm-Wine Drinkard, 9, 118n

Unilever, 163, 180; *see also* United Africa Company
Unilever House Magazine, 162, 163
Union of Agricultural Technology Workers, 92
Union of Young Democrats, 134
United Africa Company (UAC), 141, 162, 163; *see also* Unilever

University of Nigeria, Nsukka, 190

Wallace, Edgar, 8, 29, 31, 34, 35, 52, 54, 55, 56, 60, 61, 64, 85, 86, 89–90, 104, 117, 160, 176, 188, 192
  Bosambo of the River, 43, 44, 46
  The People of the River, 40, 42, 43, 47
  Sanders of the River, 45–6, 47–51, 54n, 83
warrant chief, 4, 18, 22, 24
Waugh, Evelyn, 8, 54–5, 56
waziri, 61
Weekly Tale Teller, 35
West African Pilot, 134, 145–6, 187
Western Assembly, 133, 135
Western Emergency, 135, 136, 142, 156, 164
Western Region, 21, 22, 23, 110, 132, 135, 136, 170n, 177

Yari, Labo, 190
  Climate of Corruption, 190
Yoruba, 14, 21, 132, 133, 138
  language, 12, 13, 92n, 116

Zik Group, 134

EU representative:
Easy Access System Europe
Mustamäe tee 50, 10621 Tallinn, Estonia
Gpsr.requests@easproject.com